German Heritage BAKING

Konditorei and Kaffeehaus Goldene Waage (the Golden Scale Coffee House) is the type of café I remember from my childhood. As the old bakers retire, the few cafés that remain are treasures. Photo credit: my son Derek Worchel.

German Heritage
BAKING

Time-Honored Recipes, Traditional Techniques, and Culinary Secrets

Photography by Heidrun Metzler

VOLUME I

HEIDRUN METZLER

German Heritage Baking: Time-Honored Recipes, Traditional Techniques, and Culinary Secrets

Copyright ©2024 by Heidrun Metzler.

All rights reserved. No part of this book may be reproduced in any form or by any other means, either electronically or mechanically, including photocopying, recording, or by any information storage and retrieval system without permission in writing.

ISBN:
978-0-9837438-1-1 (print)
978-0-9837438-2-8 (ebook)

First Edition Printing 2024

Library of Congress Control Number: 2024923289

Book Design by Michelle M. White

Also by Heidrun Metzler:
Skeeter's Dreams; a children's picture book
First edition 2011, Second edition 2014

Published by Metzler Books
Heidrun Metzler Worchel
P.O. Box 1373, Honokaa, HI 96727, U.S.A.
heidrunmetzler.com

Printed and Distributed by Print Bind Ship, Taylor, Michigan, United States

Dedication

This book is for my husband and children.

*It is also for the new bakers of my children's generation,
for those friends who patiently asked about and tested recipes,
and for all bakers (new and old) who love flavorful, creative baking.*

*Finally, this book is for the women who inspired me and taught me
the art of German baking–my mother, aunt, and grandmother.*

CONTENTS

PREFACE *1*
INTRODUCTION *5*

CHAPTER 1
MÜRBETEIGE
19

CHAPTER 2
COOKIES
117

View of the village Erling and the mountains, taken from the Andechs Monastery restaurant.

CHAPTER 3
SPONGE CAKE-BASED TORTES
175

CHAPTER 4
TOPPINGS, FILLINGS, AND GARNISHES
239

ACKNOWLEDGMENTS *269*
BAKING UTENSILS AND BAKING PANS *271*
INDEX *272*
ABOUT THE AUTHOR *275*

The Römerplatz (Römer Square) in Frankfurt. The city's town offices have been located within the square since 1405. In the photo are old Fachwerk houses and Old Nikolai Church.

In my hometown of Oberursel, entering the Old Town (*Altstadt*) area feels like going back in time. Fachwerk houses from the year 1444 are still standing and preserved to this day.

PREFACE

I grew up in Oberursel, Germany, a town near Frankfurt. In our home, my mother was a constant baker. She made a pastry or tart for four o'clock coffee time and fancy cakes on Sundays. She never wanted to be caught without a cake to offer if someone came calling. My aunt and grandmother lived close by, just a few easy kilometers by bike. They, too, were passionate and joyful bakers. From these women, I learned to bake. My grandmother, who lived through difficult times when ingredients were scarce, showed me that a baker could make a lot from very few ingredients if they just had the right knowledge. All three gave me lessons in choosing good-quality ingredients and practicing patience in time and technique.

For the bakers in my family, inspiration often came from the produce around us. We had cherry, plum, mirabelle, and apple trees. Raspberry bushes, currants, and rhubarb grew in the garden. Pick-your-own strawberry fields were just around the corner. In the summer, my brothers, cousins, and I ventured into the forest for wild fruit and nuts, devouring some straight from the bushes and carrying the rest back home to see what pastry could emerge. Looking forward to the different produce ripening in due season turned into a great game of anticipation for certain cakes and pies. We had chickens, too, for fresh eggs, and early in my life, there was a nearby dairy farm where we bought fresh milk.

On special occasions, I took the train to one of the many cafés in downtown Frankfurt. Called *Konditoreien*, these beautiful cafés make elaborate pastries and cakes, similar to the French pâtisseries. These trips developed my palate for what baked goods are supposed to taste like. I savored flaky-crust tarts with vanilla cream topped with glazed fresh raspberries or cherries; Linzer tortes made with ground almonds and hazelnuts and a spread of red currant jelly; and Sachertorte with a moist chocolate interior, marzipan lining

PREFACE

the exterior, and snappy tempered chocolate glaze enveloping it all. One of my favorites was a tall, good old-fashioned covered apple pie with lemon-sugar glaze and a dollop of whipped cream. There were cheesecakes made with quark (a German fresh cheese) and layered cakes filled with nut or fruit cream and decorated with piped buttercream. Of course, there was also cherry brandy-infused Black Forest torte, a combination of chocolate sponge cake, cherry filling, and a generous whipped cream layer adorned with piped rosettes, each with a cherry on top. Oh, the agony of selection!

The pastries were not packed with sugar but with a delicate balance of fruit, nuts, buttery crusts, and just enough sweetness to still taste all the intricate combinations of flavors. It became my objective to learn how to bake such delectable treats.

As I traveled and grew older, I gathered inspiration, developing more recipes and perfecting the ones I had from my family. I changed ratios here and there and experimented with new flavors and combinations. The tiniest variations enhanced recipes distinctively and left tasters asking for seconds and thirds. It could be as simple as the addition of a liqueur or swapping nut meal for some or all of the all-purpose flour. When I moved to the States in 1978, new friends noticed these variations and often remarked that they had never tasted anything quite like my homemade baked goods.

They asked for recipes, but I was hesitant to give them out until I knew I could give directions that work for all bakers, novice and experienced alike. I wanted to preserve, as clearly as possible, the generations' worth of inherited tips, techniques, and ingredient knowledge, along with the profound joy of fresh pastries prepared well in one's own kitchen. Over decades, I collected my notes and ideas, and this book on German heritage baking is the result.

There is modern updating throughout the book, but by and large, the spirit lies in the hands-in-flour, old-world approach taught to me by my mother, aunt, and grandmother. It is an approach that has proven time and again to turn out delicious goods.

A BAKER'S NOTE

The intention of this book is to give bakers the recipes and tools to produce delicious and successful German-inspired desserts, specifically Mürbeteige (shortcrusts), cookies, and sponge cake-based tortes, along with accompanying glazes, fillings, and creams. Tools relevant to all the book's chapters are covered in the main introduction. Chapter introductions provide additional tools needed for handling specific types of dough and batter. Ideally, bakers will read through the main introduction as well as chapter introductions before diving into the recipes. But if you read nothing else, thumb to page 7 and look over the passage called "Four Crucial Variables in Baking." Keeping these variables in mind will make all the difference to baking success.

I wish everyone *viel Spass beim Backen*!
(Translation: lots of fun baking)
Heidrun

INTRODUCTION

I designed this book with both new and experienced bakers in mind.

My vision is that when new bakers open this book and start reading, they will think, *I can bake this recipe!* The confidence to dive in and start creating will naturally follow. New bakers will feel this encouragement even with the long recipes. There are, undeniably, some recipes that require dedications of time and careful attention, but they are not necessarily difficult. New bakers do not need to shy away from a raspberry almond tart or a covered pie; with straightforward directions, assembling a Black Forest torte is easy. Be assured that there are short, simple recipes too. It was also important to me to include the tips and notes that are often forgotten and go unmentioned but that make a big difference in the success of a recipe. In talking with friends and family about recipes gone wrong, I often discover that only a small detail needs adjustment: a different rack placement, a few minutes less or more of mixing depending on the dough type, a looser measure on the flour. These are precisely the details I want to make clear in the recipes.

When experienced bakers open the book, I hope they glean fresh insight from the German-inspired techniques and ingredients. Many of the recipes are versatile enough for customization by experienced bakers. Bakers might, for example, swap a suggested glaze for another option from this book or from their own repertoire. The possibilities for variation are up to the baker. I have suggested variations frequently in the headnotes to encourage the creative mind.

Most of all, I hope all bakers enjoy the recipes and return to them again and again. My goal is for bakers to have fun with the process, short or long, but the long recipes especially will give a sense of amazement and accomplishment. The fun of it all is a gift I took from my loved ones as I watched them whipping egg whites with

INTRODUCTION

gusto and sneaking licks of batter to ascertain whether the flavorings were just right. Relish the process, experiment and imagine, then savor the creations. If a cake, pie, or batch of cookies turns out a little ugly, a little overdone, a little underdone, too dense, too gooey, sloped, caved, excessively puffy, or otherwise flawed, eat it anyway (it will, in all likelihood, still be tasty), and while eating, jot down a note to adjust flour, liquids, or flavors the next time around. Baking is a living art. It needs the cook's care and creativity. Read the recipes well and follow them but also make sure to bring yourself to them. They need you.

HOW THIS BOOK IS ORGANIZED

This book contains four chapters. Three of those focus on specific dough and batter types: Mürbeteig (shortcrust) dough, cookie dough, and sponge cake batter. The fourth chapter offers glazes, sauces, fillings, frostings, icings, and garnishes. Each chapter begins with an introduction specific to the needs of its particular recipes. Read these introductions before getting started. I know there is the temptation to think, "I can skip these parts and wing it." Well, yes—the second time. Reading through the chapter introductions on the first go-round will save many hassles as well as the sticky task of flipping pages back and forth when wrist-deep in dough. Giving a few careful minutes to the chapter introduction will equip bakers with the information they need to approach all recipes in that chapter. As you get into the individual recipes, remember to read each one start to finish before beginning. Getting an overview of the whole process is essential to organization and timing.

The rest of this main introduction covers the "Four Crucial Variables in Baking," "Common Ingredients," and "Common Techniques."

Videos with technique demonstrations are an additional feature of this book. The video showcases are accessible on my Vimeo channel where they are organized to correspond with the chapters of this book. Clear references to the video showcases appear in each chapter introduction and at relevant points throughout the book. To view an introductory showcase of a selection of baked goods, see vimeo.com/showcase/6576524.

INTRODUCTION

FOUR CRUCIAL VARIABLES IN BAKING

Four main variables play a major role in successful baking: measuring the flour correctly, understanding flour brands and how to adjust for the different moisture-absorbing capacities between brands, adjusting for oven rack placement, and understanding the impact of different types of baking pans.

1. How to Measure Flour

The recipes in this book give flour measurements by cup, since that is the preferred way of measuring in the United States. Unless otherwise noted in a recipe, always measure the flour un-sifted and fill the cup scantly. To get the scant measure, dip out a cup of flour and then shake off some of the flour so the cup measures in between three-fourths full and full to the rim. After measuring the flour scantly, proceed with the recipe, sifting the flour when the directions give cue.

A half cup, quarter cup, and eighth cup are measured true.

Measuring with cups instead of weighing out the ingredients in grams has certain disadvantages. Some bakers may measure a cup very full while others level the flour with a knife, which can compact the flour. With a compacted measure, a baker could easily end up with one-eighth to one-fourth cup too much flour, which will produce a dense or dry texture. The scant measure protects baked goods from this problem. Adding more flour to a soft, loose dough is much easier than adjusting liquid ingredients to get a lumpy dough back to the correct consistency.

To safeguard against circumstances when bakers accidentally compact the flour or use a highly moisture-absorbent brand, many recipes will reserve some flour before getting started with the process of combining ingredients. This is primarily to prevent adding too much flour. The baker will judge the dough or batter consistency at the end of mixing to see if the reserved flour will be needed. Cues in the recipe provide guidance to help judge consistency. Because flour measurements are so important, chapter introductions also include reminders with flour information relevant to that chapter's dough or batter.

VIDEO SHOWCASE
Baking with Heidrun
vimeo.com/showcase/6576524

2. Flours Vary in Liquid Absorption

Most recipes in this book use unbleached all-purpose flour. Unbleached flour is a natural flour and may not look as white as bleached flour, but since bleached flour is processed with bromine and chlorine to achieve a white look, I prefer the natural color of the grain. Flour for baking Mürbeteige and cakes typically has a protein content of three grams per one-fourth cup (twelve grams per one cup); some pastry flours have even less. Each flour brand absorbs water and other liquids with different capacities, and it is necessary to adjust the flour amount in a recipe according to the brand used. It is often best to find a favorite flour and use it consistently. In doing so, bakers grow accustomed to the adjustments that are needed for a particular brand.

INTRODUCTION

It is my recommendation that bakers start with a brand they are familiar with, providing it has no more than three grams of protein per one-fourth cup (twelve grams per one cup). For example, Gold Medal flour meets this protein count. Protein information is available on the ingredients list of the packaging. Bakers should use their chosen brand (with no more than three grams of protein per one-fourth cup) consistently while growing familiar with the dough and batter consistencies. Once familiar with a recipe, it is easy to switch to other flour brands and make adjustments to the flour amount as necessary to achieve proper consistency (see *"Guidelines to Adjust Flour Amounts"* later in this section).

In the U.S., flour milling is not standardized, and every brand varies. Thus, every flour brand we buy has its own characteristics. This variation is a difference between U.S. and European flour. In Europe, each country has milling standards to which flour mills have to adhere. Flour types have numbers to indicate the protein content and whether the grain is milled with or without the bran. The bran is the outer layer of the wheat kernel. The kernel also consists of the inner white endosperm and the germ, which is the part that grows into a new plant after fertilization. In the processing of the grain, the bran is removed from the kernel, and then partial bran may be added back to the grains before milling. The heavier the flour, the more bran that was added back. Flours from light whole wheat to entire whole wheat flour can be achieved this way. In Europe, these flours are numbered, indicating which types are most suited for which baked good. Lower-number flours have less bran; higher-number flours have more bran.

The number system makes it easy to tell which flour type is best for which type of dough or batter.

The numbers for the German flour are derived by burning one hundred grams of flour at 900°C. What is left are the minerals, and this ash is weighed. The higher the number, the more mineral content in the flour, meaning the flour was milled with partial to whole bran. For example, type 405 flour is a low number on the German scale. It is milled with only the white endosperm (no bran) and has only 405 milligrams of minerals in one hundred grams of flour. Type 405 has a powder-like texture, smoother than flours milled with bran, and is used for delicate baked goods, including pound and sponge cakes, sweet yeast cakes, shortcrusts, and cookies. In my experience in American markets, all-purpose flour with three grams of protein per one-fourth cup is most similar to type 405. Type 550 is for white breads, rolls, and pizza doughs and can be used for sweet yeast cakes as well. Some health-conscious bakers will use type 550 instead of 405 even for their delicate baked goods (550 is milled with some bran) or if they prefer the heavier texture. Type 1050 is wheat flour for breads. There are many more types of flour. The heavier types are grainier, and when rubbed between fingers, the varied feel of smooth and coarse in the flour is obvious. For bread baking, flour types are often mixed to achieve the desired taste and texture, and breads range from light white to heavier whole grain. Vollkorn flour (whole grain flour) is the heaviest. It is milled with the entire wheat kernel and has no type number; it is simply called whole grain flour.

France uses a different numbering system. A few flour types include T45 for shortcrusts, cakes, and

INTRODUCTION

cookies; T55 for white breads, rolls, pizza doughs, and sweet yeast cakes; and T65 for baguettes. Italy has Tipo numbers for flours, including Tipo 00, 0, 1, and 2. Lower numbers have a finer grind than higher numbers.

With these standards in each country, the baker can rely on the numbers and know the flour was milled to these specifications. The countries adhere to their own numbering system, and you will not see the French or Italian numbering system in Germany and vice versa since each country must follow milling specifications for each type of flour. For example, if 00 Italian flour is available in the grocery store in Germany or France, it will have been imported from Italy. The specifications on how to mill flour white or whole wheat are governed by each country's milling laws, and the numbering system pertains to the milling specifications of each country; therefore, the numbering labels are not interchangeable between countries.

Since I have written this book, imported German flours milled to German standards are available online in the United States. They are excellent sources of strong, tasty flour. The websites germanshop24.com and europeandeli.com are well worth exploring for their flours.

Guidelines to Adjust Flour Amounts: Because flour milling is not standardized in the U.S., bakers have to know how to adjust the flour amounts for a recipe to accommodate the specific characteristics of different flour brands. For one brand, you may use exactly the amount indicated in the recipe. For another brand, you may have to use one-fourth cup less for every two cups of flour called for in the recipe. Yet another flour may be highly absorbent compared to other brands and will need even less flour. Some specialty flours like French flour T45 are very close to the absorbency of American all-purpose brands containing three grams of protein per one-fourth cup of flour.

As a general rule, no matter which flour is used, bakers must always be observant to the look, texture, and taste of their work. If a recipe comes out a bit dry for your preference, cut back on the flour the next time. If a recipe comes out too loose and falls apart, add one-eighth to one-fourth cup more flour the next time. Bear in mind that a little added flour goes a long way. Pencil in notes on what you did differently and date the notes. I promise after one or two times of using a favorite flour, you will get baked goods exactly as you fancy.

INTRODUCTION

3. How to Adjust for Oven Rack Placement

Ovens are made in varying sizes and have anywhere from three to seven rungs for rack placement. Heat distribution is also a variable factor. The heat distribution in German ovens is split between the bottom and top coils. In U.S. ovens, the heat generally comes from the bottom coils only, with the top coils kicking in just during preheating or when the oven temperature drops significantly, for example, when the door is open for too long while adjusting a rack or baking pan. These variances have an impact. While my mother in Germany bakes most of her cakes on low rungs, I bake them in the middle or just below the middle in U.S. ovens. Perhaps there are a few cakes that I bake lower with an added cookie sheet underneath to keep the crust from getting too dark.

Even as I have worked to translate German recipes to U.S. kitchens, differing oven sizes containing from three to seven rungs make it difficult to give precise rung placement instructions. I did my best to find the correct rung placement for baking in every oven, and I have used generalized terms to direct a wide variety of bakers who are using a wide variety of ovens. These terms will be one of the following: bottom third of oven, middle of oven, top third of oven.

Individual recipes in this book also offer guidelines for troubleshooting to prevent the tops and bottoms of cakes, pies, and cookies from burning. Some recipes recommend covering just the outer rim of the cake or pie's top to prevent darkening around the edges. Some recipes (such as the Pecan Pie) recommend covering the entire top of the pie with aluminum foil, loosely placed, for the last part of the bake time. A few recipes suggest placing a cookie sheet on the rung below the baking rack to prevent the pastry's bottom from excessive darkening.

With oven rack placement, as with flour measurements, the baker's observation is essential. If you find that the bottom and sides of baked goods consistently get too dark and the top stays pale, the baking rack needs to be placed one rung higher. If the bottom and sides are consistently underbaked, but the entire top (not just the outer rim, which can be easily covered with a pie crust shield—see page 22, "About Pie Crust Shields") gets too brown, then lower the rack by one rung the next time.

4. The Impact of Different Baking Pans

There are many different baking pans on the market, from dark to light metal, to plain aluminum pans, to pans that utilize aluminum with a nonstick coating. Light color metals bake lighter crusts, and dark color metals bake faster and produce darker crusts. There are also nonstick coated steel pans, ceramic pans, glass pans, and silicone forms on the market. Each pan will bake differently, and in general, baking times can vary by ten to fifteen minutes. Therefore, when baking for the first time in a new pan, it is a good idea to set the timer fifteen minutes early and check on the doneness every five minutes thereafter to determine the baking time for that particular pan. For recipes with very short bake times, like cookies, for example, set the timer two minutes early.

In Summary of the Four Crucial Variables

Just as in cooking, there will be some experimenting until bakers find the right amount and type of flour for their taste, the right rung placement in their

INTRODUCTION

home's oven, and the proper baking time for their pans. In this book, I aimed to get as close as I could to ensure consistent baking results. However, due to these four variables, individual decisions have to be made, and I am sure every baker—novice and experienced—is very capable of doing so.

COMMON INGREDIENTS

These ingredients are used in recipes across chapters of this book. Ingredients included here are those that may be unusual or have a particularity that warrants special explanation. Some of the chapter introductions contain additional information about ingredients especially important to that chapter. Some recipes also include ingredient information when noteworthy for that recipe.

Almond Paste

This is a smooth paste traditionally made in Germany of almonds, powdered sugar, and a splash of rose water. Some almond paste preparations may also contain egg whites, honey, some type of syrup, and/or added flavors. U.S. markets often have almond paste available, but store-bought almond paste can sometimes grow hardened or brittle in the packaging, which can make mixing or rolling the paste difficult. Some brands are more pliable than others. If the texture is a problem, combine with one teaspoon of almond extract to make the paste workable. Another option is to remove the almond paste from the packaging, heat in the microwave for twenty seconds, and knead to a soft, workable consistency. Marzipan may be used as a substitute for almond paste. However, be aware that marzipan has a higher sugar content than almond paste. The two almond paste brands readily available in most grocery stores are Odense and Solo, and others are available online.

Baking Powder

Choose an aluminum-free brand. I have had good, consistent results with Rumford brand.

Chocolate

Always use good-quality chocolate for baking and garnishing. Growing up with European chocolates will spoil one's taste in chocolate forever. Fortunately, there are many good-quality European brands readily available to American bakers in stores and online. I have had good success with many of these brands. Lindt from Switzerland has chocolate bars that come in different cocoa butter percentages. Callebaut from Belgium has chocolate chips (called callets) in various percentages of cocoa butter as well, including couverture for glazing cakes. Ghirardelli is an American chocolate manufacturer owned by Lindt that makes

INTRODUCTION

excellent baking chocolate. Chocolove, a company based in Boulder, Colorado, uses Belgian chocolate that is also excellent for baking. Bakers may wish to explore additional chocolate options in their local markets or available online.

Cornstarch and Potato Starch

Tried-and-true brands of cornstarch that have been around for generations have good binding strength and yield excellent results. I use Argo brand with good results. If using a brand with less binding strength, you may need an extra one-half to one tablespoon of cornstarch in recipes. Potato starch may be harder to locate in stores than cornstarch, but it can be obtained easily online or in health food stores. I have found Bob's Red Mill potato starch to work well.

Cream Cheese

Use regular or one-third less fat cream cheese. Fat-free cream cheese does not blend as smoothly.

Eggs

Unless otherwise indicated in a recipe, the egg size is large.

Kirschwasser

Also called cherry water or kirsch, this is a cherry brandy. For best outcomes, use a good-quality kirschwasser. Other brandy flavors such as pear or raspberry can be substituted for kirschwasser as long as they complement the recipe. These types of spirits are hard to find in the U.S. While visiting Oregon, I was lucky to find Clear Creek Distillery in Hood River (hrdspirits.com). Their fruit brandy is as tasty as German brandies. Clear Creek Distillery's brandies are available in select liquor stores and online.

Jams and Jellies

Whether using apricot, red currant, raspberry, or another fruit variety, choose good-quality jams and jellies. The quality makes a difference in taste. Wilkin & Sons and Bonne Maman are two brands I have used in a variety of desserts with good results.

Powdered Sugar

Powdered sugar is milled granulated sugar. It is also called confectioners' sugar or 10x sugar, which means the sugar is fine and sifted ten times. The sweetness of powdered sugar depends on the amount of added starch. Starch is added to prevent the sugar from clumping. The more starch, the less sweet the sugar will be. It is best to buy a good-quality powdered sugar with little starch. In recipes, always start with a little less powdered sugar than called for, to account for the different levels of sweetness. Taste while working and add more if desired. In my experience, tried-and-true brands that have been around for generations, for example, Domino, yield excellent results.

Quark

Quark is a soft cheese, made when milk thickens by fermentation. It has a smooth texture and a mellow flavor, a bit like Greek yogurt but milder. It is a common dairy ingredient in Germany and readily available in stores there. Quark used to be nearly impossible to locate in the States, but natural food stores and some chain retailers now have begun to carry it. In my experience, Vermont Creamery brand quark is available in markets and works

INTRODUCTION

well in baking. Quark can also be made at home. The old-fashioned method—the one my grandmother used—lets unpasteurized raw milk sit on the counter for a few days in a covered bowl. Once the liquid (the whey) begins to separate, scoop the solids into a cheesecloth and tie the cloth to a kitchen cabinet knob with a bowl underneath to catch drips. Let it drip there for a few hours because quark should be as dry as possible. Refrigerate the quark to let it drip overnight. Finally, give the cheesecloth a good wring, and the quark is ready to use in recipes. Making quark at home is a bit harder today than it used to be because it is almost impossible to find fresh unpasteurized cow's milk. However, there are enzymes available to make quark at home with pasteurized milk. These enzymes are available online through specialty retailers like culturesforhealth.com. For a video demonstration of making your own quark, see vimeo.com/showcase/10470112.

Vanilla Sugar

Vanilla sugar is a popular ingredient in German baking. In the States, vanilla sugar can be hard to find in local grocery stores, though some areas now carry it readily. It is also available online through German specialty companies. Bakers can easily make their own vanilla sugar by slicing one vanilla bean open and placing it into a small jar with three cups of powdered sugar or granulated sugar. For stronger flavor, use one vanilla bean per one cup sugar. The sugar will take on the vanilla flavor after two to three days. When it is time to refresh the sugar, check if the vanilla still has flavor. Add another vanilla bean if needed. Scraping out the pulp of a vanilla bean and mixing it with sugar is another method. If using this method, make sure to sift the sugar after mixing in the vanilla seed to remove any lumps. Homemade vanilla sugar may be weaker than commercial brands. Bakers may need to double the amount of vanilla sugar in recipes if using a homemade version, depending on the strength. When using vanilla sugar in recipes, it can always be added at the same time as the plain granulated or powdered sugar.

VIDEO SHOWCASE
Fillings and Garnishs
vimeo.com/showcase/10470112

COMMON TECHNIQUES

These techniques are used in recipes in several chapters of the book. Chapter introductions contain additional information about techniques particularly important to that chapter.

Blanching Almonds

Blanching removes the skin from an almond. Place the almonds into a pot and cover with water. Bring to a simmer and simmer for about two minutes. Take off heat and let the almonds and water cool in the pot until the water is still warm but almonds are cool enough to handle, about five minutes. Test one almond first: Place it on a dish towel and rub with the towel or take the almond between fingers and squeeze gently. The almond should pop out of the skin easily. Work quickly to squeeze each almond from its skin; leave other almonds in the still-warm water while working. If they cool too much, peeling will become difficult. Work in a place with a

INTRODUCTION

backsplash, or the almonds will fly off the counter. Let blanched almonds dry on a kitchen towel. When completely dry, they can be ground into almond meal or into finer flour. Blanched almond flour or meal has a milder flavor and lighter texture than unblanched. Whole blanched almonds can also be used as a garnish on pies, cakes, cookies, or a gingerbread house.

Grinding Whole Nuts into Nut Meal and Nut Flour

Freshly ground nuts impart more flavor than store-bought nut meals and flours. Nut meals are milled more coarsely while nut flours are milled more finely. Nut meals are suitable for recipes with a medium or medium-to-fine grind. Nut flours, which have a fine or super-fine grind, are best as a substitution for all-purpose flour (for example, to make gluten-free crusts and cakes). The consistency of store-bought nut meals and nut flours varies by brand and the method used to mill the product. Many commercially ground nut meals and flours available in the States are much finer than what home bakers can produce with their kitchen machines. The finer the milling, the more absorbent the meal or flour will be. For example, one cup of whole nuts, coarsely ground at home, produces about one and one-third cups of meal, which will have the same absorbency as one cup of finely ground, store-bought meal. Store-bought, super-fine nut flour will be even more absorbent.

It is my recommendation to grind nuts at home whenever possible. Grinding nuts yourself is the best way to get the correct consistency. There are nut grinders on the market that can grind both medium and fine, not just fine. Options include hand-crank nut grinders and electric grinders for nuts and spices. Handheld coffee grinders with a propeller-type blade (not a burr grinder) work also. If using an electric grinder, fill halfway. Pulse to grind for medium-consistency nut meal. For fine consistency or for nut flour to replace all-purpose flour in cakes and pastries, hold the button down to grind, stop and stir, then grind again until finely milled.

In recipes calling for nut flour or nut meal, start with less and adjust as needed depending on the consistency of the nut flour or meal. Try to avoid substituting nut meal for nut flour in a recipe and vice versa. Doing so may change the consistency of a batter or dough and impact the texture of the baked product. If substitution cannot be avoided, remember to take into account the different absorption capacities. The varying absorbency is more of a worry with nut flour than it is with nut meal.

INTRODUCTION

Roasting Nut Meal and Nut Flour

Roasting nut meal and nut flour gives a deeper flavor. Heat a skillet over medium to medium-high. Add the meal or flour into the skillet and flatten it down with a spatula. Stir and flip the meal or flour regularly, for about five minutes, so it toasts evenly. If smoke starts to develop, the skillet is too hot. If that happens, remove from heat for a brief time and continue stirring, then return to heat as needed, with the temperature reduced as needed. Aim for golden brown, not dark brown. If the meal or flour darkens too much, it will become bitter. Know that nut flour is finer than nut meal and can burn easier.

Roasting Whole Nuts

Place whole nuts onto an ungreased cookie sheet. Place sheet on a rack in the top third of the oven (one rung above middle) and bake at 350°F for about ten to fifteen minutes. Shake and turn halfway through the roasting process. Let cool, then grind into nut meal.

Browning Crumbs

The German word for a crumb topping is "streusel," which means "dough strewn about." Streusel is heavy in sugar and butter, which is why the crumbs taste so good and add a special touch to pastries. Crumb toppings on cakes and pies should bake only to golden brown. If crumbs start to get too brown during baking, especially around the pan's edges, cover the rim for the last twenty minutes with a pie crust shield (see page 22, "About Pie Crust Shields"). This kind of shield works with cakes too. The shield will protect the crumbs around the edges, where heat concentrates. On the other hand, if the cake or pie is done but the crumbs have not browned to your liking, broil for thirty seconds. Watch closely and do not leave. The crumbs can look pale for several seconds and then burn quickly.

Melting Chocolate

Use good-quality chocolate chips or chocolate bar (broken into pieces) (see page 11 in the "Common Ingredients"). Melt chocolate in a microwave or on the stovetop in a double boiler or bain-marie. For both methods, watch carefully as chocolate will not be usable if it overheats and seizes (balls up).

If melting in a microwave, heat for thirty to forty seconds. Stop and stir. Then heat for another thirty to forty seconds. Some solid pieces will remain, but they will dissolve while stirring. The chocolate

Bain-marie or double boiler

INTRODUCTION

is done when it stirs easily and has a smooth consistency. Depending on the microwave, time can vary by ten seconds. Start with the lower time and increase if necessary. In my own microwave, I have good luck microwaving for thirty seconds, stirring the chocolate, then microwaving for an additional forty seconds.

If melting chocolate in a double boiler or bain-marie, fill water in the bottom pot, just enough so the water doesn't touch the upper pot. Bring water to a low simmer and then place the chocolate into the top pot. Stir frequently and carefully to achieve the smooth consistency. Take care not to get any water in the chocolate. Chocolate can seize up into a ball and be rendered useless if overheated or even a drop of water falls into the chocolate.

Straining Jam, Preserves, or Marmalade

Certain types of jam, preserves, and marmalade have seeds or lumps, which some bakers prefer to remove for a smoother texture. To remove, strain through a small strainer, pushing and stirring with the back of a spoon. Occasionally scrape the underside of the strainer to loosen up any accumulation.

Whipping Egg Whites

First, always make sure that hands, mixing bowls, and beaters are free of egg yolk, oil, and butter, or the egg whites will not whip. Copper bowls work best for whipping egg whites. Recipes may call for egg whites whipped to soft peaks, firm peaks, or stiff peaks. Whipping egg whites to soft peaks will take a very short time with an electric mixer on medium to high speed. Whipping to firm peaks takes a bit longer. Whipping to stiff peaks takes the longest.

While learning to judge the peaks, use the whisk test. Scoop up some of the whipped whites with a whisk and turn it over. Soft peaks are the loosest. They hold their shape on the end of the whisk, but the top will flop over like a droopy elf's hat. Firm whites should hold a more defined peak than soft whites, but the peak will still fall over slightly at the

Soft peaks

Firm peaks

Stiff peaks

INTRODUCTION

top. Stiff peaks are the sharpest. They should stand straight up on the whisk like a witch's hat. Be vigilant. It is easy to overbeat the egg whites with an electric mixer. Overbeaten egg whites will look curdled and flake away in chunks rather than having a smooth consistency. Overbeaten egg whites can be saved by adding a new egg white and beating just enough to get the smooth look back.

The freshness of the eggs will also impact whipping. The fresher the eggs, the faster they whip. Fresh eggs will whip up in just over a minute and are less likely to end up over-whipped.

Zesting Lemons

Use a rasp-style grater or zester to rasp off the outer rind, avoiding the white membrane.

Disclaimer

Throughout the recipes in this book, I mention the names of certain brands of ingredients solely to identify those that I have used and determined to provide good results for successful desserts. Your results may vary based on your experimentation with other brands or based on your personal preference. None of the owners of the brands mentioned contributed to, sponsored, endorsed, or should be understood by mention of their brand names to be associated with this book or the recipes or instructions in it.

MÜRBETEIGE 1

The word "Mürbeteig" (the plural form in German is "Mürbeteige") is compounded from the words *mürbe* and *teig* and translates from German to English as "shortcrust." This translation is not exact. *Teig* means dough. Translations for the word *mürbe* are soft, tender, delicate, easily falls apart, or crumbly. These words help us to envision the consistency of this type of dough. While shortcrust typically contains just flour, butter, a little salt, and perhaps some ice-cold water, Mürbeteig traditionally contains butter, sugar, flour, a dash of salt, egg, and sometimes a small amount of baking powder and flavoring. The result is a delicate yet durable pastry crust, ready to use as a canvas for pies, tarts, and cheesecakes.

Throughout this chapter, the precise ratio of ingredients in the Mürbeteig varies by recipe to complement the taste and texture of the filling and to provide for the size of the baking pan, as well as the dough needed for lattice or top crusts. Nevertheless, the technique for forming the dough is consistent, and every recipe in this chapter begins with that technique. The General Tips and Tricks portion of this introduction explains the technique.

Apple Crumb Pie 25	Pumpkin Cheesecake 69
Covered Apple Pie .29	Pear Frangipane Tart .72
Apple Pie 33	Apricot Almond Cream Tart 77
Mixed Berry Pie 38	Raspberry Almond Tart 81
Strawberry Rhubarb Pie 43	Almond Hazelnut Mini Tarts 85
Pumpkin Pie 48	Linzer Torte 89
Pecan Pie 52	Tarte Tatin 94
Ricotta Cheesecake 56	Apfelstrudel (Apple Strudel) 102
Traditional German Cheesecake with Quark . . . 60	Almond or Hazelnut Crust 109
Liliko'i Cheesecake 64	Cherry Turnovers 112

CHAPTER 1

PREPARATION TIME

For new bakers, preparing a Mürbeteig may take upward of fifteen minutes. Once bakers have grown accustomed to the technique, they can have a Mürbeteig crust prepared in under five minutes. Working quickly is important to keep the butter cool, but do not let time force too much pressure. Leisure is a great luxury in baking.

Mürbeteig dough also needs time to chill before molding it into the baking dish or pan. For each recipe in this chapter, chill dough for thirty minutes, except for the *Apfelstrudel* (Apple Strudel) dough, which rests under a heated pot for thirty minutes instead. Preparing the fillings will usually take about that length of time, for some pies, a bit longer. For that reason, always prepare the crust before preparing the filling.

Recipes that call for a lattice or top crust will take additional time. Be patient with rolling, cutting, and transferring the dough in those recipes. Should the dough get sticky, form it into a ball and refrigerate for ten to fifteen more minutes, then reroll. Repeat this process more than once if need be. Shrug off those first attempts; sprinkle more flour onto the dough, rolling pin, and blade; and have another go.

GENERAL TIPS AND TRICKS

How to Measure Flour

Flour measurements for all Mürbeteig recipes are based on unbleached all-purpose flour with protein content of three grams per one-fourth cup (twelve grams per one cup). Measure the flour un-sifted and fill the cup scantly. To get the scant measure, dip out a cup of flour and then shake off some of the flour so the cup measures somewhere between three-fourths full and full to the rim. Before getting started with a Mürbeteig recipe, please read "Four Crucial Variables in Baking" starting on page 7, with special attention to the first variable's extended explanation on measuring flour, as well as the "Guidelines to Adjust Flour Amounts" (see page 9).

For Mürbeteig recipes, always set aside one-fourth cup of the measured flour to use as needed while forming the dough. Reserving some of the measured flour is a safeguard against adding too much flour into the dough. Bakers will judge the dough texture as they work to determine whether the reserved flour is needed. Reserved flour may be necessary if the dough is very sticky. Many factors can contribute to sticky dough, including humidity in the environment and quality of the ingredients. These factors vary from kitchen to kitchen, so be flexible to the dough's needs as you bake. Also keep in mind that different brands of flour have different capacities for liquid absorption, which affects how much of the reserved flour the dough will need. In all likelihood, bakers will need all the reserved flour. However, when using different flour brands, bakers may need only some of the reserved flour or none at all.

Keep Extra Flour Nearby

In addition to the flour amount called for in the recipe ingredients, have a small bowl with extra flour on hand to use as needed while rolling out the dough and pressing it into the form. Sprinkle the extra flour, sparingly and only as much as needed, onto the dough, work surface, rolling pin, and/or hands if the dough becomes sticky during this process.

MÜRBETEIGE

Technique to Prepare Mürbeteig Dough

A video demonstration of the start-to-finish process of making a Mürbeteig crust is available at vimeo.com/showcase/10471286. An additional video of the specific technique to cut butter (explained later in this section) is also included. Cold butter is essential for successful Mürbeteig. To keep butter cold, bakers need to work efficiently and limit the dough's contact with warm hands. The work surface and a metal dough scraper will be great allies in the effort to keep butter cold while cutting and incorporating it.

VIDEO SHOWCASE
Mürbeteig
vimeo.com/showcase/10471286

VIDEO SHOWCASE
How to Cut Butter
vimeo.com/886179797

A pastry or cutting board, preferably marble, will be the work surface. The bigger the board, the better. Use it as an all-in-one space to measure out, cut, and combine. First, sift the flour onto the board and make a well (a deep indentation) in the middle. Add the sugar, egg, and flavorings into the well's center, and then it is time to get the chilled butter. Place the cold butter on the board, alongside the well. Loosely roll the butter in the flour at the edges of the well. Dip the dough scraper into the flour too. This will prevent the butter from sticking to the metal as it cuts.

How to Cut Butter: A video demonstration of the technique described here is available at vimeo.com/886179797.

Cut the sticks of butter, lengthwise, into three sections. Loosely dip the butter sections in the flour. Dip the blade into the flour again. Stack the butter sections back together and repeat the cuts so that you have nine thin, rectangular strips. Keeping the strips stacked, start at one end to cut one-fourth-inch to one-half-inch pieces until all the butter is cut. Sprinkle the butter chunks over the edge of the flour well.

Once the butter is cut and sprinkled around the edge, use the dough scraper to stir the egg in the well's center gently as if scrambling it and then carefully begin to collapse the flour walls into the well's center. This will prevent the egg from running away. Using the blade, chop the butter pieces on the well's edge while working them into the flour. Ingredients will naturally spread out over the board as they are worked and combined. Scrape them back to center and continue chopping. Patience is crucial. Use the dough scraper as long as possible, until the butter pieces are at least half their size or smaller, before continuing by hand.

Finish combining the dough with your hands. Squeeze, gather, and press the dough. It may take several minutes before a ball forms. When butter pieces are barely visible, use the heel of your hand to push the dough out on the work surface and then fold it back on itself. Have fun with this part. Spending time with the dough and really working it is how bakers get to know the dough. It connects bakers to what they are creating. Over time, you will be able to tell when the dough is combined fully by its feel. You will gain an innate sense for

CHAPTER 1

whether the dough is too sticky and needs a sprinkle of more flour or a rest in the refrigerator, or if it is just right.

If the dough continues to stick to the work surface and hands after working for a few minutes to combine ingredients and the butter is mostly incorporated, add another tablespoon of flour. On the other hand, if the dough has too much flour, is brittle, and does not hold together as a ball, add milk or water, but be restrained because even a small amount of liquid can make the dough too sticky again. To avoid the battle of too dry and then too sticky, opt for adding more butter instead of more liquid. Adding more butter when necessary generally seems to work out better in most circumstances.

About Pie Crust Shields

If a crust's edge appears to be darkening too much during baking before the filling is done, a pie crust shield will protect the edges. Inexpensive pie crust shields are available at culinary retailers, home goods stores, and most all-purpose stores. Some crafty bakers also construct their own out of aluminum foil. For a homemade ten-inch pie crust shield, cut aluminum foil into a circle fourteen inches in diameter. Then cut out a six-inch circle in the middle.

About Work Surfaces

A cold surface is needed for working Mürbeteig dough. A marble stone board is best to keep the dough cool.

About Baking Pans and Pie Dishes

Some of the recipes in this chapter bake in a springform pan, an aluminum cheesecake pan with a removable bottom, or a special tart or torte pan. Other recipes call for baking in a pie dish. Options abound when it comes to size, material, and shape of pie dishes. Buying a quality dish from a kitchen store rather than just picking one up at the grocery store makes a big difference. In general, for both baking pans and pie dishes, dark metal or carbon-coated metal will bake pies and cakes five to ten minutes faster than ceramic or uncoated aluminum. In the end, it does not really matter what type of pan or dish the baker uses, as long as they adjust baking time depending on the material and as long as the pan or dish is deep enough for the recipe.

An aluminum cheesecake pan with a removable bottom is my personal favorite for my tall cheesecakes and the traditional German Covered Apple Pie, which has more of a cake-like shape. My favorite dish for big pies is an off-white porcelain clay stoneware dish with blue accenting stripes and scalloped edges. It measures 10 x 2½ inches and bakes up crunchy, golden crusts with plenty of room for deep fillings. I often leave the pie in it for cooling and serving because the porcelain clay does not scratch the way metal does when cutting and serving slices. I bought the dish at a country western store in Texas that has been around since 1899. It looks old-fashioned and reminds me of the times when pies were cooked over the open fire hearth. It was a sentimental buy that turned out to be my best pie dish. For smaller, shallower pies, I have a metal quiche pan that measures 9½ x 2 inches, and I have a red ceramic dish with gently ridged edging that measures 9 x 2 inches. These two dishes have straight sides so I can fit a ten-inch crust recipe in them. Most nine-inch pans have slanted sides, which reduces the diameter at the bottom. Those

MÜRBETEIGE

pie pans will not hold all the filling, and the crust will be thicker. Pie recipes in this book are for ten-inch pie dishes.

However, since I wrote this book, a variety of nine-inch pie dishes are being sold more and more by retailers. Therefore, I am including ingredients for a basic nine-inch crust recipe here. If you have a shallow or slanted nine-inch pie dish, this crust can be substituted for any of the Mürbeteig doughs in this chapter. There will be filling left over, of course, but the next tip addresses that issue. This nine-inch pie crust recipe is for a bottom crust only. For a nine-inch pie with a top crust or lattice, double the recipe. Alternatively, make the bottom crust with the first recipe and the lattice with the second recipe. The second recipe swaps the egg for water, which creates a sturdier crust for lattice.

NINE-INCH PIE CRUST RECIPE

¾ cup all-purpose flour (protein 3 grams per ¼ cup; see page 7)

¼ teaspoon baking powder

⅛ cup sugar

1 egg

4 tablespoons butter

1 teaspoon vanilla, or 2 teaspoons vanilla sugar

To prepare the crust, use the method described previously in "Technique to Prepare Mürbeteig Dough" (see page 21), then follow the instructions in any recipe. If baking the crust without filling, bake for 20 minutes at 325°F on a rack in the middle of the oven. If baking the crust with a filling, bake according to the time and temperature instructions provided for the filling you are preparing.

SPECIAL CRUST RECIPE FOR STURDY LATTICE

¾ cup all-purpose flour (protein 3 grams per ¼ cup; see page 7)

¼ teaspoon baking powder

⅛ cup sugar

3 tablespoons water

4 tablespoons butter

1 teaspoon vanilla, or 2 teaspoons vanilla sugar

To prepare the dough, use the method described previously in "Technique to Prepare Mürbeteig Dough" (see page 21). Bake according to the time and temperature instructions provided for the pie you are preparing. This crust produces a sturdy lattice that holds its shape well.

What to Do with Extra Filling

If there is extra filling, try to repurpose it. Extra fruit fillings can be heated in a saucepan to a slow boil (stirring all the while) and puréed to use as a topping on ice cream, oatmeal, yogurt, or waffles. Bake extra pumpkin pie filling on its own into soft pumpkin bites in muffin tins lined with cupcake paper or mix it into pancake or waffle batter. Transform extra custard-type fillings, like that of the Apricot Almond Cream Tart, into pancakes, as well, with the addition of flour. Innovate. A tasty creation will likely come of it.

CHAPTER 1

Bakers can also freeze leftover filling of any kind in freezer bags to have on hand for puff pastry turnovers, which are a fast treat when unexpected guests come. To make the turnovers, buy puff pastry sheets, let thaw, and roll out to a larger and thinner square shape of 15 x 15 inches. Cut into nine squares (each measuring 5 x 5 inches). Imagine a diagonal line running through each square, creating two equal-sized triangles. Add a tablespoon of filling near, but slightly offset from, that imaginary center line. Brush all sides with an egg white wash, fold over to create a triangle, press the edges together, and bake. The last recipe of this chapter makes turnovers from puff pastry and a cherry filling. Bakers can adapt that recipe for leftover pie fillings or any other fillings of their choosing.

VIDEO SHOWCASE
Mürbeteig
vimeo.com/showcase/10471286

RECOMMENDED TOOLS

- Large pastry board (marble preferred), wooden cutting board, or butcher block
- Metal dough scraper or broad, non-serrated knife
- Pie crust shield
- Springform pan
- Pie dishes, good quality
- Measuring spoons
- Measuring cups
- Sifter
- Silicone baking mat, with marked sizing rings (to help with measuring when rolling out dough)
- Pastry sock (to slip over rolling pin and prevent dough from sticking)
- Lemon zest rasp
- Cake lifter (called a *kuchenretter* in German), very useful for lifting whole pies from springform bases
- Pastry wheel cutter (for recipes with lattice)

APPLE CRUMB PIE

It does not take exotic ingredients or a complex technique to produce a stunning and satisfying apple pie. This pie makes use of common kitchen staples—you may very well have all the items in your pantry at this very moment. Meanwhile, the crumb topping and the glaze in the filling add impressive touches with minimal fuss. For the apples, if you live in an area with a specialty produce store or, better yet, with orchards growing European heirloom apples, you may be able to find Gravenstein, Belle de Boskoop, Renette, or Pippins such as Cox's Orange. These are the preferred varieties to bake with in Europe. Braeburn or Granny Smith also make a good choice, either on their own or mixed with Jonathan, Winesap, Golden Delicious, Pink Lady, Fuji, or Jonagold. Different apple varieties give different results and can be fun to experiment with. If serving the pie hot, consider adding a scoop of ice cream or an extra drizzle of glaze to melt over the slices. The pie is equally delicious served cold or at room temperature.

APPLE CRUMB PIE

BAKING PAN
10 x 3-inch springform pan, buttered and floured

Baking time may be shortened if a steel-based pan is used rather than aluminum; dark pans bake faster than light pans.

BAKING TEMPERATURE
350°F

BAKE TIME
1 hour and 25 minutes

RACK PLACEMENT
bottom third of oven, just below middle

Place a heavy cookie sheet on bottom rung to keep crust from getting too dark.

YIELD
one 10-inch pie

INGREDIENTS

FOR CRUST

2 ¼ cups unbleached all-purpose flour (protein 3 grams per ¼ cup; see page 7), plus extra for working dough

1 teaspoon baking powder

Pinch of salt (about ⅛ teaspoon or less)

⅔ cup sugar

1 egg

12 tablespoons (1 ½ sticks) unsalted butter, cold

FOR FILLING

8 medium apples (about 2 ½ to 3 pounds)

Juice of 1 small lemon (about 2 tablespoons)

FOR FILLING GLAZE

4 ounces apricot or raspberry jam

2 tablespoons orange liqueur or *kirschwasser*

FOR CRUMBS

1 ¾ cups unbleached all-purpose flour (protein 3 grams per ¼ cup; see page 7)

½ teaspoon cinnamon

1 cup sugar

12 tablespoons (1 ½ sticks) unsalted butter, cold

MÜRBETEIGE

DIRECTIONS

1. Prepare the crust: Set aside ¼ cup of the measured flour to use as needed while working the dough and pressing it into the form. Sift the remaining flour and baking powder onto a large marble or wooden board. Form a well in the middle and sprinkle the salt around the edge. Add the sugar and egg into the well. Cut the butter into small pieces, approximately ¼ to ½ inch (see page 21, "How to Cut Butter," in "Technique to Prepare Mürbeteig Dough"). Distribute the pieces over and around the flour. Using the tip of a metal dough scraper, stir the egg as if gently scrambling. Begin carefully pushing the dry ingredients into the well's center. Work to combine all ingredients, first with the dough scraper and then with your hands, until a ball of dough forms. Add flour sparingly or chill as necessary if the dough becomes too sticky.

2. Refrigerate the dough for 30 minutes.

3. Position a rack in the bottom third of the oven (just below middle) and preheat to 350°F. Butter and flour the pan in preparation for assembly. Set aside.

4. Prepare the filling: Peel, core, and quarter the apples. Cut the quarters, lengthwise, into thirds. Place into a large bowl and sprinkle with lemon juice to prevent browning. Stir to coat. Set aside.

5. Prepare the filling glaze: Whisk together the jam and the orange liqueur or kirschwasser. Set aside.

6. Prepare the crumb dough: Sift the flour and cinnamon onto a large marble or wooden board. Make a well in the middle and add the sugar. Cut the butter into small pieces, approximately ¼ to ½ inch (see page 21, "How to Cut Butter," in "Technique to Prepare Mürbeteig Dough"). Distribute the pieces over and around the flour. Work the butter into the dry ingredients, first with a metal dough scraper, then finish with your hands (see tip 1). Alternatively, use a large bowl and form crumbs by hand without a metal dough scraper.

~ TIP 1 ~

At first, it may seem like there is too much flour. Keep at it, and the crumbs will begin to form. If the crumbs are very buttery, sprinkle over a bit more flour, a little at a time. If they are too buttery, they will run flat during baking. If there is too much flour, cut up 1 to 2 more tablespoons of butter to add; one tablespoon goes a long way.

7. Form crumbs: Squeeze fistfuls of dough into palms to combine the ingredients. Crumble the mixture and further incorporate the butter pieces by grabbing fistfuls of dough and squeezing against palms, while moving thumbs upward and fingers downward along the palm. The dough will fall onto the work surface in chunks. Keep doing this motion, picking up dough, squeezing and crumbling with fingers against palms, and letting pieces drop as you go along. Pieces should range in size from coarse

APPLE CRUMB PIE

graham cracker crumbs to small peas to some as large as dimes. Crumbs need not be perfectly uniform in size. Variety produces a rustic effect.

8. Mold dough into pan: Slice the chilled dough horizontally into four discs. Lay the discs into the prepared pan so they lean partially against the sides. The pieces may overlap. With flour-dipped fingers, push the dough out, rather than pressing it down, to cover the pan evenly. Pull dough up on the sides about three-fourths of the way. Even out any thin spots to get the dough to a fairly consistent thickness.

9. Assemble for baking: Starting at the crust's edge, arrange the apple slices in overlapping concentric circles with the core-side facing the pan's center. There will be more than one layer of apples. Keep layering until all the apples are used, or until you nearly reach the top of the crust. Spoon the filling glaze over the apples. Sprinkle the crumbs over the top.

10. Bake for 1 hour and 25 minutes, until the crumbs are golden brown (see tip 2). Insert a wooden skewer gently between the crust and rim to check doneness. The crust should be firm and should lift away from the rim without leaving dough on the skewer. Also insert the skewer through the pie's center. There may be some juice on it, but it should not present underbaked dough. The apples should be soft. Serve hot or cold.

~ TIP 2 ~

If crumbs start to get too brown during baking, especially around the edges, cover the rim for the last 20 minutes with a pie crust shield (see page 22, "About Pie Crust Shields"). The shield will protect the crumbs around the edges, where heat concentrates. On the other hand, if the pie is done but the crumbs have not browned to your liking, broil for 30 seconds. Watch closely and do not leave. The crumbs can look pale for several seconds and then burn quickly.

COVERED APPLE PIE

Growing up in Germany, I spent birthdays, holidays, and special occasions with my extended family. On these occasions, my mother, aunt, and grandmother all pitched in with the baking. Knowing my love of pastries, they joked and wagered on which dessert I would choose. "Oh, I think Heidrun is going to have the cheesecake," my mom would say, lobbying for her pastry. "No, she will pick the apple pie," my aunt would parry in favor of her dessert. I loved (and continue to love) my mom's cheesecake, but my aunt was right. If there was an apple pastry on the table, that's the one I would always go for first. Of course, sampling cheesecake was next, but apple pastries were my number one love. They still are.

This pie is one of my all-time favorite apple treats. It's a tall, fat, cakey pie stuffed to the rim and bursting with a mix of apple varieties. The currants (or raisins) give a surprising pop of sweet mixed with the savory slivers of almonds. You will need about three pounds of apples total. The recipe suggests a combination of Pink Lady, Granny Smith, and Fuji for a mix of sweet and tangy, but take liberty with your own taste. The pie is forgiving. If using just one apple variety, Braeburns make a tasty pie. Apples should be just ripe or slightly under ripe. Some regions in the U.S. with apple orchards grow European heirloom apples. If you can find them, you might try some of the favorite varieties we bake with in Europe. These include Gravenstein, Belle de Boskoop, Renette, or Pippins such as Cox's Orange.

COVERED APPLE PIE

BAKING PAN
10 x 3-inch springform pan, buttered and floured

Baking time may be shortened if a steel-based pan is used rather than aluminum; dark pans bake faster than light pans.

BAKING TEMPERATURE
350°F

BAKE TIME
1 hour and 25 minutes to 1 hour and 35 minutes

RACK PLACEMENT
bottom third of oven

Place a heavy cookie sheet on bottom rung to keep crust from getting too dark.

YIELD
one 10-inch pie

INGREDIENTS

FOR CRUST

2 ½ cups unbleached all-purpose flour (protein 3 grams per ¼ cup; see page 7), plus extra for working dough

2 ½ teaspoons baking powder

Pinch of salt (about ⅛ teaspoon or less)

⅔ cup sugar

2 eggs

1 teaspoon vanilla sugar, or ½ teaspoon vanilla extract

16 tablespoons (2 sticks) unsalted butter, cold

FOR FILLING

3 pounds Braeburn apples; or 3 pounds apples of different varieties, for example:
    3 Pink Lady apples (1 pound)
    3 Granny Smith apples (1 pound)
    3 to 4 Fuji apples (1 pound)

3 tablespoons lemon juice or lime juice

½ cup sliced or thinly slivered almonds (thickly slivered almonds will remain somewhat crunchy)

2 teaspoons cinnamon

½ cup dried currants or raisins

1 tablespoon rum

1 tablespoon almond liqueur, or 1 teaspoon almond extract

2 tablespoons cornstarch

½ cup sugar

FOR SUGAR GLAZE

1 ½ cups powdered sugar

3 teaspoons lemon juice

3 teaspoons rum or water

MÜRBETEIGE

DIRECTIONS

1. Prepare the crust: Set aside ¼ cup of the measured flour to use as needed while working the dough, pressing it into the form, and rolling the top crust. Sift the remaining flour and baking powder onto a large marble or wooden board (see tip 1). Form a well in the middle and sprinkle the salt around the edge. Add the sugar, eggs, and vanilla into the well. Cut the butter into small pieces, approximately ¼ to ½ inch (see page 21, "How to Cut Butter," in "Technique to Prepare Mürbeteig Dough"). Distribute the pieces over and around the flour. Using the tip of a metal dough scraper, stir the egg as if gently scrambling. Begin carefully pushing the dry ingredients into the well's center. Work to combine all ingredients, first with the dough scraper and then with your hands, until a ball of dough forms. Add flour sparingly or chill as necessary if the dough becomes too sticky.

~ TIP 1 ~

This dough has a good bit of flour. It may even initially feel like there is too much flour, but keep at it, squeezing the dough with the palms of your hands, folding, and pushing it down. Remember this recipe makes more dough than others because there must be enough for both bottom and top crusts.

2. Refrigerate the dough for 30 minutes.

3. Make the filling: Peel, core, and quarter the apples. Cut the apple quarters in half, lengthwise, and then start chopping from one end into small pieces, about ¼ inch in size. A food processor julienne disc or small french fry disc works well also. Place the apple pieces into a large mixing bowl. Stir in the lemon juice or lime juice. Add the slivered almonds, cinnamon, dried currants or raisins, rum, and almond liqueur or almond extract. Mix thoroughly. Sift in the cornstarch. Mix again and set aside. Save the sugar for step 6.

4. Position a rack in the bottom third of the oven. Preheat to 350°F. Butter and flour the pan in preparation for assembly.

5. Mold bottom crust into pan: Remove dough from the refrigerator. Slice off two-thirds. Place the remaining one-third back into the refrigerator. Slice the two-thirds piece horizontally into three discs. Lay the discs into the prepared pan so they lean partially against the sides. The pieces may overlap. With flour-dipped fingers, push the dough out, rather than pressing it down, to cover the pan evenly. Pull the dough up the pan's side about three-fourths of the way. Even out any thin spots to get the dough to a fairly consistent thickness.

6. Add the sugar into the filling, give it a stir, and spread into the crust.

7. Roll top crust: Dust a marble or wooden board with flour. Remove the remaining dough from the refrigerator. Rub flour onto the rolling pin and work surface and sprinkle flour sparingly

COVERED APPLE PIE

over the dough if necessary. Roll the dough until it is slightly bigger than the diameter of the pan. The rolled dough should be ¼-inch thick or less. Gently loosen the bottom of the dough from the board with a flour-dipped dough scraper, and transfer to the top of the pie (see tip 2). Press along the edges to form a seal between the top and bottom crusts. Make a cross-shaped slit in the middle of the top crust for a vent.

~ TIP 2 ~

Use a rolling pin for assistance. Place the rolling pin on top of the dough at the edge. As you loosen the dough, roll it over the rolling pin and then unroll it over the filling. If the dough sticks to the board or tears during transfer, gather it back into a ball, sprinkle a bit more flour onto the dough, board, and rolling pin, and try again. Do not worry if you have to attempt rolling and transferring a couple times.

8. Bake for 1 hour and 25 minutes to 1 hour and 35 minutes, until the top is golden brown (see tip 3). Insert a wooden skewer gently between the crust and rim to check doneness. The crust should be firm and lift away from the rim without leaving dough on the skewer. Also insert the skewer through the pie's center. The apples should be soft, and the top and bottom crusts should be set. There may be a little juice on the skewer, but it should be mostly clean.

~ TIP 3 ~

If the pie starts to get too brown during baking, especially around the edges, cover the rim for the last 20 minutes with a pie crust shield (see page 22, "About Pie Crust Shields"). The shield will protect the edge, where heat concentrates.

9. Serve the pie while still warm or after cooling. Brush with sugar glaze before serving.

Directions for Sugar Glaze

Whisk together the powdered sugar, lemon juice, and rum or water to a thick but still fluid consistency. If a thicker icing is desired, add more powdered sugar. If too thick, add more liquid, just a few drops at a time.

APPLE PIE

This pie is a near twin to the Covered Apple Pie. It uses the same flavors and ingredients, but there is a crucial difference in the size. The Covered Apple Pie bakes in a 10 x 3-inch springform pan. In appearance, that pie is more like a cake. In Germany, pies are much taller than most Americans think of when they hear "pie," and German pies traditionally bake with more filling. The taste will win anyone over. Shallower pies are more common in North America and Britain. I don't know what it is about pies in America, but whenever a baker says, "I'll make a pie," heads go up and eyes twinkle. So, here is a recipe designed for a shallower dish than the pan used in the Covered Apple Pie. The dimensions of this recipe are more in line with the American concept of pie. I felt it important to include both.

For the apples, if you live in an area with a specialty produce store or, better yet, with orchards growing European heirloom apples, you may be able to find Gravenstein, Belle de Boskoop, Renette, or Pippins such as Cox's Orange. These are the preferred varieties to bake with in Europe. Otherwise pick apples with a bright, citrusy taste such as Fuji, Pink Lady, Granny Smith, Koru, Jonagold, or Gala. A mix of several varieties pronounces the apple most efficiently. The recipe also holds back on sugar to highlight the natural fruit flavor. Limited sugar is how we like it in Germany. If you crave more sweetness, add sugar to taste in the filling. But use a deft hand as there is also a sugar glaze with the recipe. Extra garnishes of whipped cream and powdered sugar or ice cream will bring more sweetness too. The slivered

APPLE PIE

almonds may also be unusual to some American eaters, perhaps an acquired texture. They remain a little al dente. If that texture is not desired, omit them or chop into even finer slices. Finally, do not neglect the egg wash over the lattice. It gives the crust a crunchy finish.

BAKING PAN
10 x 2-inch ceramic pie dish, buttered and floured

BAKING TEMPERATURE
350°F

BAKE TIME
1 hour and 25 minutes

RACK PLACEMENT
middle of oven

If using a metal pie dish instead of ceramic, place a heavy cookie sheet on bottom rung to keep crust from getting too dark and to catch overflowing juices.

YIELD
one 10-inch pie (see page 23 for a 9-inch pie crust)

INGREDIENTS

FOR CRUST (see *note* at end of recipe)

1 ⅔ cups unbleached all-purpose flour (protein 3 grams per ¼ cup; see page 7), plus extra for working dough

¾ teaspoon baking powder

Pinch of salt (about ⅛ teaspoon or less)

½ cup sugar

1 egg

1 teaspoon vanilla sugar, or ½ teaspoon vanilla extract

8 tablespoons (1 stick) unsalted butter, cold

FOR FILLING

4 to 5 large apples (2 pounds)

5 tablespoons lemon juice

⅓ cup sugar

2 teaspoons cinnamon

¾ cup slivered almonds

⅔ cup dried currants or raisins

1 tablespoon rum

1 tablespoon almond liqueur, or 1 teaspoon almond extract

2 tablespoons cornstarch or potato starch

FOR EGG WASH

1 egg white

1 teaspoon almond extract

FOR SUGAR GLAZE

1 cup powdered sugar

1 teaspoon lemon juice

3 teaspoons rum or water, or 1 ½ teaspoons of each

MÜRBETEIGE

DIRECTIONS

1. Prepare the crust: Set aside ¼ cup of the measured flour to use as needed while working the dough, pressing it into the form, and making lattice. Sift the remaining flour and baking powder onto a large marble or wooden board (see tip 1). Form a well in the middle and sprinkle the salt around the edge. Add the sugar, egg, and vanilla into the well. Cut the butter into small pieces, approximately ¼ to ½ inch (see page 21, "How to Cut Butter," in "Technique to Prepare Mürbeteig Dough"). Distribute the pieces over and around the flour. Using the tip of a metal dough scraper, stir the egg as if gently scrambling. Begin carefully pushing the dry ingredients into the well's center. Work to combine all ingredients, first with the dough scraper and then with your hands, until a ball of dough forms. Add flour sparingly or chill as necessary if the dough becomes too sticky.

~ TIP 1 ~

This dough has a good bit of flour. It may even initially feel like there is too much flour, but keep at it, squeezing the dough with the palms of your hands, folding, and pushing it down. This recipe makes more dough than some of the others because there must be enough for both the bottom crust and the lattice.

2. Refrigerate the dough for 30 minutes.

3. Make the filling: Peel, core, and quarter the apples. Cut the apple quarters in half, lengthwise, and then start chopping from one end into small pieces, about ¼ inch. A food processor julienne disc or small french fry disc works well also. Place apples into a large mixing bowl. Stir in the lemon juice. Add the sugar, cinnamon, slivered almonds, dried currants or raisins, rum, and almond liqueur or almond extract. Mix thoroughly. Sift in the cornstarch or potato starch. Mix again and set aside.

4. Position a rack in the middle of the oven and preheat to 350°F. Butter and flour the dish in preparation for assembly. Set aside.

5. Mold bottom crust into dish: Remove dough from the refrigerator. Slice the chilled dough horizontally into three discs. Leave one disc in the refrigerator. Lay the other two discs into the prepared dish so they lean partially against the sides. The pieces may overlap. With flour-dipped fingers, push the dough out, rather than pressing it down, to cover the dish evenly. Pull the dough up the dish's sides about three-fourths of the way. Even out any thin spots for a fairly consistent thickness.

6. Give the filling a quick stir and then spread into the crust.

7. Prepare the first layer of lattice: Lightly dust a marble or wooden board with flour. Remove half of the remaining dough from the refrigerator. Rub flour onto the rolling pin and work surface and sprinkle sparingly over the dough if necessary. Roll out the dough until it matches

APPLE PIE

the diameter of the pie dish (see tip 2). The rolled dough should be ¼-inch thick or less. Dip a pastry cutter in flour. Slice the rolled dough into strips, each about 1 inch wide (see tip 3).

~ TIP 2 ~

To assist in estimating diameter, it is helpful to roll out the dough on a nonstick pastry mat with measured circles, to overturn another pan of the same size and lightly press the rim into the rolled-out dough, or to have a ruler on hand.

~ TIP 3 ~

There are different types of pastry wheel cutters available that readily cut lattice strips.

8. Assemble lattice: Lift one strip at a time by sliding a floured dough scraper under it. Starting at the pie's edge with the shortest strip, lay strips diagonally on top of the filling. Keep the strips about ¾ inch apart. If a strip is too short or breaks during transfer, simply add on more dough. Once the pie is baked and garnished, the seam will not show (see tip 4).

~ TIP 4 ~

Laying lattice strips is delicate work, refined with practice. Strips may break for a variety of reasons. The dough may be rolled too thin; it may not have enough flour; it may be too soft or too warm. The lifting tool or work surface may not have enough flour or may be too warm. Regardless of the reason, do not fret. It is better to have a few strips break than to end up with too much flour, which will produce a dry dough in the lattice.

9. When the first layer is finished, take the rest of the dough from the refrigerator. Repeat the process of rolling out and slicing the dough. Finish the lattice by laying the second layer of strips diagonally across the first, in the opposite direction. The pattern should produce diamond-shaped gaps showing the filling. If there is leftover dough, roll into a thin rope and place around the pie's edge or fashion into a bow to lay in the middle.

10. Make the egg wash: Whisk together the egg white and the almond extract until foamy. Brush over the lattice and the pie's edge.

MÜRBETEIGE

11. Bake for 1 hour and 25 minutes. Use a pie crust shield after the first 50 minutes (see page 22, "About Pie Crust Shields"). When the pie is done, the lattice should be golden brown. Insert a wooden skewer gently between the crust and rim to check doneness. The crust should be firm and lift away from the rim without leaving dough on the skewer. Also insert the skewer through the lattice into the pie's center. The skewer should come out clean of dough, but it may show a little juice from the filling. The apples should be soft.

12. Serve the pie while still hot or after cooling. Brush with sugar glaze before serving.

Directions for Sugar Glaze

Whisk together the powdered sugar, lemon juice, and rum or water to a thick but still fluid consistency. If a thicker icing is desired, add more powdered sugar. If too thick, add more liquid, just a few drops at a time.

....

Note: This pie dough recipe makes a bottom crust and a top lattice. If you prefer a woven lattice design, use the sturdier lattice recipe on page 23 for the top crust. To make a bottom crust only from this Apple Pie recipe, use half the crust ingredients except the egg (use 1 whole egg). You may need a little extra flour (about ⅛ to ¼ cup) in the bottom crust to accommodate the whole egg.

MIXED BERRY PIE

This simple pie highlights the bright berry flavors of springtime and summer, and it gives bakers the freedom to enjoy those flavors year-round by using frozen produce. If berries are plentiful in your local area, consider picking and freezing your own mixes, or simplify matters with ready, store-bought frozen mixes. The pie is wonderful for serving as a seasonal brunch item or as an afternoon treat. A scoop of vanilla ice cream or big dollop of fresh whipped cream makes a nice finishing touch.

MÜRBETEIGE

BAKING PAN
10 x 2-inch pie dish, buttered and floured

BAKING TEMPERATURE
350°F

BAKE TIME
1 hour and 30 minutes to 1 hour and 35 minutes

RACK PLACEMENT
middle of oven

Place a heavy cookie sheet on bottom rung to catch overflowing juices.

YIELD
one 10-inch pie (see page 23 for a 9-inch pie crust)

INGREDIENTS

FOR CRUST (see *note* at end of recipe)

1 ½ cups unbleached all-purpose flour (protein 3 grams per ¼ cup; see page 7), plus extra for working dough

1 teaspoon baking powder

Pinch of salt (about ⅛ teaspoon or less)

⅓ cup sugar

1 egg

1 teaspoon vanilla powder, or ½ teaspoon vanilla extract, or pulp of ¼-inch piece of vanilla bean

8 tablespoons (1 stick) unsalted butter, cold

FOR FILLING

8 cups frozen mixed berries (2 ½ pounds), add 1 extra cup for fresh berries

¼ cup lemon juice or lime juice

2 tablespoons orange liqueur, optional

1 ¼ cups sugar

6 tablespoons potato starch, use 5 tablespoons for fresh berries

FOR SUGAR GLAZE

1 cup powdered sugar

2 teaspoons lemon juice

2 teaspoons rum or water, or 1 teaspoon of each

FOR DUSTING (in place of glaze)

⅓ cup powdered sugar

MIXED BERRY PIE

DIRECTIONS

1. Prepare the crust: Set aside ¼ cup of the measured flour to use as needed while working the dough, pressing it into the form, and making lattice. Sift the remaining flour and baking powder onto a large marble or wooden board. Form a well in the middle and sprinkle the salt around the edge. Add the sugar, egg, and vanilla into the well. Cut the butter into small pieces, approximately ¼ to ½ inch (see page 21, "How to Cut Butter," in "Technique to Prepare Mürbeteig Dough"). Distribute the pieces over and around the flour. Using the tip of a metal dough scraper, stir the egg as if gently scrambling. Begin carefully pushing the dry ingredients into the well's center. Work to combine all ingredients, first with the dough scraper and then with your hands, until a ball of dough forms. Add flour sparingly or chill as necessary if the dough becomes too sticky.

2. Refrigerate the dough for 30 minutes.

3. Position a rack in the middle of the oven and preheat to 350°F. Butter and flour the dish in preparation for assembly. Set aside.

4. Make the filling: Place the frozen berries into a large mixing bowl (see tip 1). Add the lemon juice or lime juice, and optional orange liqueur. Mix well. In a separate bowl, add the sugar and sift in the potato starch. Mix thoroughly. Do not add the sugar and potato starch to the mixed berries until step 6.

~ TIP 1 ~

To help reduce the amount of liquid in the berries, remove them from the freezer before beginning the recipe. Place them in a bowl, sprinkle with sugar, and let sit at room temperature, stirring occasionally, until defrosted. The sugar will draw out the juice. When ready to make the filling, use a large, slotted spoon to transfer the berries, without the juice, into a clean bowl. Then proceed with the recipe.

5. Mold dough into dish: Slice the chilled dough horizontally into three discs. Leave one disc in the refrigerator. Lay the other two discs in the prepared dish so they lean partially against the sides. The pieces may overlap. With flour-dipped fingers, push the dough out, rather than pressing it down, to cover the dish evenly. Pull the dough three-fourths of the way up the dish's sides. Even out any thin spots to get the dough to a fairly consistent thickness.

6. Stir the sugar and potato starch mixture into the berry filling and mix with any juices that have settled to the bottom. There should be some juice, but if there is a lot, drain the excess (see tip 2). Spread the filling into the crust. The mixture should come to a little more than three-fourths of the way up to the rim of the crust (see tip 3).

MÜRBETEIGE

~ TIP 2 ~

Adding the sugar mixture to the filling just before spreading it into the crust will help reduce the amount of liquid drawn from the berries. If a lot of liquid pools in the filling, another option is to transfer the filling, mixed with the sugar and starch, to a large pot and briefly cook over high heat, while stirring constantly. Cook just enough so that the filling gels partially and will not soak the crust. The liquid will thicken further as the pie bakes.

~ TIP 3 ~

Take care not to overfill the crust. The berries give off liquid during baking. This liquid will concentrate by the time the pie is done, but it can spill over and burn on the crust's edge and the bottom of the oven if the filling rises too high.

necessary. Roll out the dough until it matches the diameter of the dish (see tip 4). The rolled dough should be ¼ inch thick or less. Dip a pastry cutter in flour. Slice the rolled dough into strips, each about 1 inch wide (see tip 5).

~ TIP 4 ~

To assist in estimating diameter, it is helpful to roll out the dough on a nonstick pastry mat with measured circles, to overturn another pan of the same size and lightly press the rim into the rolled-out dough, or to have a ruler on hand.

~ TIP 5 ~

There are different types of pastry wheel cutters available that readily cut lattice strips.

8. Assemble lattice: Lift one strip at a time by sliding a floured dough scraper under it.

7. Prepare the first layer of lattice: Lightly dust a marble or wooden board with flour. Remove half of the remaining dough from the refrigerator. Rub flour onto the rolling pin and work surface, and sprinkle flour sparingly over the dough if

MIXED BERRY PIE

Starting at the pie's edge with the shortest strip, lay strips diagonally on top of the filling. Keep the strips about 1 inch apart. If a strip is too short or breaks during transfer, simply add on more dough. Once the pie is baked and garnished, the seam will not show (see tip 6).

~ TIP 6 ~

Laying lattice strips is delicate work, refined with practice. Strips may break for a variety of reasons. The dough may be rolled too thin; it may not have enough flour; it may be too soft or too warm. The lifting tool or work surface may not have enough flour or may be too warm. Regardless of the reason, do not fret. It is better to have a few strips break than to end up with too much flour, which will produce a dry dough in the lattice.

9. When the first layer is finished, take the remaining dough from the refrigerator. Repeat the process of rolling out and slicing the dough. Finish the lattice by laying the second layer of strips diagonally across the first, in the opposite direction. The pattern should produce diamond-shaped gaps showing the filling. If there is leftover dough, roll into a thin rope and place around the pie's edge or fashion into a bow to lay in the middle.

10. Bake for about 1 hour and 30 minutes to 1 hour and 35 minutes, until the lattice is golden brown. Cover the rim with a pie crust shield for the last 25 minutes if the edges get too dark (see page 22, "About Pie Crust Shields"). Insert a wooden skewer gently between the crust and rim to check doneness. The crust should be firm and should lift away from the rim without leaving dough on the skewer. Also insert the skewer through the lattice into the pie's center. The skewer should come out clean of dough, but it may show a little juice from the filling. Allow pie to settle and cool.

11. Once cooled, brush with glaze or dust with powdered sugar before serving.

Directions for Sugar Glaze

Whisk together the powdered sugar, lemon juice, and rum or water to a thick but still fluid consistency. If a thicker icing is desired, add more powdered sugar. If too thick, add more liquid, just a few drops at a time.

. . . .

Note: This pie dough recipe makes a bottom crust and a top lattice. If you prefer a woven lattice design, use the sturdier lattice recipe on page 23 for the top crust. To make a bottom crust only from this Mixed Berry Pie recipe, use half the crust ingredients except the egg (use 1 whole egg). You may need a little extra flour (about ⅛ to ¼ cup) in the bottom crust to accommodate the whole egg.

STRAWBERRY RHUBARB PIE

Rhubarb is a staple in German gardens. My grandmother, aunt, and mom always had it growing. Some days, I joined my grandmother to weed and harvest in her garden, which grew in a designated patch in the farm fields. In Germany, all farm fields are outside the villages. Even farmers have their acreages away from their houses. Farmers usually live around the edge of the village with easy access to their fields. Roads in between acres are paved to create passage for tractors and farm equipment. Urban sprawl is controlled this way, and the fields are open for everyone to enjoy as long as traffic stays on the designated pathways. Horses and any non-motorized wheels such as bikes are also allowed. These acreages are split into fields, about the size of a football field or larger. Crops grown on these fields range from corn to flax to wheat, rye, and barley. There are patches of sugar beets and rapeseed for oil. Over hundreds of years, the fields have been sold and resold. On the edges of the fields, there are usually one hundred to two hundred smaller plots, about the size of a large backyard. These plots are designated for people living in the villages with no gardens of their own. My grandmother rented one of these plots.

Being out there and working in the sunshine with the breezes flowing over the vast acreage was a quiet, thoughtful, meditative, and productive time. I loved the connection with nature and the earth. The garden was beautifully laid out with raised beds so we could walk in between the rows and easily tend to the vegetables. I now have rhubarb growing in my garden in Hawaii. It is easy to grow.

STRAWBERRY RHUBARB PIE

As long as it is planted in well-drained soil, it should do well. When I look after it, I am transported back to Germany and to the feel of working the earth with my grandmother.

Whether in the garden or in the market, pick rhubarb stalks that are vibrant in color and of medium to small size. Those are the most tender. Bigger stalks tend to be too tough and woody for this pie.

BAKING PAN
10 x 2-inch pie dish, buttered and floured

BAKING TEMPERATURE
350°F

BAKE TIME
1 hour and 20 minutes to 1 hour and 35 minutes

RACK PLACEMENT
middle of oven

Place a heavy cookie sheet on bottom rung to keep crust from getting too dark and to catch overflowing juices.

YIELD
one 10-inch pie (see page 23 for a 9-inch pie crust)

INGREDIENTS

FOR CRUST (see *note* at end of recipe)

1 ½ cups unbleached all-purpose flour (protein 3 grams per ¼ cup; see page 7), plus extra for working dough

1 teaspoon baking powder

Pinch of salt (about ⅛ teaspoon or less)

⅓ cup sugar

1 egg

1 teaspoon vanilla sugar, or ½ teaspoon vanilla extract, or pulp of ¼-inch piece of vanilla bean

8 tablespoons (1 stick) unsalted butter, cold

FOR FILLING

6 to 7 stalks rhubarb (1 pound)

2 pounds strawberries

¼ cup lemon juice or lime juice

2 tablespoons orange liqueur, optional

¾ cup sugar

5 tablespoons cornstarch

FOR SUGAR GLAZE

1 cup powdered sugar

2 teaspoons lemon juice

2 teaspoons rum or water, or 1 teaspoon of each

FOR DUSTING (in place of glaze)

⅓ cup powdered sugar

MÜRBETEIGE

DIRECTIONS

1. Prepare the crust: Set aside ¼ cup of the measured flour to use as needed while working the dough, pressing it into the form, and making lattice. Sift the remaining flour and baking powder onto a large marble or wooden board. Form a well in the middle and sprinkle the salt around the edge. Add the sugar, egg, and vanilla into the well. Cut the butter into small pieces, approximately ¼ to ½ inch (see page 21, "How to Cut Butter," in "Technique to Prepare Mürbeteig Dough"). Distribute the pieces over and around the flour. Using the tip of a metal dough scraper, stir the egg as if gently scrambling. Begin carefully pushing the dry ingredients into the well's center. Work to combine all ingredients, first with the dough scraper and then with your hands, until a ball of dough forms. Add flour sparingly or chill as necessary if the dough becomes too sticky.

2. Refrigerate the dough for 30 minutes.

3. Prepare the filling: Peel the rhubarb and cut into thin slices, about 1¼ inches or less (see tip 1). Clean, hull, and halve regular-sized strawberries; third or quarter large strawberries. Place rhubarb and strawberries into a large bowl and add the lemon juice or lime juice and the optional orange liqueur. Stir to distribute evenly. In a separate bowl, add the sugar and sift in the cornstarch. Mix well. Set both bowls aside. Do not add the sugar and cornstarch to the rhubarb and strawberries until step 6.

~ TIP 1 ~

Peeling rhubarb is similar to stringing green beans. No special tools are needed—just your hands and a small knife. Simply grasp the threads between knife and thumb and pull them down the stalk.

4. Position a rack in the middle of the oven and preheat to 350°F. Butter and flour the dish in preparation for assembly.

5. Mold dough into dish: Slice the chilled dough horizontally into three discs. Leave one disc in the refrigerator. Lay the other two discs in the prepared dish so they lean partially against the sides. The pieces may overlap. With flour-dipped fingers, push the dough out, rather than pressing it down, to cover the dish evenly. Pull the dough all the way up to the top of the dish's rim. Even out any thin spots to get the dough to a fairly consistent thickness.

6. Stir the sugar and cornstarch mixture into the rhubarb and strawberries, and then spread the filling into the crust (see tip 2). Depending on the shape of the pie dish, there may be filling left over (see page 23, "What to Do with Extra Filling"). The mixture should come to a little more than three-fourths of the way up to the rim of the crust (see tip 3).

STRAWBERRY RHUBARB PIE

~ TIP 2 ~

Adding the sugar mixture to the filling just before spreading it into the crust will help reduce the amount of liquid drawn from the strawberries and rhubarb. Some juice can be poured out if the sugar mixture draws out too much liquid. If a lot of liquid pools in the filling, another option is to transfer the filling, mixed with the sugar and starch, to a large pot and briefly cook over high heat, while stirring constantly. Cook just enough so that the filling gels partially and will not soak the crust. The liquid will thicken further as the pie bakes.

~ TIP 3 ~

Take care not to overfill the crust. The rhubarb and strawberries give off liquid during baking. This liquid will concentrate by the time the pie is done, but it can spill over and burn on the crust's edge and the bottom of the oven if the filling rises too high.

7. Prepare the first layer of lattice: Lightly dust a marble or wooden board with flour. Remove half of the remaining dough from the refrigerator. Rub flour onto the rolling pin and work surface, and sprinkle flour sparingly over the dough if necessary. Roll out the dough until it matches the diameter of the dish (see tip 4). The rolled dough should be ¼ inch thick or less. Dip a broad, non-serrated knife or pastry cutter in flour. Slice the rolled dough into strips, each about 1 inch wide (see tip 5).

~ TIP 4 ~

To assist in estimating diameter, it is helpful to roll out the dough on a nonstick pastry mat with measured circles, to overturn another pan of the same size and lightly press the rim into the rolled-out dough, or to have a ruler on hand.

~ TIP 5 ~

There are different types of pastry wheel cutters available that readily cut lattice strips.

8. Assemble lattice: Lift one strip at a time by sliding a floured dough scraper under it. Starting at the pie's edge with the shortest strip, lay strips diagonally on top of the filling. Keep the strips about 1 inch apart. If a strip is too short or breaks during transfer, simply add on more dough. Once the pie is baked and garnished, the seam will not show (see tip 6).

~ TIP 6 ~

Laying lattice strips is delicate work, refined with practice. Strips may break for a variety of reasons. The dough may be rolled too thin; it may not have enough flour; it may be too soft or too warm. The lifting tool or work surface may not have enough flour or may be too warm. Regardless of the reason, do not fret. It is better to have a few strips break than to end up with too much flour, which will produce a dry dough in the lattice.

MÜRBETEIGE

9. When the first layer is finished, take the remaining dough from the refrigerator. Repeat the process of rolling out and slicing the dough. Finish the lattice by laying the second layer of strips diagonally across the first, in the opposite direction. The pattern should produce diamond-shaped gaps showing the filling. If there is leftover dough, roll into a thin rope and place around the pie's edge or fashion into a bow to lay in the middle.

10. Bake for about 1 hour and 20 minutes to 1 hour and 35 minutes. Cover the rim with a pie crust shield for the last 25 minutes if the edges get too dark (see page 22, "About Pie Crust Shields"). When the pie is done, the lattice should be golden brown. Insert a wooden skewer gently between the crust and rim to check doneness. The crust should be firm and lift away from the rim without leaving dough on the skewer. Also insert the skewer through the lattice into the pie's center. The skewer should come out clean of dough, but it may show a little juice from the filling. The rhubarb and strawberries should be soft. Allow pie to settle and cool.

11. Once cooled, brush with sugar glaze or dust with powdered sugar before serving.

Directions for Sugar Glaze

Whisk together the powdered sugar, lemon juice, and rum or water to a thick but still fluid consistency. If a thicker icing is desired, add more powdered sugar. If too thick, add more liquid, just a few drops at a time.

. . . .

Note: This pie dough recipe makes a bottom crust and a top lattice. If you prefer a woven lattice design, use the sturdier lattice recipe on page 23 for the top crust. To make a bottom crust only from this Strawberry Rhubarb Pie recipe, use half the crust ingredients except the egg (use 1 whole egg). You may need a little extra flour (about ⅛ to ¼ cup) in the bottom crust to accommodate the whole egg.

PUMPKIN PIE

This pie is a fusion of German fundamentals and American tradition. It is a creamy, decadent, delightful pie spiced with autumn flavors. The optional sour cream, a German influence, comes highly recommended to make for a richer, more rounded filling. To enhance the experience, cook your own pie pumpkin (see *note* at end of recipe). It is quite easy and will fill your home and heart with warmth. The pie is equally beautiful served plain or garnished with a dollop of fresh whipped cream, a sprinkle of crushed pecans, and/or a drizzle of pure maple syrup.

MÜRBETEIGE

BAKING PAN
10 x 2-inch pie dish, buttered and floured

BAKING TEMPERATURE
325°F

BAKE TIME
1 hour and 35 minutes to 1 hour and 40 minutes

RACK PLACEMENT
middle of oven

Place a heavy cookie sheet on bottom rung to keep crust from getting too dark.

YIELD
one 10-inch pie (see page 23 for a 9-inch pie crust)

INGREDIENTS

FOR CRUST

1 cup unbleached all-purpose flour (protein 3 grams per ¼ cup; see page 7), plus extra for working dough

¾ teaspoon baking powder

Pinch of salt (about ⅛ teaspoon or less)

¼ cup sugar

1 egg

1 teaspoon vanilla sugar, or ½ teaspoon vanilla extract

5 tablespoons unsalted butter, cold

FOR FILLING

3 eggs

2 cups cooked and puréed fresh pumpkin (see *note* at end of recipe), or 1 (15- or 16-ounce) can pumpkin purée

4 ounces cream cheese (⅓ less fat or regular), at room temperature

1 cup granulated sugar

⅓ cup packed dark brown sugar

1 tablespoon cornstarch

1 teaspoon vanilla sugar or vanilla extract, or pulp of 1-inch piece of vanilla bean

3 teaspoons pumpkin spice

2 teaspoons cinnamon

⅛ teaspoon ground cloves

1 ½ to 2 tablespoons lemon juice (perhaps more depending on strength of flavor)

Zest of ½ lemon (about 1 teaspoon)

¼ teaspoon baking lemon oil, optional

1 tablespoon orange liqueur, optional

½ cup sour cream, optional

PUMPKIN PIE

DIRECTIONS

1. Prepare the crust: Set aside ¼ cup of the measured flour to use as needed while working the dough and pressing it into the form. Sift the remaining flour and baking powder onto a large marble or wooden board. Form a well in the middle and sprinkle the salt around the edge. Add the sugar, egg, and vanilla into the well. Cut the butter into small pieces, approximately ¼ to ½ inch (see page 21, "How to Cut Butter," in "Technique to Prepare Mürbeteig Dough"). Distribute the pieces over and around the flour. Using the tip of a metal dough scraper, stir the egg as if gently scrambling. Begin carefully pushing the dry ingredients into the well's center. Work to combine all ingredients, first with the dough scraper and then with your hands, until a ball of dough forms. Add flour sparingly or chill as necessary if the dough becomes too sticky.

2. Refrigerate the dough for 30 minutes.

3. Position a rack in the middle of the oven and preheat to 325°F. Butter and flour the dish. Set aside.

4. Separate the eggs for the filling (see tip): Place the whites in a large mixing bowl and the yolks in a small bowl. Whip the egg whites to firm peaks and set aside.

~ TIP ~

Bakers can make the pie with or without whipping the egg whites, but the consistency will change depending on the choice. The air from the whipped egg whites will make the filling fluffier. Whole, unwhipped eggs will make the filling denser and less airy, but no less tasty. If whipping the egg whites, test their readiness by scooping up some of the whites with a whisk and turning it over. The whites should hold a peak, but the peak will fall over slightly at the very top, like an elf's hat.

5. Make the filling: Blend the pumpkin and soft cream cheese with an electric mixer until combined. Mix the egg yolks briefly with a fork and pour into the pumpkin mixture. Blend again. Add the granulated sugar and brown sugar into the mixture and sift in the cornstarch. Blend to combine, about 2 to 3 minutes. Add the vanilla, pumpkin spice, cinnamon, and cloves. Blend once more. Mix in the lemon juice and zest to taste. There should be a hint of lemon but not an overpowering bite. Add the optional lemon oil and optional orange liqueur, if using, and blend. Fold in the optional sour cream.

6. Give the egg whites a few strokes with a wire whisk to whip up any liquid that may have formed at the bottom of the bowl. Slide the whites over the pumpkin mixture and fold in gently to incorporate.

7. Mold dough into dish: Flatten the chilled dough a bit and lay into the prepared dish. With flour-dipped fingers, push the dough out, rather than pressing it down, to cover the dish evenly. Pull the dough about three-fourths of the way up the

MÜRBETEIGE

dish's sides. Even out any thin spots to get the dough to a fairly consistent thickness.

8. Assemble for baking: Pour the filling into the crust. Keep about 1 inch of dough above the filling to allow room for the filling to expand.

9. Bake for 1 hour and 35 minutes to 1 hour and 40 minutes, until the filling appears set. Use a pie crust shield after the first 50 minutes (see page 22, "About Pie Crust Shields"). When the pie is done, the filling in the center and the filling around the edges should be at an even level. Insert a wooden skewer into the pie's center. The skewer should come out clean. Also insert the wooden skewer gently between the crust and rim to check doneness. The crust should be firm and lift away from the rim without leaving dough on the skewer. Place the dish on a rack to cool. Serve the pie at room temperature or cooler.

. . . .

Note: Buy two pie pumpkins to make enough for the filling. They are smaller than carving pumpkins and have more flesh. Halve the pumpkins and scrape out the seeds and strings. Save the seeds for roasting later as a snack. Lightly oil a baking pan that has edges high enough to catch the pumpkins' liquid (at least ½ inch high). Place the pumpkins, cut-side down, in the pan. On a rung just lower than the middle of the oven, cook at 325°F for 45 minutes to 1 hour, or until a knife cuts through smoothly. For example, one pie pumpkin weighing 2 pounds, 6 ounces and the other 1 pound, 8 ounces take 45 minutes to bake. Do not overcook. Let cool and then scoop out the pulp. Mash the pulp with an electric mixer or by hand. If working by hand, strain the pulp through a colander after mashing to ensure a smooth texture. If pulp is left over, freeze it for the next pie. Cook the pumpkin the day before to decrease the amount of work on the day of baking the pie.

PECAN PIE

When I moved to Texas, I found the best tasting pecans. I did not know that Texas had so many pecan groves, but I learned that the soil and the weather make it ideal for growing pecans. We lived in Austin, and I found out that before 1937, there were old groves in the valley. Then flood control dams were built, the Highland Lakes were created, and the valley flooded. To this day, some of those farms and trees are still visible underwater. It seems pecans are such a regional favorite that there are even novelty pecan confections marketed to travelers passing through the Austin airport. I will never forget picking up a box of "Armadillo Droppings" made by the Armadillo Candy Company. In actuality, they are caramel pecan praline treats. The story reproduced on the box from the Armadillo Candy Company goes something like this: Maria was cooking dinner for the farmhands one day, and while she was making caramel with pecans, an armadillo came and pushed over her bucket. She had to abandon her cooking and chase away the armadillo. In the meantime, the pecan treats ended up getting gooey and browner than usual, and when the men came in from the ranch, they asked, "What are you cooking there, Maria?" Promptly she answered, "Armadillo droppings."

I love a good-humored Texas story!

I was very intrigued by the pecan pie and the taste of these fresh nuts, but the filling was too heavy for my preference. Changing the often-used corn syrup to maple syrup, cutting down on the amount of syrup, and adding ground pecans into the filling with a layer of almond paste to line the crust transformed a regular pecan pie into a delicate creation. The whipped egg whites bring extra lightness and richness to the filling. The result is absolutely delightful. If you want to experiment with a different kind of pecan pie, this is your pie. Take care to lay the pecans as recommended—like sunbeams that extend from the pie's center. It does not take much time, and the design produces a stunning finish of warmth and abundance.

MÜRBETEIGE

BAKING PAN
10 x 2 ½-inch springform pan or 10 x 2-inch pie dish, buttered and floured

Baking time may be shortened if a steel-based pan is used rather than aluminum; dark pans bake faster than light pans.

BAKING TEMPERATURE
325°F

BAKE TIME
1 hour and 20 minutes

RACK PLACEMENT
bottom third of oven, just below middle

Place a heavy cookie sheet on bottom rung to keep crust from getting too dark.

YIELD
one 10-inch pie

INGREDIENTS

FOR CRUST

1 cup unbleached all-purpose flour (protein 3 grams per ¼ cup; see page 7), plus extra for working dough

½ teaspoon baking powder

Pinch of salt (about ⅛ teaspoon or less)

⅓ cup sugar

1 medium egg

5 tablespoons unsalted butter, cold

FOR FILLING

2 eggs

1 ½ cups freshly ground pecan meal (about 2 cups pecan halves if grinding yourself, see page 14 for technique; store-bought pecan meal is less flavorful)

½ cup packed light brown sugar

¼ cup maple syrup

½ cup heavy whipping cream

1 tablespoon orange liqueur, almond liqueur, or coffee liqueur (for a flavor variation)

FOR LINING THE CRUST

7 ounces (200 grams) almond paste

2 tablespoons powdered sugar (for rolling out almond paste, not all may be needed)

FOR TOPPING

1 ½ cups pecan halves

PECAN PIE

DIRECTIONS

1. Prepare the crust: Set aside ¼ cup of the measured flour to use as needed while working the dough and pressing it into the form. Sift the remaining flour and baking powder onto a large marble or wooden board. Form a well in the middle and sprinkle the salt around the edge. Add the sugar and egg into the well. Cut the butter into small pieces, approximately ¼ to ½ inch (see page 21, "How to Cut Butter," in "Technique to Prepare Mürbeteig Dough"). Distribute the pieces over and around the flour. Using the tip of a metal dough scraper, stir the egg as if gently scrambling. Begin carefully pushing the dry ingredients into the well's center. Work to combine all ingredients, first with the dough scraper and then with your hands, until a ball of dough forms. Add flour sparingly or chill as necessary if the dough becomes too sticky.

2. Refrigerate the dough for 30 minutes.

3. Separate the eggs for the filling: Place the egg whites in a medium-sized mixing bowl and the yolks in a small bowl. Whip the egg whites to firm peaks. Set aside.

4. Grind the pecans in a nut mill, coffee mill, or food processor until they are the texture of coarse meal. If using store-bought pecan meal, skip this step.

5. Make the filling: Using an electric mixer or food processor, blend the pecan meal with the brown sugar, maple syrup, unwhipped heavy whipping cream, and egg yolks until fluffed and creamy, about 45 to 60 seconds. Scoop ¼ cup of the pecan mixture into a small bowl and stir in the orange liqueur, almond liqueur, or coffee liqueur. Add to the remaining pecan mixture and stir thoroughly. This process will distribute the liqueur flavor evenly.

6. Give the egg whites a few strokes with a wire whisk to whip up any liquid that may have formed at the bottom of the bowl. Slide the whites over the pecan mixture and fold in gently to incorporate.

7. Position a rack in the bottom third of the oven (just below middle) and preheat to 325°F. Butter and flour the dish in preparation for assembly.

8. Dust a board and rolling pin with powdered sugar. Roll out the almond paste to the size of the bottom of the pie dish.

9. Mold dough into dish: Slice the chilled dough horizontally into three discs. Lay the discs into the prepared dish so they lean partially against the sides. The pieces may overlap. With flour-dipped fingers, push the dough together and out, rather than pressing it down, to cover the dish evenly. Pull the dough three-fourths of the way up the dish's sides. Even out any thin spots to get the dough to a fairly consistent thickness.

MÜRBETEIGE

10. Assemble for baking: Lay the rolled-out almond paste on top of the crust. It should cover the bottom, but not the sides. Pour in the filling and arrange the pecan halves on top. Start with one pecan in the very center. From there, lay the pecans in four lines, shaped like a cross, to divide the pie into quarters. Starting at the center pecan again, lay another row of pecans in the middle of each quarter to create eighths. The rows should run from the center pecan to the crust's edge like sunbeams. Next, lay another row in between the eighths to make sixteenths. Fill in with as many pecans as space allows to cover the entire pie.

11. Bake for 1 hour and 20 minutes. Check the pie after 1 hour to 1 hour and 10 minutes. If the pecans start browning too much, cover the whole pie with aluminum foil (see tip). To check doneness, insert a wooden skewer through the pie's center. There may be a few kernels of filling on it, but it should not present underbaked dough. Also insert the skewer gently between the crust and rim. The crust should be firm and lift away from the rim without leaving dough on the skewer. Serve warm, room temperature, or cooled.

~ TIP ~

To prevent the pecans from getting too brown, cut out a round aluminum foil cover, 14 inches in diameter. Tap the middle to create a slight dome shape and place cover over entire pie. Leave the foil loose. Sealing the edges will trap steam and alter the baking. Remember, the foil will become hot, so do not handle it without mitts when checking on the pie or removing it.

RICOTTA CHEESECAKE

This cheesecake comes together quite easily, with a filling that is astoundingly simple to make. Really, the filling is a quick affair of measuring and mixing, and the addition of the flavorful apricots offers a sweet, tangy complement to the rich dairy blend. Make sure to leave enough time for the cheesecake to cool to room temperature or lower before serving. Cooling allows the flavors to harmonize and the texture to settle into one creamy bite. Cheesecake will keep in the refrigerator for days and develop even more flavor.

MÜRBETEIGE

BAKING PAN
10 x 3-inch springform pan, buttered and floured

Baking time may be shortened if a steel-based pan is used rather than aluminum; dark pans bake faster than light pans.

BAKING TEMPERATURE
350°F

BAKE TIME
1 hour and 25 minutes to 1 hour and 40 minutes

RACK PLACEMENT
bottom third of oven

Place a heavy cookie sheet on bottom rung to keep crust from getting too dark.

YIELD
one 10-inch cake

INGREDIENTS

FOR CRUST

1 ½ cups unbleached all-purpose flour (protein 3 grams per ¼ cup; see page 7), plus extra for working dough

1 ½ teaspoons baking powder

Pinch of salt (about ⅛ teaspoon or less)

½ cup sugar

1 egg

1 teaspoon vanilla sugar, or ½ teaspoon vanilla extract

8 tablespoons (1 stick) unsalted butter, cold

FOR FILLING

1 (15- or 16-ounce) can apricots, packed in light syrup

1 cup part-skim ricotta

3 eggs

8 ounces cream cheese (⅓ less fat or regular), at room temperature

1 ¼ cups sugar

1 cup sour cream

1 tablespoon vanilla sugar, or 1 teaspoon vanilla extract

½ cup lemon juice

4 tablespoons cornstarch

RICOTTA CHEESECAKE

DIRECTIONS

1. Prepare the crust: Set aside ¼ cup of the measured flour to use as needed while working the dough and pressing it into the form. Sift the remaining flour and baking powder onto a large marble or wooden board. Form a well in the middle and sprinkle the salt around the edge. Add the sugar, egg, and vanilla into the well. Cut the butter into small pieces, approximately ¼ to ½ inch (see page 21, "How to Cut Butter," in "Technique to Prepare Mürbeteig Dough"). Distribute the pieces over and around the flour. Using the tip of a metal dough scraper, stir the egg as if gently scrambling. Begin carefully pushing the dry ingredients into the well's center. Work to combine all ingredients, first with the dough scraper and then with your hands, until a ball of dough forms. Add flour sparingly or chill as necessary if the dough becomes too sticky.

2. Refrigerate the dough for 30 minutes.

3. Position a rack in the bottom third of the oven and preheat to 350°F. Place a heavy cookie sheet on bottom rung. Butter and flour the pan in preparation for assembly. Set aside.

4. Drain the apricots into a colander and set aside.

5. Mix the filling: Using a high-speed blender or an electric mixer or food processor, first blend the ricotta with one of the eggs to a smooth, creamy consistency (see tip). Then add the remaining two eggs and the cream cheese and blend until smooth. Add the sugar and mix until mostly dissolved. Add the sour cream, vanilla, and lemon juice and blend until smooth. Sift the cornstarch over the mixture. Blend again. The consistency will be like heavy cream.

~ TIP ~

Ricotta cheese can have a grainy texture; therefore, I prefer blending ingredients for the filling in a high-speed blender.

6. Mold dough into pan: Slice the chilled dough horizontally into four discs. Lay the discs into the bottom of the prepared pan so they lean partially against the sides. The pieces may overlap. With flour-dipped fingers, push the dough out, rather than pressing it down, to cover the pan evenly. Pull the dough about two-thirds of the way up the pan's side. Even out any thin spots for a fairly consistent thickness.

7. Assemble for baking: Pour about half of the filling into the crust. Distribute the apricots over the filling. Pour the rest of the filling on top. Push down any apricots that may have floated up. Check the crust's rim. The filling needs room to rise during baking. Keep crust ¼ inch above the filling. Push it down gently if it is higher.

MÜRBETEIGE

8. Bake for 1 hour and 25 minutes to 1 hour and 40 minutes. Cover the rim with a pie crust shield for the last 25 minutes if the edges get too dark (see page 22, "About Pie Crust Shields"). The cake is ready when the middle is level with the sides and is of a light golden color. The crust will be a darker color. To check doneness, insert a wooden skewer through the cake's center. There may be a few kernels of filling on it, but it should not present underbaked dough. The filling may jiggle a little when the pan is moved, but it should be mostly set. Also insert the skewer gently between the crust and rim. The crust should be firm and lift away from the rim without leaving dough on the skewer. Open the oven door and allow cake to cool for 10 minutes. Then place cake on the counter and allow to cool on a wire rack for at least 30 minutes before removing the pan's metal rim. Use a *kuchenretter* (cake lifter) to lift cake from the pan's base, and continue cooling on a wire rack to room temperature before serving, or refrigerate to cool further.

TRADITIONAL GERMAN CHEESECAKE WITH QUARK

This is my mother's original cheesecake recipe. The filling is delicious quark (see page 12), a common dairy ingredient in Germany. This recipe uses restraint in the sugar quantity to avoid overpowering the quark. For those who crave sweeter fillings, add more sugar to taste. Another option my mother thought of to bring extra flavor to the cake is stirring raisins into the filling or adding a layer of apricots. As with other cheesecakes, allow sufficient time to cool between baking and serving. The cake is best if refrigerated overnight. Flavors develop further as it chills, and the quark filling stays delicious for several days. For a video demonstration of making your own quark, see vimeo.com/showcase/10470112.

VIDEO SHOWCASE
Fillings and Garnishes
vimeo.com/showcase/10470112

MÜRBETEIGE

BAKING PAN
10 x 3-inch springform pan, buttered and floured

Baking time may be shortened if a steel-based pan is used rather than aluminum; dark pans bake faster than light pans.

BAKING TEMPERATURE
350°F

BAKE TIME
1 hour and 25 minutes to 1 hour and 35 minutes

RACK PLACEMENT
bottom third of oven

Place a heavy cookie sheet on bottom rung to keep crust from getting too dark.

YIELD
one 10-inch cake

INGREDIENTS

FOR CRUST

1 ½ cups unbleached all-purpose flour (protein 3 grams per ¼ cup; see page 7), plus extra for working dough

1 ½ teaspoons baking powder

Pinch of salt (about ⅛ teaspoon or less)

½ cup sugar

1 egg

1 teaspoon vanilla sugar, or ½ teaspoon vanilla extract

8 tablespoons (1 stick) unsalted butter, cold

FOR FILLING

36 ounces quark

⅛ to ¼ cup milk

3 eggs

1 cup sugar

1 tablespoon lemon zest

2 tablespoons lemon juice

5 tablespoons cornstarch

TRADITIONAL GERMAN CHEESECAKE WITH QUARK

DIRECTIONS

1. Prepare the crust: Set aside ¼ cup of the measured flour to use as needed while working the dough and pressing it into the form. Sift the remaining flour and baking powder onto a large marble or wooden board. Form a well in the middle and sprinkle the salt around the edge. Add the sugar, egg, and vanilla into the well. Cut the butter into small pieces, approximately ¼ to ½ inch (see page 21, "How to Cut Butter," in "Technique to Prepare Mürbeteig Dough"). Distribute the pieces over and around the flour. Using the tip of a metal dough scraper, stir the egg as if gently scrambling. Begin carefully pushing the dry ingredients into the well's center. Work to combine all ingredients, first with the dough scraper and then with your hands, until a ball of dough forms. Add flour sparingly or chill as necessary if the dough becomes too sticky.

2. Refrigerate the dough for 30 minutes.

3. Position a rack in the bottom third of the oven and preheat to 350°F. Place a heavy cookie sheet on bottom rung. Butter and flour the pan in preparation for assembly. Set aside.

4. Mix the filling: Using an electric mixer or food processor, blend the quark, milk, eggs, sugar, lemon zest, and lemon juice until smooth (see tip). Sift the cornstarch over the mixture. Blend again. The consistency will be like heavy cream. Set aside.

~ TIP ~

The amount of milk needed depends on the dryness of the quark. Start with ⅛ cup of milk. Add another ⅛ cup if needed to reach the desired consistency.

---

5. Mold dough into pan: Slice the chilled dough horizontally into four discs. Lay the discs into the bottom of the prepared pan so they lean partially against the sides. The pieces may overlap. With flour-dipped fingers, push the

MÜRBETEIGE

dough out, rather than pressing it down, to cover the pan evenly. Pull the dough up almost to the rim's edge. Even out any thin spots for a fairly consistent thickness.

6. Assemble for baking: Pour the filling into the crust. The filling will come up higher than it does in other cheesecakes—nearly to the rim. Keep crust ¼ inch above the filling.

7. Bake for 1 hour and 25 minutes to 1 hour and 35 minutes. Cover the rim with a pie crust shield for the last 20 minutes if the edges get too dark (see page 22, "About Pie Crust Shields"). The cake is ready when the middle is level with the sides and is of a light golden color. The crust will be a darker color. To check doneness, insert a wooden skewer through the cake's center. There may be a few kernels of filling on it, but it should not present underbaked dough. The filling may jiggle a little when the pan is moved, but it should be mostly set. Also insert the skewer gently between the crust and rim. The crust should be firm and lift away from the rim without leaving dough on the skewer. Allow cake to cool for at least 30 minutes before removing the pan's metal rim. Use a *kuchenretter* (cake lifter) to lift cake from the pan's base, and continue cooling on a wire rack to room temperature before serving, or refrigerate to cool further.

LILIKO'I CHEESECAKE

Liliko'i is the name used for passion fruit in Hawaii, where the fruit grows abundantly. The vines also grow in South America and are often sold as climbers in nurseries around the world. When I lived in Virginia and in Texas, I planted these vines as summer climbers. In Texas, I planted the vine by my koi pond, tucked in an outdoor corner of our limestone house. With the high temperatures, heat radiated from the limestone wall, and the vine flourished, showing off the most delicate, beautiful flowers. By the end of the fall, I noticed the first fruit, a green ball about the size of a small lemon. I had never seen fruit on any of my vines before and did not know how it was supposed to look. I picked it prematurely and was dismayed to find that no flesh had grown.

When I moved to Hawaii, the vines on our property grew as they pleased, crawling over the

MÜRBETEIGE

bamboo and macadamia nut trees. The fruit turned yellow or purple depending on the variety, and I gave them another try. The yellow fruit is acidic, like a combination of lemon and orange, and is best used in cooking or diluted as a drink. The purple fruit is mild, like pleasantly sour pineapple, and enjoyable straight from the shell. It seemed to me the liliko'i would be a complementary ingredient to replace or enhance lemon juice in any pastry recipe, especially those with dairy fillings. Dairy fillings take on flavor well and lend themselves to experimentation. To add liliko'i flavor to other cheesecake recipes, pour half a cup of liliko'i juice into the filling and spread the glaze from this recipe over the top. After trying the liliko'i in cheesecakes, test it out in this book's other recipes that have fillings. Even though it is not mentioned in other recipes, I often add liliko'i to brighten the flavors or to substitute for another kind of citrus.

Even in non-tropical environments, health-conscious grocery stores often carry liliko'i or passion fruit concentrate and juice, and liliko'i products are also available online. If using a store-bought

concentrate or purée, read the instructions on the packaging. The brand may recommend thinning the product with water. While experimenting, tinker with the juice-to-water ratio to achieve the desired intensity. Taste test the liliko'i product before starting and continue tasting periodically while working to determine whether it needs sweetening or diluting. I recommend this tasting while preparing both the cheesecake filling and the glaze. As with other cheesecakes, allow sufficient time to cool between baking and serving. The cake is best if refrigerated overnight.

BAKING PAN
10 x 3-inch springform pan, buttered and floured

Baking time may be shortened if a steel-based pan is used rather than aluminum; dark pans bake faster than light pans.

BAKING TEMPERATURE
350°F

BAKE TIME
1 hour and 35 minutes to 1 hour and 45 minutes

RACK PLACEMENT
bottom third of oven

Place a heavy cookie sheet on bottom rung to keep crust from getting too dark.

YIELD
one 10-inch cake

LILIKOʻI CHEESECAKE

INGREDIENTS

FOR CRUST

1 ½ cups unbleached all-purpose flour (protein 3 grams per ¼ cup; see page 7), plus extra for working dough

1 ½ teaspoons baking powder

Pinch of salt (about ⅛ teaspoon or less)

½ cup sugar

1 egg

1 teaspoon vanilla sugar, or ½ teaspoon vanilla extract

8 tablespoons (1 stick) unsalted butter, cold

FOR FILLING

16 ounces thick Greek yogurt

8 ounces cream cheese (⅓ less fat or regular), at room temperature

1 ¼ cups sugar

4 ounces sour cream

2 eggs

2 teaspoons vanilla sugar, or 1 teaspoon vanilla extract

2 tablespoons lemon juice

½ cup lilikoʻi juice (see *note 1* at end of recipe)

5 tablespoons cornstarch

FOR LILIKOʻI GLAZE

1 cup water

½ cup thawed-from-frozen lilikoʻi/passion fruit juice, or ⅔ cup fresh lilikoʻi juice (see *note 2* at end of recipe)

2 tablespoons potato starch (for a translucent glaze), or 2 tablespoons cornstarch (for an opaque glaze)

5 tablespoons sugar (adjust sugar as needed, but keep taste on the tangy side)

DIRECTIONS

1. Prepare the crust: Set aside ¼ cup of the measured flour to use as needed while working the dough and pressing it into the form. Sift the remaining flour and baking powder onto a large marble or wooden board. Form a well in the middle and sprinkle the salt around the edge. Add the sugar, egg, and vanilla into the well. Cut the butter into small pieces, approximately ¼ to ½ inch (see page 21, "How to Cut Butter," in "Technique to Prepare Mürbeteig Dough"). Distribute the pieces over and around the flour. Using the tip of a metal dough scraper, stir the egg as if gently scrambling. Begin carefully pushing the dry ingredients into the well's center. Work to combine all ingredients, first with the dough scraper and then with your hands, until a ball of dough forms. Add flour sparingly or chill as necessary if the dough becomes too sticky.

MÜRBETEIGE

2. Refrigerate the dough for 30 minutes.

3. Position a rack in the bottom third of the oven and preheat to 350°F. Place a heavy cookie sheet on bottom rung. Butter and flour the pan in preparation for assembly. Set aside.

4. Mix the filling: Using an electric mixer or food processor, blend the Greek yogurt, cream cheese, and sugar until sugar is mixed in well and starts to dissolve. Add sour cream, eggs, vanilla, lemon juice, and liliko'i juice and mix until smooth. Sift the cornstarch over the mixture. Blend again. The consistency will be like heavy cream.

5. Mold dough into pan: Slice the chilled dough horizontally into four discs. Lay the discs into the bottom of the prepared pan so they lean partially against the sides. The pieces may overlap. With flour-dipped fingers, push the dough out, rather than pressing it down, to cover the pan. Pull the dough up 1¾ to 2 inches on the sides of the pan. Even out any thin spots for a fairly consistent thickness.

6. Assemble for baking: Pour the filling into the crust and check the rim. The filling needs room to rise during baking. Keep crust ¼ inch above the filling. Push it down gently if it is higher.

7. Bake for 1 hour and 35 minutes to 1 hour and 45 minutes. Cover the rim with a pie crust shield for the last 25 minutes if the edges get too dark (see page 22, "About Pie Crust Shields"). The cake is ready when the middle is level with the sides and is of a light golden color. The crust will be a darker color. To check doneness, insert a wooden skewer through the cake's center. There may be a few kernels of filling on it, but it should not present underbaked dough. The filling may jiggle a little when the pan is moved, but it should be mostly set. Also insert the skewer gently between the crust and rim. The crust should be firm and lift away from the rim without leaving dough on the skewer. Allow cake to cool on a wire rack for at least 30 minutes before removing the pan's metal rim. Use a *kuchenretter* (cake lifter) to lift cake from the pan's base, and continue cooling on a wire rack to room temperature before serving, or refrigerate to cool further.

8. Before serving, top with liliko'i glaze.

Directions for Liliko'i Glaze

Combine the water and liliko'i juice. In a small bowl, whisk ½ cup of the diluted juice with the potato starch until the potato starch dissolves. Pour the remaining 1 cup of diluted juice into a medium-sized saucepan over medium-high heat. Add the potato starch mixture and the sugar. Stirring constantly, bring to a boil. This takes about 2½ minutes. Turn down the heat and continue to stir, more vigorously now, until the glaze starts to bubble up and reaches a consistency slightly thicker than maple syrup (see tip).

LILIKOʻI CHEESECAKE

~ TIP ~

The glaze can bubble over or stick to the saucepan's bottom very quickly, so do not leave the saucepan unattended at any time. Once the mixture starts to bubble, stir rapidly, making sure to scrape the bottom of the saucepan to avoid sticking and burning. A flat wooden spoon works best for this task. The glaze is nearly ready when it starts to bubble, which means that it has begun to gel up. At this point, turn off the heat or reduce it to low. Continue to stir and scrape for a few more strokes to prevent burning. If making a translucent glaze, the appearance should now be transforming from milky to clear. If the glaze boils too rapidly too early, remove from heat for a moment to prevent a spill-over, then turn down heat before replacing the saucepan. If the glaze appears too thick, add a little more juice and raise the heat to bring the mixture back to a low simmer. Turn down the heat and continue stirring to reach the desired consistency.

Allow glaze to cool enough that it is not too hot to the touch. For a rustic look, simply drizzle glaze over cake. For a smooth finish, place cake onto a serving tray and pour glaze onto the center of the cake. Hold the cake in place with thumbs, pick up the tray and tilt and roll it gently so that the glaze spreads out evenly over the top. This method will eliminate the streaks caused by spreading with a spatula.

Note 1: You can use freshly squeezed juice if you live in an area where lilikoʻi grows or is obtainable through a local grocer. The fresh fruit flavor is worth it. Use ½ cup of juice for this recipe. Each fruit will yield 1 to 2 tablespoons of juice. To obtain the juice, scoop the flesh and seeds into a fine mesh strainer and press with a spoon. For a video demonstration of making lilikoʻi juice, see vimeo.com/showcase/10470112. Lilikoʻi juice is very tart; taste the filling to see if more sugar is needed. Add additional sugar, a tablespoon at a time.

VIDEO SHOWCASE
Fillings and Garnishes
vimeo.com/showcase/10470112

Note 2: If using store-bought lilikoʻi juice for the glaze, look for brands that list lilikoʻi as the first ingredient. You may only find brands that mix lilikoʻi juice with other fruit juices. Other flavors could be a vibrant complement to the recipe but try to avoid brands with added sugar or sweetener. If using freshly squeezed lilikoʻi juice in the glaze, it will need more dilution than store-bought juice. Dilute ¼ cup of fresh juice with 1¼ cups of water, then use the amount needed for the glaze. Alternatively, 2 tablespoons of lilikoʻi concentrate or purée can be substituted for juice; dilute if necessary, according to label directions. There are vendors that sell purée and concentrate online. Ordering directly from the island of Kauai, Hawaii, is an option as well. It is best to taste test for tanginess before cooking the glaze, as brands differ in acidity.

PUMPKIN CHEESECAKE

The addition of pumpkin makes this cheesecake a lovely variation for fall and winter holidays, though the lime juice allows the cake to bridge into spring and summer seasons too. The lime may seem an unusual flavor with the pumpkin, but do not overlook it. It invigorates and deepens the warm clove, cinnamon, and pumpkin spice. This cake is not overly spiced to leave room for the complementing dairy flavor. More spice can be added according to personal taste. As with other cheesecakes, allow sufficient time to cool between baking and serving. The cake is best if refrigerated overnight. This cheesecake is made with a mixture of cream cheese and quark, which is my husband's favorite. Quark may not be available in all areas and can be hard to find (see page 12). If so, substitute one and a half cups ricotta and two-thirds cup sour cream.

PUMPKIN CHEESECAKE

BAKING PAN
10 x 3-inch springform pan, buttered and floured

Baking time may be shortened if a steel-based pan is used rather than aluminum; dark pans bake faster than light pans.

BAKING TEMPERATURE
350°F

BAKE TIME
1 hour and 30 minutes to 1 hour and 40 minutes

RACK PLACEMENT
bottom third of oven

Place a heavy cookie sheet on bottom rung to keep crust from getting too dark.

YIELD
one 10-inch cake

INGREDIENTS

FOR CRUST

1 ½ cups unbleached all-purpose flour (protein 3 grams per ¼ cup; see page 7), plus extra for working dough

1 ½ teaspoons baking powder

⅛ teaspoon salt

½ cup sugar

1 egg

1 teaspoon vanilla sugar, or ½ teaspoon vanilla extract

8 tablespoons (1 stick) unsalted butter, cold

FOR FILLING

8 ounces cream cheese (⅓ less fat or regular), at room temperature

16 ounces quark (if quark is hard to find, substitute 1 ½ cups ricotta and ⅔ cup sour cream)

3 eggs

1 ½ cups granulated sugar

¼ cup packed light brown sugar

1 tablespoon vanilla sugar, or 1 teaspoon vanilla extract

1 ½ tablespoons lime juice

4 tablespoons cornstarch

1 cup pumpkin purée (for purée from fresh pumpkin, see *note* in the Pumpkin Pie recipe on page 48)

Dash of ground cloves (less than ¹⁄₁₆ teaspoon)

1 ½ teaspoons pumpkin spice

½ teaspoon cinnamon

MÜRBETEIGE

DIRECTIONS

1. Prepare the crust: Set aside ¼ cup of the measured flour to use as needed while working the dough and pressing it into the form. Sift the remaining flour and baking powder onto a large marble or wooden board. Form a well in the middle and sprinkle the salt around the edge. Add the sugar, egg, and vanilla into the well. Cut the butter into small pieces, approximately ¼ to ½ inch (see page 21, "How to Cut Butter," in "Technique to Prepare Mürbeteig Dough"). Distribute the pieces over and around the flour. Using the tip of a metal dough scraper, stir the egg as if gently scrambling. Begin carefully pushing the dry ingredients into the well's center. Work to combine all ingredients, first with the dough scraper and then with your hands, until a ball of dough forms. Add flour sparingly or chill as necessary if the dough becomes too sticky.

2. Refrigerate the dough for 30 minutes.

3. Position a rack in the bottom third of the oven and preheat to 350°F. Place a heavy cookie sheet on bottom rung. Butter and flour the pan in preparation for assembly. Set aside.

4. Mix the filling: Using an electric mixer or food processor, blend the cream cheese, quark, eggs, granulated sugar, light brown sugar, vanilla, and lime juice until smooth. Sift the cornstarch over the mixture. Blend again. Add the pumpkin purée, cloves, pumpkin spice, and cinnamon. Blend briefly until an even, light-orange color is achieved. The consistency will be like heavy cream.

5. Mold dough into pan: Slice the chilled dough horizontally into four discs. Lay the discs into the bottom of the prepared pan so they lean partially against the sides. The pieces may overlap. With flour-dipped fingers, push the dough out, rather than pressing it down, to cover the pan evenly. Pull the dough about two-thirds of the way up the pan's sides. Even out any thin spots for a fairly consistent thickness.

6. Assemble for baking: Pour the filling into the crust and check the rim. The filling needs room to rise during baking. Keep crust ¼ inch above the filling. Push it down gently if it is higher.

7. Bake for 1 hour and 30 minutes to 1 hour and 40 minutes. Cover the rim with a pie crust shield for the last 25 minutes if the edges get too dark (see page 22, "About Pie Crust Shields"). The cake is ready when the middle is level with the sides and is of a toasted orange color. The crust will have deepened in color. Insert a wooden skewer gently between the crust and rim to check doneness. The crust should be firm and lift away from the rim without leaving dough on the skewer. Also insert the skewer through the cake's center. There may be a few kernels of filling on it, but it should not present underbaked dough. The filling may jiggle a little when the pan is moved, but it should be mostly set. Allow cake to cool on a wire rack for at least 30 minutes before removing the pan's metal rim. Use a *kuchenretter* (cake lifter) to lift cake from the pan's base, and continue cooling on a wire rack to room temperature before serving, or refrigerate to cool further.

PEAR FRANGIPANE TART

This pie borrows its flavor from my family's Christmas dinners in Germany. We would fill pear halves with lingonberry jelly to serve alongside earthy game meat. Many years later, I wanted to see if the sweet, delicate pear and the woodsy tartness of lingonberries could work together in a pastry. As I was creating this pie, I reminisced over times spent in the forest, the herby scents of summer forest flora, and the bushes covered with all varieties of berries ripe for picking.

Just-ripe pears are best to complement the indulgent frangipane filling and the rich hazelnut crust. Select pears that are ready for eating and beginning to soften, but not overly soft. Mildly sweet varieties such as D'Anjou or Williams (also known as Bartlett in the United States) work well.

To enhance the fruit flavor, this recipe gives an optional lingonberry spread underneath the pears. Optional garnishes include apricot glaze and/or roasted sliced almonds.

It is preferable to make the frangipane filling the day before baking the pie and refrigerate overnight. This will save time the next day and give the frangipane a chance to thicken and develop flavor. There will be filling left over; the recipe makes one and a half cups, but only needs one and one-third cups. Leftover filling can be frozen and used later to make easy turnovers with store-bought puff pastry sheets (see page 23, "What to Do with Extra Filling"). Leftover frangipane also works well as extra richness in the filling for the Almond Hazelnut Mini Tarts (see page 85).

MÜRBETEIGE

BAKING PAN
10 x 1 ½-inch quiche or tart pan or 10 x 2-inch cheesecake or springform pan, buttered and floured

Baking time may be shortened if a steel-based pan is used rather than aluminum; dark pans bake faster than light pans.

BAKING TEMPERATURE
375°F

BAKE TIME
55 to 60 minutes

RACK PLACEMENT
middle of oven

Place a heavy cookie sheet on bottom rung to keep crust from getting too dark.

YIELD
one 10-inch pie

INGREDIENTS

FOR FRANGIPANE (ALMOND) FILLING
(yields 1 ½ cups of filling)

8 tablespoons (1 stick) unsalted butter, at room temperature and very soft (can be partially melted)

½ cup sugar

2 eggs (to add to butter), plus 1 egg yolk (to add to almond paste)

4 ounces almond paste (see page 11)

1 ½ teaspoons almond extract (preferably bitter almond extract)

⅓ cup potato starch

1 ½ cups blanched almond flour

FOR CRUST

1 ¼ cups unbleached all-purpose flour (protein 3 grams per ¼ cup; see page 7), plus extra for working dough

½ cup hazelnut meal

Pinch of salt (about ⅛ teaspoon or less)

¼ cup sugar

1 egg, plus 1 egg yolk

6 tablespoons unsalted butter, cold

FOR FRUIT

3 to 4 large fresh pears (about 2 pounds)

Juice of 1 small lemon (about 2 tablespoons)

1 teaspoon pear brandy (brandy suggestion: Clear Creek Distillery Pear Brandy, available in select liquor stores and online)

1 tablespoon unsalted butter, melted (for brushing pears before pie goes into the oven)

Ingredients continued on next page

PEAR FRANGIPANE TART

FOR OPTIONAL LINGONBERRY SPREAD

4 ounces lingonberry jam (raspberry jam can be substituted)

1 teaspoon brandy (preferably pear brandy or orange liqueur)

FOR OPTIONAL APRICOT GLAZE

3 to 4 ounces apricot jam

FOR OPTIONAL ROASTED ALMOND GARNISH

½ cup sliced almonds

1 tablespoon unsalted butter (omit if dry roasting in oven; see *note* at end of recipe)

DIRECTIONS

1. Make the frangipane filling the day before baking: In a stand mixer or with an electric mixer, cream the soft butter until creamy and fluffy, about 5 minutes. Add the sugar and mix for another 1 to 2 minutes. In a separate bowl, and mixing by hand, work the egg yolk into the almond paste, then set aside. Return to the butter mixture and add the remaining eggs, one at a time, and cream for an additional 1 minute. Add the almond and egg yolk mixture into the butter mixture and beat until incorporated. Add the almond extract and mix for 20 more seconds, until just incorporated. Sift in the potato starch and mix briefly. Working by hand with a large spoon, fold in the almond flour until blended. The mixture should be of a thick, spreadable consistency. Refrigerate overnight.

2. Prepare the crust: Set aside ¼ cup of the measured flour to use as needed while working the dough and pressing it into the form. Sift the remaining flour and hazelnut meal onto a large marble or wooden board. Form a well in the middle and sprinkle the salt around the edge. Add the sugar and the egg and egg yolk into the well. Cut the butter into small pieces, approximately ¼ to ½ inch (see page 21, "How to Cut Butter," in "Technique to Prepare Mürbeteig Dough"). Distribute the pieces over and around the flour and nut meal. Using the tip of a metal dough scraper, stir the egg and yolk as if gently scrambling. Begin carefully pushing the dry ingredients into the well's center. Work to combine all ingredients, first with the dough scraper and then with your hands, until a ball of dough forms. Add flour sparingly or chill as necessary if the dough becomes too sticky.

3. Refrigerate the dough for 30 minutes.

4. If using the optional lingonberry spread, prepare now: Mix the lingonberry jam and pear brandy. Set aside.

5. Position a rack in the middle of the oven and preheat to 375°F. Butter and flour the pan in preparation for assembly. Set aside.

MÜRBETEIGE

6. **Mold dough into pan:** Slice the chilled dough horizontally into three discs. Lay the discs into the prepared pan so they lean partially against the sides. The pieces may overlap. With flour-dipped fingers, push the dough together and out, rather than pressing it down, to cover the pan evenly. Pull the dough about 1½ inches up the sides of the pan. Even out any thin spots to get the dough to a fairly consistent thickness.

7. **Spread frangipane filling and slice and assemble pears:** Spread 1⅓ cups of the frangipane filling over the crust and set aside. Have the lingonberry spread ready, if using. Meanwhile, prepare a medium to large bowl with the lemon juice and pear brandy. Peel, halve, and core the pears. Place each pear half into the bowl and turn to coat with the lemon juice and brandy mixture to prevent the pears from browning.

With a sharp carving knife in hand, place each pear half, hollow-side down and with the stem end away from your body, onto a wooden board. You will be making long, thin cuts to create a fan shape—the fruit will remain intact at the stem end. Grasp the stem end and place the knife about ½ inch down from that end; remember the stem end will not be sliced. Start with the knife at a 20- to 30-degree angle from the board and slice by pulling the knife through the pear, all the way down to the board's surface. Make as many thin slices as possible, up to twenty slices, depending on the size of the pear. All slices should still be attached to the stem end but cut through otherwise. When finished, carefully push down on each pear half to fan the slices out.

If not using the optional lingonberry spread, place one fanned pear half in the middle of the pie, on top of the frangipane filling, and arrange the others in a circle around the center pear; stem sides should face the pie's middle. If using the optional lingonberry spread, first place a teaspoon of the spread onto the frangipane filling where each pear half will be placed, then carefully transfer the fanned pears onto

PEAR FRANGIPANE TART

the dollops of lingonberry, stem-sides facing toward the pie's middle.

Evenly brush pears with the melted butter. Finally, check the crust. If the crust extends more than 1 inch above the filling, gently push it down to about ½ inch.

8. Bake for 55 to 60 minutes, until the top is golden brown. Cover the rim with a pie crust shield for the last 20 minutes if the edges get too dark (see page 22, "About Pie Crust Shields"). Insert a wooden skewer gently between the crust and rim to check doneness. The crust should be firm and should lift away from the rim without leaving dough on the skewer. Also insert the skewer through the pie's center. The skewer should come out clean of dough, and the pears should be soft. Remove the pan's rim and let cool on a wire rack for 15 minutes. Then use a *kuchenretter* (cake lifter) to lift the pie from the pan's bottom, and let cool on a wire rack to room temperature. Continue cooling longer in the refrigerator if desired.

9. After the pie has cooled, serve as is or drizzle with optional apricot glaze and/or sprinkle with optional roasted sliced almonds (see *note* at end of recipe).

Directions for Optional Apricot Glaze

Strain the apricot jam through a strainer. In a saucepan, heat and stir until hot and smooth. Spoon evenly over pears for a thin glaze.

Note: Almonds can be roasted on the stovetop or in the oven.

Stovetop: In a skillet over medium heat, melt the butter. Add the sliced almonds and stir constantly until golden brown. Spread out on a plate to cool.

Oven: Position a rack in the top third of the oven and preheat to 350°F. Spread the sliced almonds on a cookie sheet. There is no need to butter the cookie sheet when oven roasting the almonds. Roast for 3 to 4 minutes and then stir and flip the almonds, moving the outside ones into the middle and vice versa for even roasting. Roast for another 2 to 3 minutes, or until golden brown. Watch almonds carefully. Don't over-roast. If they get too dark, the flavor becomes strong and bitter.

APRICOT ALMOND CREAM TART

With a smooth, creamy filling, this tart features a deep almond and custard flavor, with bursts of palate-teasing tartness from the apricots. The tart develops its flavor when given time to rest and tastes even better the next day. Although very tempting to eat right away, give it at least a few hours to cool before serving. For extra decoration (as shown in the recipe photograph), garnish with dollops of buttercream before serving (see *note 1* at end of recipe).

APRICOT ALMOND CREAM TART

BAKING PAN
10 x 3-inch springform pan, buttered and floured

Baking time may be shortened if a steel-based pan is used rather than aluminum; dark pans bake faster than light pans.

BAKING TEMPERATURE
375°F

BAKE TIME
55 to 60 minutes

RACK PLACEMENT
middle of oven

Place a heavy cookie sheet on bottom rung to keep crust from getting too dark.

YIELD
one 10-inch tart

INGREDIENTS

FOR CRUST

1 ¼ cups unbleached all-purpose flour (protein 3 grams per ¼ cup; see page 7), plus extra for working dough

2 teaspoons baking powder

Pinch of salt (about ⅛ teaspoon or less)

⅓ cup sugar

1 egg

2 teaspoons vanilla sugar, or 1 teaspoon vanilla extract

8 tablespoons (1 stick) unsalted butter, cold

FOR FILLING

1 ½ (15- or 16-ounce) cans apricots (about 14 to 16 apricot halves)

1 cup blanched almond meal (see *note 2* at end of recipe)

1 cup powdered sugar

2 tablespoons potato starch

1 egg

4 ounces almond paste (see page 11)

½ cup heavy whipping cream, scantly measured

Pulp of ½ of a vanilla bean, or 1 teaspoon vanilla extract, or 2 teaspoons vanilla sugar

1 teaspoon almond extract

1 tablespoon almond liqueur, optional

15 whole blanched almonds or sliced almonds, for decoration (see page 13 for blanching technique)

MÜRBETEIGE

DIRECTIONS

1. Prepare the crust: Set aside ¼ cup of the measured flour to use as needed while working the dough and pressing it into the form. Sift the remaining flour and baking powder onto a large marble or wooden board. Form a well in the middle and sprinkle the salt around the edge. Add the sugar, egg, and vanilla into the well. Cut the butter into small pieces, approximately ¼ to ½ inch (see page 21, "How to Cut Butter," in "Technique to Prepare Mürbeteig Dough"). Distribute the pieces over and around the flour. Using the tip of a metal dough scraper, stir the egg as if gently scrambling. Begin carefully pushing the dry ingredients into the well's center. Work to combine all ingredients, first with the dough scraper and then with your hands, until a ball of dough forms. Add flour sparingly or chill as necessary if the dough becomes too sticky.

2. Refrigerate the dough for 30 minutes.

3. Drain the apricots into a colander and set aside.

4. Make the filling: Measure the ground almonds into a large bowl. Sift the powdered sugar with the potato starch over the ground almonds. Mix the dry ingredients together. Crack the egg into a separate medium-sized bowl and beat as if scrambling, just long enough to incorporate the yolk and white. Using a fork or hands, work the almond paste into the egg. Mix until incorporated, breaking up lumps in the process. Once all the egg is incorporated, blend smooth with an electric mixer on medium for 1 minute. Slowly pour and mix the unwhipped heavy whipping cream into the egg and almond paste mixture; add the vanilla, almond extract, and optional almond liqueur. Pour the egg, almond, and cream mixture into the dry ingredients. With a wire whisk or large spatula, gently fold and stir until just incorporated.

5. Position a rack in the middle of the oven and preheat to 375°F. Butter and flour the pan in preparation for assembly. Set aside.

6. Mold dough into pan: Slice the chilled dough horizontally into three discs. Lay the discs into the prepared pan so they lean partially against the sides. The pieces may overlap. With flour-dipped fingers, push the dough together and out, rather than pressing it down, to cover the pan evenly. Pull the dough about 1½ inches up the side of the pan. Even out any thin spots to get the dough to a fairly consistent thickness.

7. Assemble for baking: Pour the filling into the crust and place one apricot, stone-side up, in the center. Arrange the rest, also stone-side up, in concentric circles. Ensure that none touch the pan's rim. Place one whole or sliced almond into the curved middle of each apricot. The apricots will resemble little cradles or boats for the almonds. If the crust extends more than ½ inch above the filling, gently push it down.

8. Bake for 55 to 60 minutes, until filling appears set and golden brown. Cover the rim with a pie crust shield for the last 20 minutes if the edges get too dark (see page 22, "About Pie Crust Shields"). If necessary, cover the entire

APRICOT ALMOND CREAM TART

tart loosely with aluminum foil shaped into a dome (see tip). Insert a wooden skewer gently between the crust and rim to check doneness. The crust should be firm and lift away from the rim without leaving dough on the skewer. Also insert the skewer through the tart's center. There may be a few kernels of filling on it, but it should not present wet filling or underbaked dough. Place pan on a rack to cool. After about an hour, transfer to the refrigerator to continue cooling for a few hours or overnight before serving.

~ TIP ~

Cut out a round piece of foil (14 inches in diameter), tap the middle to create a slight dome shape, and place over the entire tart. Leave the foil loose. Sealing the edges will trap steam and alter the baking. Remember, the foil will become hot, so do not handle it without mitts when checking on the tart or removing it.

Note 1: To garnish with buttercream, use the lemon buttercream from the Lemon, Lilikoʻi, or Chocolate Buttercream recipe on page 252. Ensure the buttercream chills for 1½ to 2 hours before piping. It must be semi-soft and able to hold its shape. After the tart has baked and cooled as directed, pipe a dollop of buttercream onto the almond in each apricot half. Use a large or extra-large open star tip (such as Wilton 4B or 1M, or another tip of a similar size) for piping. Leftover buttercream can be stored in the refrigerator for several days to a week.

Note 2: A good ⅔ cup or a scant ¾ cup of whole blanched almonds makes 1 cup ground almonds. Store-bought almond flour will be less flavorful. See page 13 for blanching technique and page 14 for grinding technique. If absolutely necessary, a scant 1 cup of store-bought almond flour can be substituted; avoid super finely milled almond flour.

RASPBERRY ALMOND TART

This tart has an enchanting variety of texture and taste. Between the crust and the fluffy almond filling lies a sweet and tart spread of raspberry jelly and whole raspberries. Sprinkled on top is a layer of roasted sliced almonds. The layers give slices a gorgeous profile, and the tastes of rich almond filling and fresh berry make this a perfect tart for any season. The tart's distinct almond flavor comes through by working the almond paste into the filling. This step adds time to the recipe, but it also transforms the tart with a rounded, delicate taste sure to win over any guest, inevitably leading to requests for more.

RASPBERRY ALMOND TART

BAKING PAN
10 x 2-inch springform pan, buttered and floured

Baking time may be shortened if a steel-based pan is used rather than aluminum; dark pans bake faster than light pans.

BAKING TEMPERATURE
350°F

BAKE TIME
55 to 60 minutes, cover with pie crust shield after 35 minutes

RACK PLACEMENT
middle of oven

Place a heavy cookie sheet on bottom rung to keep crust from getting too dark.

YIELD
one 10-inch tart

INGREDIENTS

FOR CRUST

1 ⅓ cups unbleached all-purpose flour (protein 3 grams per ¼ cup; see page 7), plus extra for working dough

1 teaspoon baking powder

¼ cup almond flour

⅓ cup powdered sugar

Pinch of salt (about ⅛ teaspoon or less)

1 egg, plus 1 egg yolk

7 tablespoons unsalted butter, cold

FOR ALMOND FILLING

1 ⅔ cups blanched almond meal (see *note 1* at end of recipe)

¼ cup potato starch

3 eggs

1 cup powdered sugar

8 ounces almond paste (see page 11)

1 tablespoon almond extract

Pulp of 1 vanilla bean, or 1 tablespoon vanilla extract

4 tablespoons unsalted butter, melted

FOR RASPBERRY FILLING

4 ounces raspberry jelly or jam

1 cup fresh raspberries

Sugar to taste (about 1 to 3 tablespoons)

FOR ROASTED ALMOND GARNISH

½ cup sliced almonds

1 tablespoon unsalted butter (omit if dry roasting in oven; see *note 2* at end of recipe)

FOR DUSTING

¼ cup powdered sugar

MÜRBETEIGE

DIRECTIONS

1. Prepare the crust: Set aside ¼ cup of the measured flour to use as needed while working the dough and pressing it into the form. Sift the remaining flour, baking powder, almond flour, and powdered sugar onto a large marble or wooden board. Form a well in the middle and sprinkle the salt around the edge. Add the egg and egg yolk into the well. Cut the butter into small pieces, approximately ¼ to ½ inch (see page 21, "How to Cut Butter," in "Technique to Prepare Mürbeteig Dough"). Distribute the pieces over and around the flour. Using the tip of a metal dough scraper, stir the egg and yolk as if gently scrambling. Begin carefully pushing the dry ingredients into the well's center. Work to combine all ingredients, first with the dough scraper and then with your hands, until a ball of dough forms. Add flour sparingly or chill as necessary if the dough becomes too sticky.

2. Refrigerate the dough for 30 minutes.

3. Make the almond filling: In a large bowl, mix the almond meal with the potato starch. Set aside. Separate the eggs. Place the whites into a large bowl and the yolks into a small bowl. With an electric mixer, whip the egg whites until soft peaks form. Sift the powdered sugar over the egg whites and mix on slow to medium speed to incorporate, until smooth and silky. Set aside.

   In a separate large mixing bowl, add the almond paste. Knead the egg yolks, one at a time, into the almond paste. Once all the yolks are incorporated, blend smooth with an electric mixer, adding the almond extract and vanilla while mixing. By hand and with a wire whisk, carefully blend one-third of the egg whites into the almond paste mixture, breaking up lumps if any appear. Incorporate the next third in the same way, and then the final third. Once incorporated, add the almond meal and potato starch mixture, and fold carefully until blended. Drizzle the melted butter over the filling and fold, gently, until incorporated. Set aside until assembling for baking.

4. Position a rack in the middle of the oven and preheat to 350°F. Butter and flour the pan in preparation for assembly.

5. Prepare the raspberry filling: If the raspberry jelly contains seeds, strain through a sifter to remove them and then set the jelly aside in preparation for assembly. Wash the raspberries and shake dry in a towel. Do not add the sugar until step 7.

6. Mold dough into pan: Slice the chilled dough horizontally into four discs. Lay the discs into the bottom of the prepared pan so they lean partially against the sides. The pieces may overlap. With flour-dipped fingers, push the dough out, rather than pressing it down, to cover the pan evenly. Pull the dough three-fourths of the way up the pan's rim. Even out any thin spots for a fairly consistent thickness.

7. Assemble for baking: Spread the jelly over the crust. Spread one-third of the almond filling onto the jelly. Add sugar to taste to the

RASPBERRY ALMOND TART

raspberries, then place the raspberries on top of the filling. Spread the remainder of the almond filling to cover the raspberries.

8. Bake for 55 to 60 minutes. Cover the rim with a pie crust shield if the edges get too dark—check the edges for darkening after 35 minutes of bake time and then every 5 to 10 minutes, until the tart is done (see page 22, "About Pie Crust Shields"). The tart is ready when the filling's top is a light golden brown. The crust will have deepened in color. Insert a wooden skewer gently between the crust and rim to check doneness. The crust should be firm and lift away from the rim without leaving dough on the skewer. Also insert the skewer through the tart's center. There may be a few kernels of filling or a little raspberry juice on it, but it should not present wet filling or under-baked dough. Cool on a wire rack to room temperature.

9. After the tart cools, roast the sliced almonds (see *note 2* at end of recipe). Sprinkle roasted sliced almonds over the tart and dust with powdered sugar before serving.

Note 1: Some stand mixers have special attachments for grinding nuts. A coffee mill with a blade grinder will also work but do not use a burr grinder style of mill. To prepare homemade almond meal in a coffee mill, measure out 1¼ cups blanched almonds. This amount will produce the 1⅔ cups of almond meal needed for the recipe. Pour some of the almonds into the coffee mill until it is filled halfway, and then pulse twelve to fifteen times to grind the almonds. Repeat filling the mill halfway twice more to grind the remaining almonds. Almond meal is coarser in texture than almond flour.

Note 2: Almonds can be roasted on the stovetop or in the oven.

Stovetop: In a skillet over medium heat, melt the butter. Add the sliced almonds and stir constantly until golden brown. Spread out on a plate to cool.

Oven: Position a rack in the top third of the oven and preheat to 350°F. Spread the sliced almonds on a cookie sheet. There is no need to butter the cookie sheet when oven roasting the almonds. Roast for 3 to 4 minutes and then stir and flip the almonds, moving the outside ones into the middle and vice versa for even roasting. Roast for another 2 to 3 minutes, or until golden brown. Watch almonds carefully. Don't over-roast. If they get too dark, the flavor becomes strong and bitter.

ALMOND HAZELNUT MINI TARTS
(baked in a muffin pan)

This recipe was an experiment I tried on a whim, thinking it would be nice to have pies readymade as individually sized tarts. They turned out splendidly. The tarts bake in a muffin pan, which concentrates the heat to give each little tart a beautifully domed and caramelized top, a golden crust, and a gooey center. The filling is a simple but irresistible medley of nutty flavors. Garnish options at the end of the recipe include an easy whipped cream topping or fresh hazelnut buttercream frosting. The mini tarts are also delicious plain with powdered sugar sifted over the top. Be warned—the handheld size makes these treats all the easier to grab and devour.

ALMOND HAZELNUT MINI TARTS

BAKING PAN
12-cup muffin pan, with cups 2 ½ inches in diameter, buttered and floured

BAKING TEMPERATURE
350°F for 10 minutes; reduce to 325°F for remaining time

BAKE TIME
35 to 40 minutes

RACK PLACEMENT
middle of oven

YIELD
twelve 2 ½-inch tarts

INGREDIENTS

FOR CRUST

1 cup unbleached all-purpose flour (protein 3 grams per ¼ cup; see page 7), plus extra for working dough

½ teaspoon baking powder

Pinch of salt (about ⅛ teaspoon or less)

¼ cup sugar

1 egg

1 teaspoon vanilla sugar, or ½ teaspoon vanilla extract

5 tablespoons unsalted butter, cold

FOR FILLING

1 cup hazelnut meal

3 eggs

1 cup almond meal

¾ cup sugar

¼ cup heavy whipping cream

⅓ cup frangipane, optional (see *note 1* at end of recipe)

1 tablespoon orange liqueur

2 teaspoons vanilla extract

DIRECTIONS

1. Prepare the crust: Set aside ¼ cup of the measured flour to use as needed while working the dough and pressing it into the form. Sift the remaining flour and baking powder onto a large marble or wooden board. Form a well in the middle and sprinkle the salt around the edge. Add the sugar, egg, and vanilla into the well. Cut the butter into small pieces, approximately ¼ to ½ inch (see page 21, "How to Cut Butter," in "Technique to Prepare Mürbeteig Dough"). Distribute the pieces over and around the flour. Using the tip of a metal dough scraper, stir the egg as if gently scrambling. Begin carefully pushing the dry ingredients into the well's center. Work to combine all ingredients, first with the dough scraper and then with your hands, until a ball of dough forms. Add flour sparingly or chill as necessary if the dough becomes too sticky.

MÜRBETEIGE

2. Refrigerate the dough for 30 minutes.

3. Roast the hazelnut meal: Heat a skillet over medium to medium-high. Add the hazelnut meal into the skillet and flatten it down with a spatula. Toast the hazelnut meal for about 5 minutes, to a light brown color, then stir and flip regularly to brown evenly. If smoke starts to develop, the skillet is too hot. If that happens, remove from heat for a brief time and continue stirring, then return to heat as needed, with the temperature reduced as needed. Aim for golden brown, not dark brown. If the hazelnut meal darkens too much, it will become bitter. Spread out hazelnut meal on a plate to cool to room temperature.

4. Position a rack in the middle of the oven and preheat to 350°F. Butter and flour each cup in the muffin pan. Set aside.

5. Separate the eggs: Place the egg whites in a large mixing bowl and the yolks in a small bowl. Whip the egg whites to firm peaks.

6. Make the filling: Using an electric mixer or food processor, blend the roasted hazelnut meal, almond meal, sugar, unwhipped heavy whipping cream, and egg yolks until fluffed and creamy, about 45 to 60 seconds. Add the optional frangipane (if using) and mix until incorporated. Place ¼ cup of the mixture in a small bowl and stir in the orange liqueur and vanilla. Add back to the remaining mixture and stir thoroughly. This process will distribute the liqueur and vanilla flavors evenly.

7. Give the egg whites a few strokes with a wire hand whisk to whip up any liquid that may have formed at the bottom of the bowl. Slide the whites over the nut meal mixture and fold in gently to incorporate.

8. Roll and cut the dough: Roll out the dough to about ⅛-inch thickness. Use a 3-inch cookie cutter or drinking glass to cut out twelve circles. Gently press the circles into the muffin pan cups. Keep the crusts short of the rims so they have room to rise during baking.

9. Assemble for baking: Scoop filling into each crust, keeping it a little short of the crust's edge so the filling has room to bake up.

10. Bake for 35 to 40 minutes (350°F for 10 minutes, then reduce to 325°F for remaining time). The tarts are done when the tops appear golden brown and crackly. Cool tarts in pan on a wire rack to room temperature. Once cooled, pop the tarts out of the cups with a fork. Serve plain and dusted with powdered sugar or with hazelnut buttercream or easy whipped cream topping.

ALMOND HAZELNUT MINI TARTS

FOR HAZELNUT BUTTERCREAM

28 tablespoons (3 ½ sticks) unsalted butter, at room temperature and very soft but not melted

4 eggs, at room temperature

1 ½ cups sugar

8 teaspoons lemon juice

1 whole vanilla bean (or at least ½ of a vanilla bean), split down the middle

Zest of 1 small lemon (about 2 teaspoons)

4 tablespoons orange liqueur (for example, Grand Marnier)

1 ½ cups finely ground hazelnut meal (or ¾ cup each hazelnut meal and almond meal), roasted (see *note 2* at end of recipe)

Directions for Hazelnut Buttercream

Follow the directions for the lemon buttercream in the Lemon, Lilikoʻi, or Chocolate Buttercream recipe (page 252). Before the final step to refrigerate the buttercream, take out ⅓ cup of the buttercream and mix it with the orange liqueur, then add back to the remaining buttercream and fold in to incorporate. Fold in the finely ground and roasted nut meal for a full-bodied, delicate nut taste. Proceed with the final step to refrigerate the buttercream. When ready to use the buttercream, remove from the refrigerator and let sit at room temperature until softened enough for easy piping; stir every so often to ensure even softening. This recipe makes enough buttercream to frost twelve tarts.

FOR EASY WHIPPED CREAM TOPPING

4 cups unwhipped heavy whipping cream

1 ¾ cups powdered sugar, sifted

¾ cup finely ground hazelnut meal (or ⅜ cup each hazelnut meal and almond meal), roasted (see *note 2* at end of recipe)

Directions for Easy Whipped Cream Topping

Whip the cream with the powdered sugar to stiff peaks. Sprinkle the finely ground and roasted nut meal on top and fold under to incorporate. Pipe the topping onto the tarts. This recipe makes enough whipped cream to top twelve tarts.

. . . .

Note 1: The frangipane (almond paste) brings extra indulgence to the filling. Use the frangipane filling recipe in the Pear Frangipane Tart (page 72). That recipe yields 1½ cups of filling. Leftover filling can be frozen and used later, either as additions to more Almond Hazelnut Mini Tarts or as filling in easy turnovers with store-bought puff pastry sheets (see page 23, "What to Do with Extra Filling").

Note 2: For homemade ground nut meal, use a nut grinder or coffee mill (with a blade grinder, not a burr grinder; see page 14, "Grinding Whole Nuts into Nut Meal and Nut Flour"). Fill the grinder or coffee mill only halfway; work in batches as needed.

To roast the finely ground nut meal, follow the directions in step 3 of the mini tart recipe. Let roasted nut meal cool to room temperature before incorporating into the whipped cream topping.

LINZER TORTE

The Linzer torte is a source of great pride for its namesake town of Linz, Austria, where written recipes of this nutty, spiced, jelly-filled cake date back to the seventeenth century. However, modern home bakers, even novices, should not let the Linzer torte's revered history nor its delicate appearance intimidate them. The torte is remarkably sturdy and versatile.

This recipe's crust has a mix of all-purpose flour, ground almonds, and ground hazelnuts. Grind the nuts at home for fresh flavor and ideal nut meal consistency. Commercially available ground almonds and hazelnuts are milled more finely, which may produce a dry consistency in this crust.

While a raspberry variation is offered, this recipe recommends the traditional red currant jelly filling. The red currant provides a vibrant, slightly tart flavor, something like a mix of raspberry, gooseberry, lingonberry, and cranberry. Currants are small berries wrapped in shiny, translucent skin. Look for a good-quality red currant jelly, free of corn syrup and watered-down juice. The first ingredient should be red currants. If the jelly is difficult to find, visit a gourmet store or specialty grocer, or order online. Alternatively, make your own jelly if red currants are available in your local area. Raspberry jelly makes an excellent second choice. To garnish, use either a hot apricot glaze or simply give the torte a powdered sugar dusting.

LINZER TORTE

BAKING PAN
10 x 1-inch fluted tart pan, preferably with removable bottom; or 10 x 2 ½-inch aluminum springform pan, buttered and floured

Baking time may be shortened if a steel-based pan is used rather than aluminum; dark pans bake faster than light pans.

BAKING TEMPERATURE
350°F

BAKE TIME
25 to 35 minutes

RACK PLACEMENT
middle of oven

YIELD
one 10-inch torte

INGREDIENTS

FOR CRUST

1 ½ cups unbleached all-purpose flour (protein 3 grams per ¼ cup; see page 7), plus ¼ cup extra for working dough and cutting lattice

⅔ cup medium-fine ground almonds (not as fine as almond flour) (a good ½ cup whole nuts if grinding yourself, see page 14 for technique)

⅔ cup coarsely ground hazelnuts (a good ½ cup whole nuts if grinding yourself, see page 14 for technique)

¼ teaspoon good-quality Dutched cocoa (for example, Droste brand), optional

1 ½ teaspoons cinnamon

1/16 teaspoon ground cloves

2 teaspoons lemon zest (about 1 small or ½ large lemon), freshly grated and loosely measured

Pinch of salt (about ⅛ teaspoon or less)

¾ cup sugar

1 egg

1 tablespoon rum

9 tablespoons (1 ⅛ sticks) unsalted butter, cold

FOR FILLING

¾ cup (8 ounces) red currant jelly or raspberry jelly

1 tablespoon *kirschwasser* (preferred, see page 12; orange liqueur can be substituted)

FOR OPTIONAL HOT APRICOT GLAZE (to garnish)

4 ounces apricot jelly

4 tablespoons water

2 tablespoons sugar

FOR DUSTING (in place of hot apricot glaze)

⅓ cup powdered sugar

MÜRBETEIGE

DIRECTIONS

1. Prepare the crust: Set aside the extra ¼ cup of flour to use as needed while working the dough, pressing it into the form, and making lattice. Sift the remaining flour into a large bowl. Add the ground almonds, ground hazelnuts, cocoa (if using), cinnamon, ground cloves, and lemon zest. Stir to combine. Turn out the dry ingredients onto a large marble or wooden board and shape into a mound. Form a deep well in the middle and sprinkle the salt around the edge. Add the sugar, egg, and rum into the well. Cut the butter into small pieces, approximately ¼ to ½ inch (see page 21, "How to Cut Butter," in "Technique to Prepare Mürbeteig Dough"). Distribute the pieces over and around the flour. Using the tip of a metal dough scraper, stir the egg as if gently scrambling. Begin carefully pushing the dry ingredients into the well's center. Work to combine all ingredients, first with the dough scraper until the butter is cut into very small bits, then continue with your hands, until a ball of dough forms. Add flour sparingly or chill as necessary if the dough becomes too sticky.

2. When the dough forms a smooth ball, place on a plate, cover with plastic wrap, and refrigerate for 30 minutes.

3. Make the filling: If using seeded raspberry jelly, strain the jelly through a strainer, working with the back of a spoon to push the jelly through. Scrape off excess underneath the strainer. Red currant jelly does not need to be strained. Whisk the jelly with the kirschwasser or orange liqueur.

4. Position a rack in the middle of the oven and preheat to 350°F. Butter and flour the tart pan or springform.

5. Mold dough into pan: Slice the chilled dough horizontally into three discs. Lay two discs into the prepared pan so they lean partially against the sides. The pieces may overlap. Leave the third disc in the refrigerator. With flour-dipped fingers, push the dough out, rather than pressing it down, to cover the pan evenly. Pull the dough up about ¾ inch on the sides of the pan. Even out any thin spots to get the dough to a fairly consistent thickness.

6. Spread the jelly mixture over the crust and set the pan aside.

7. Prepare the first layer of lattice: Lightly dust a marble or wooden board with flour. Remove half of the remaining dough from the refrigerator. Rub flour onto the rolling pin and work surface, and sprinkle sparingly over the dough if necessary. Roll out the dough until it matches the diameter of the pan (see tip 1). The rolled dough should be ¼ inch thick or less. Dip a pastry cutter in flour and slice the rolled-out dough into strips, each about 1 inch wide (see tip 2).

~ TIP 1 ~

To assist in estimating diameter, it is helpful to roll out the dough on a nonstick pastry mat with measured circles, to overturn another pan of the same size and lightly press the rim into the rolled-out dough, or to have a ruler on hand.

LINZER TORTE

~ TIP 2 ~
There are different types of pastry wheel cutters available that readily cut lattice strips.

---

8. Assemble lattice: Lift one strip at a time by sliding a floured dough scraper under it. Starting at the torte's edge with the shortest strip, lay strips diagonally on top of the jelly. Keep the strips about 1 inch apart. If a strip is too short or breaks during transfer, simply add on more dough. Once the torte is baked and garnished, the seam will not show (see tip 3).

~ TIP 3 ~
Laying lattice strips is delicate work, refined with practice. Strips may break for a variety of reasons. The dough may be rolled too thin; it may not have enough flour; it may be too soft or too warm. The lifting tool or work surface may not have enough flour or may be too warm. Regardless of the reason, do not fret. It is better to have a few strips break than to end up with too much flour, which will produce a dry dough in the lattice.

---

9. When the first lattice layer is finished, take the remaining dough from the refrigerator. Repeat the process of rolling out and slicing the dough strips. Finish the lattice by laying the second layer of strips diagonally across the first, in the opposite direction. The pattern should produce diamond-shaped gaps showing the jelly filling. Check the crust's edge. If it extends much higher than

MÜRBETEIGE

the lattice, gently push it down to be about ¼ inch higher than the filling.

If there is leftover dough, roll into a thin rope and place around the torte's edge or fashion into a bow to lay in the middle.

10. Bake for 25 to 35 minutes, until the lattice is golden brown; the edges may be darker. Insert a wooden skewer through the lattice into the center to check doneness. The skewer may show some jelly, but it should not present underbaked dough. Allow torte to settle and cool on a wire rack for 20 minutes. Remove rim and use a *kuchenretter* (cake lifter) to lift torte from the pan's base, and continue cooling on the wire rack.

11. Once cooled, brush with hot apricot glaze or dust with powdered sugar.

Directions for Hot Apricot Glaze

Strain the apricot jelly through a strainer, working with the back of a spoon to push the jelly through. Scrape off excess underneath the strainer. Set aside.

Measure the water and sugar into a small saucepan. While stirring, bring the mixture to a low boil and cook until sugar is dissolved. Add the apricot jelly and cook a few more seconds while stirring. Continue stirring until smooth.

TARTE TATIN

While visiting France in my younger years, I had the pleasure of tasting tarte Tatin twice and will never forget it. During cooking, the juices from the apples mix with the fresh caramel to create a syrupy sauce unrivaled by any other apple pie. The tarte is legendary, and there have been many stories about how it originated and why the crust bakes on top of the apples rather than beneath them. According to legend, tarte Tatin originated in the late 1800s, an invention of Stéphanie and Caroline Tatin, who owned the Hôtel Tatin in the small town of Lamotte-Beuvron, located in the countryside of Sologne, France. Caroline operated the business, and Stéphanie took care of the cooking. She cooked everything on a small, wood-fired stovetop in the hotel's busy kitchen. A popular version of the legend says that in this hectic environment, Stéphanie one day forgot to put the crust into the pan before adding the apples, so she laid it over the top instead. But others say that similar tartes were already a tradition in Sologne and that the Tatin sisters were merely putting their own spin on a regional favorite.

No matter how the tarte came to be, it is indeed a special dessert. I experimented with many techniques to produce caramel of the proper consistency and color that would do the tarte justice. I gather the tarte was originally cooked in a Dutch oven with coals on top of the lid. Heat directly underneath the sugar and butter would form the caramel as the tarte cooked, and the crust would turn brown from the hot coals on the lid. At least in theory, it is very probable. In our modern kitchens, this method would prove difficult. After much experimenting, I recommend doing some of the preparation on the stovetop before transferring the tarte to the oven to bake.

During this preparation, the caramel will heat on the stovetop for a surprising forty to fifty minutes, total time. First cook the sugar—alone in the pan—to liquify it and to achieve the desired caramel color, and then add the butter and continue cooking until a smooth caramel forms. Then place the apples into the caramel and continue cooking on the stovetop. This is the best way to get the caramel cooked down and soaked into the apples. Meanwhile, the juice from the apples mingles into the caramel to produce a harmony of flavor and a sticky consistency like syrup. After this cooking, the apples will essentially be done, and all that remains is to lay on the crust and bake the tarte to a golden brown.

Crucial to the success of the tarte is using the right apple. The apple has to hold its shape and not turn to sauce while cooking in the caramel. The apple should be firm and sweet. It should not be dry, but neither should it have an overabundance of juice as most eating apples do. In Europe, we have many varieties of apples that lend themselves to this kind of preparation: Belle de Boskoop, Cox's Orange Pippin, Renette, Braeburn, and Calville. All these will hold their shape and are high in vitamin C with a tangy, earthy citrus flavor. In the U.S., it is hard to come by these varieties. Experimenting with the apples available here in Hawaii, the best apple I could find for this tarte is the Braeburn. If a store has both smaller and larger varieties of Braeburns, choose the smaller variety rather than the larger variety. The small Braeburn apples are an older variety, whereas the larger ones seem to be a newer hybrid that lacks in substance and flavor.

MÜRBETEIGE

Also important to the tarte Tatin's success is using the right pan. Stovetop cooking and oven baking both occur in the same pan. Using a copper tarte Tatin pan is best. Avoid the ones coated with tin on the inside; tin's melting point is 449.5°F. Copper pans lined with stainless steel are recommended. Heavy-duty enameled cast-iron pans are an option as well. It is preferable to use enameled pans with a light-colored interior so that it is easy to watch the changing color of the caramel. The pan must have a lid.

Note that the tarte Tatin's crust must be prepared first and refrigerated for at least two hours before starting the rest of the recipe, so plan time accordingly. The crust can be left in the refrigerator longer—overnight or up to two days. For an authentic taste, this crust uses European butter and flour. The Irish butter has a higher cream content than American-brand butters and is available in most grocery stores. French T45 flour is available at online stores.

This French caramelized apple tarte should be served warm and as is—without crème fraîche, whipped cream, or ice cream—so as not to take away from the deliciously complex flavor. However, I will leave that to the baker's discretion. This recipe may seem lengthy, but it was necessary to include the timing for making the caramel and simmering apples to have guaranteed success. Once made one time, it is easy to skip some of the reading.

TARTE TATIN

BAKING PAN
9 ½-inch copper tarte Tatin pan or enameled cast-iron pan

STOVETOP COOKING TIME
about 40 to 50 minutes

BAKING TEMPERATURE
400°F

BAKE TIME
30 to 35 minutes

RACK PLACEMENT
middle of oven

YIELD
one 9 ½-inch tarte

SPECIAL TOOLS
Heat-resistant spatula

Thick oven mitts (for handling the pan on the stovetop and for transferring pan to oven)

Serving dish with some depth (for flipping the tarte)

INGREDIENTS

FOR CRUST

1 cup French T45 flour (farine de blé), plus extra for working dough

¼ teaspoon baking powder

⅛ cup sugar

1 teaspoon vanilla extract

3 tablespoons water

⅛ teaspoon salt

4 tablespoons unsalted Irish butter, cold

FOR APPLES

3 pounds Braeburn apples (about 6 to 8 medium apples; 12 if the apples are small)

3 tablespoons lemon juice

FOR CARAMEL

4 tablespoons unsalted butter, softened to room temperature and cut into 3 pieces

1 tablespoon lemon juice

Pulp of ½ to 1 vanilla bean

1 cup sugar

1/16 teaspoon salt, optional

FOR TOPPING APPLES, ONCE ARRANGED IN THE PAN

¼ cup sugar

2 tablespoons unsalted butter, softened to room temperature and cut into flakes

MÜRBETEIGE

DIRECTIONS

1. Prepare the crust: Set aside ¼ cup of the measured flour to use as needed while working the dough and rolling it into shape. Sift the remaining flour and baking powder onto a large marble or wooden board. Form a well in the middle. Add the sugar, vanilla extract, and water into the well and sprinkle the salt around the edge. With a spatula, incorporate some of the flour into the well to absorb some of the water. Cut the butter into small pieces, approximately ¼ to ½ inch (see page 21, "How to Cut Butter," in "Technique to Prepare Mürbeteig Dough"). Distribute the butter pieces over and around the flour. Work to combine all ingredients, first with a metal dough scraper and then with your hands, until a smooth ball of dough forms. It may seem a bit dry at first but keep working the dough.

2. Refrigerate the dough for 2 hours or overnight. This dough can stay in the refrigerator up to two days. Remove dough from the refrigerator when starting to prepare the apples. Removing the dough will let it warm up while working through the next steps and will make it easier to roll in step 11.

3. Prepare the apples: Peel, core, and quarter the apples and place into a large bowl. Pour lemon juice over the apples; toss to coat.

4. Position a rack in the middle of the oven and preheat to 400°F.

5. Prepare to make the caramel: Cream the soft butter pieces with an electric mixer. Drizzle the lemon juice into the butter, add the vanilla, and mix. Set aside to use in step 7.

If possible, make the caramel in the copper tarte Tatin pan or enameled cast-iron pan you will use to bake the tarte; doing so will save transferring the caramel in step 8. It is best to use a pan that has a white or light metal color bottom to see the sugar turn into the amber caramel color.

Select the appropriately sized burner to match the pan size and set the stovetop dial to 4 to 6, assuming that the dial reads from a low of 0 to a high of 10. Every stovetop is different, so adjust heat and time accordingly throughout the next steps.

6. Make the caramel: Pour the sugar into the pan. If using the salt, add in now with the sugar. After 5 to 6 minutes, the sugar will start to melt and liquify. A few puddles will begin to form, mostly in the middle of the pan. When that happens, gently push the outside sugar inward so that the sugar melts evenly. Use a heat-resistant spatula to scrape down the sides of the pan efficiently.

Continue stirring gently for 2 minutes. Stirring may create lumps. Flatten these lumps with the spatula, let them melt, and then stir as more of the sugar liquifies. Once the sugar has liquified completely, keep stirring until the liquid turns an amber color, about 2 more minutes (see tip 1). Timing is crucial at this stage so the caramel does not become bitter. If smoke appears

TARTE TATIN

during the browning process, move the pan off the burner and examine the color. Reduce heat and brown more if needed. When a dark amber color is achieved, pull the pan from the burner. Keep the burner on but reduce heat to 3 on the dial. Allow the burner to cool down while continuing to work in the pan off the heat.

~ TIP 1 ~

One important detail to know is that however brown the sugar is before the butter goes in, that is the color the caramel will stay. Sometimes bakers will pull the caramel too early out of fear that the caramel could brown too much during baking and perhaps take on a very dark color and bitter taste. However, that is not the case, so do not add the butter while the sugar is still very light. Doing so will produce a pale caramel.

7. Add the butter mixture: With the pan off the heat, add the soft butter mixture and keep stirring. As soon as the sugar thickens and drags, replace the pan onto the burner, which should still be set to 3 on the dial. If necessary, increase the heat to 5 to 6 on the dial briefly until the caramel melts again, then reduce to 3. The mixture should look foamy and be simmering vigorously but should not be splattering. Stir and cook until the butter incorporates fully, a smooth layer of caramel forms, and the bottom becomes tacky. At this point, stir for about 5 more minutes and then turn off the burner until step 10.

8. With thick oven mitts on, pull the pan from the heat and transfer onto a heatproof surface on the counter. If this is the pan you will use for baking, continue work in the same pan. If this is not the tarte pan you will use for baking, pour the caramel into the tarte pan now. Arrange the apples on top of the caramel, taking care not to burn fingers. Begin by placing apples, core-side up, around the edge of the pan (see tip 2). Work inwards, placing the apples in concentric circles. Pack apples as tightly as possible to hold the circular pattern. When you get to the middle, and there is no longer room for the final apple pieces to lie flat, stand the apple pieces upright, with one in the middle and the others forming a circle around it. Lay the rest of the pieces, core-side down, into the gaps of the circular rows around the pan, so that cut-side meets cut-side. Slice a few pieces to fit into remaining gaps, if necessary. Pack in as many apple pieces as the pan possibly allows.

~ TIP 2 ~

It can be helpful to hold the apples around the edges a little and push them up while fitting the apples in the interior and middle. The apples will not stay all the way up and will try to slide down, but with agile hands, you can keep them propped up against the sides some. Attending to the apples this way makes for a thicker, prettier look when the tarte is turned over after baking.

MÜRBETEIGE

9. Sprinkle the ¼ cup sugar and distribute the butter flakes over the apples.

10. Place the pan containing the caramel and apples back on the burner and set the heat dial to 4. After about 3 minutes, the caramel will begin to simmer in the pan, all around, not just in the middle. It should not simmer so vigorously that it splatters out. If that happens, reduce the heat. Cook at a steady simmer for 5 minutes. This process softens the apples and adds juice to the caramel, which thins it. Because of this juice, the caramel will need time to reduce and thicken to a consistency like thin syrup; later the consistency will firm up even more when the tarte has baked and cooled. After 5 minutes, turn the dial back to 2, cover the pan with the lid, and let the apples and caramel cook at medium simmer for about 8 to 10 more minutes; watch and adjust the dial for the appropriate heat to keep the medium-strength simmer going but do not allow the caramel to splatter out. As the apples soften on the bottom, occasionally lift the lid and push apples down lightly with a spatula to get an even height, especially for the taller slices in the middle. After the 8 to 10 minutes, remove the lid and raise the dial to 5 (see tip 3). Simmer vigorously for 3 minutes, then reduce heat to 3 to 4 and simmer 6 more minutes or up to 15 minutes if needing to evaporate more liquid; be careful not to let apples cook down so much that they become sauce. The caramel should appear syrup-like. Turn off the heat and transfer the pan to a heatproof surface on the counter.

~ TIP 3 ~
The burst of high heat near the end of the stovetop cooking is important for the reduction of the sauce.

11. Roll out the dough to form the crust: This dough requires very little or no flour for rolling out. If the dough is still cold and too hard to roll, slice into four discs. Spread the discs onto the work surface so that they touch or overlap slightly. Roll out the dough until it is slightly bigger than the size of the tarte pan, about 11 inches. Transfer to the pan by folding the dough over the rolling pin and wrapping it halfway around; do not overlap. Lift the dough with the rolling pin and the help of a dough scraper or large spatula. Transfer the dough over the apples and carefully unroll, letting the dough drape over the apples (see tip 4). Work carefully as the pan is very hot. With a spatula, trim off any excess dough by pushing down on the rim of the pan. Discard the fallen-off remnants. Use the spatula to push and seal the dough around the edges to cover the apples completely, tucking the dough between the apples and the rim. With a knife, make 4 to 6 slits in the middle of the dough, like a simple star, to serve as a vent.

TARTE TATIN

~ TIP 4 ~

Using a *kuchenretter* (cake lifter) can help with the dough transfer. With this method, unroll the dough onto the kuchenretter. Hold the kuchenretter over the apples and flip it upside down. This method produces a smooth, even drape of the dough over the apples.

12. Bake for 30 to 35 minutes, until the crust is golden brown. To check doneness, insert a fork between the edge of the pan and the crust to ensure that the caramel has jelled into a thick sauce and that the apples have soaked up the caramel (see tip 5). Place on a wire rack for 30 minutes to 1 hour. Cooling time varies depending on the type of baking pan used; copper pans cool more quickly than cast-iron. Place in refrigerator for an additional 30 to 45 minutes or until liquid has set. The pan will still be slightly warm to the touch.

~ TIP 5 ~

Because apples vary in their juiciness, here are a few adjustments if necessary. If after baking the caramel looks like a watery sauce and it appears the apples are swimming in it and the juices are coming up to the crust, place the pan back on the stovetop burner. Do not put the lid on the pan. Turn the heat dial to 3 and allow the sauce to simmer for 5 to 8 minutes to evaporate and reduce the juices. Let cool on a wire rack until the pan feels just warm and the juices have thickened, then proceed with turning the tarte over onto a serving dish. On the other hand, if it appears after baking that the juices have all been absorbed by the apples, the pan can be turned over after just 15 minutes of cooling.

Turn the tarte over onto a serving dish with some depth, not flat like a plate, to prevent overflow from the sauce. To turn, place the dish over the crust and then, with a firm grip, flip the dish and pan simultaneously. The crust will now be on the bottom and the apples on the top.

The apples should be nicely coated with the jelled caramel, and there should be no runny liquid. If, however, the tarte came out too early or the cooling time was not long enough before flipping, there may be liquid pooling around the tarte. If so, do this: Place a large spatula over one edge of the tarte, holding it firmly against the tarte and taking care that the tarte remains in place on the dish. Tilt the dish at a 30- to 45-degree angle to let the liquid run into a pot. Heat this liquid on medium-low heat on the stove to caramelize it again (see tip 6). Once thickened, use a spoon to spread the caramel evenly over the apples to give the tarte its shine.

MÜRBETEIGE

~ TIP 6 ~

Adding agar agar powder or flakes to the liquid helps to thicken it successfully and more quickly. If using agar agar powder, add 1 teaspoon per ½ cup liquid (use a good-quality brand that does not smell or taste fishy; I have good results with Living Jin brand). If using agar agar flakes, add 1 tablespoon per ½ cup of liquid. Simmer vigorously for 3 minutes.

Tarte Tatin tastes best warm. The tarte can be reheated at any time. Set oven to 250°F to 300°F to reheat.

....

Reference for the tarte Tatin legend:

Wells, Patricia. "Fare of the Country; As French As Tarte Tatin." *The New York Times*, 24 March 1985, https://www.nytimes.com/1985/03/24/travel/fare-of-the-country-as-french-as-tarte-tatin.html

APFELSTRUDEL (APPLE STRUDEL)

Apfelstrudel is often associated with German and Austrian baking. Growing up in the state of Hessen, near Frankfurt, I was used to apple cakes in abundance, but when venturing south into Bavaria and Austria, it was always a treat to see more and more strudels in the cafés. There is nothing like going into the café at four o'clock in the afternoon to the greeting of delicate pastry and apple cinnamon in the air. Whipped cream is always served along with apple strudel, but an alternative favorite of mine is vanilla sauce. Though apple is among the most well-known fillings, strudel dough lends itself to a variety of fillings. Not only are there fruit, nut, poppy seed, and cheese fillings but also vegetables with béchamel sauce, ham and cheese, or ground beef with onions and peppers. Strudel dough is very versatile, and this beautiful pastry can be used for dessert or dinner.

When I started writing this book, adding strudel was not part of my plan. I thought perhaps it would require too much patience, and stretching the dough is intimidating. Nevertheless, when I started telling my friends and acquaintances the book was finished, many of them asked: "Is there an apple strudel recipe?" Having this much request, I made the decision to include one.

I think of the strudel dough as a shell that keeps the filling together. The recipe provides methods to prepare the dough either by hand or with a stand mixer. If working by hand, the preparation begins like a Mürbeteig, which is why the recipe appears in this chapter, but there is the extra step of stretching the dough thin. To make this fine, pliable dough, Italian pasta flour is recommended. After kneading the dough, letting it rest under a warm pot for thirty minutes is important. Resting under a warm pot is another distinction between strudel dough and Mürbeteig; the latter rests in the refrigerator for thirty minutes. After resting, the strudel dough must be stretched to avoid a thick texture and doughy taste inside the roll. The stretching process of drawing and pulling out the dough is delicate, and while holes that tear occasionally can be fixed, these patches stay somewhat thicker. So, it is best to aim for a steady, slow stretch so as to repair the dough as little as possible. Once the dough is stretched, it is filled and rolled. To create the thin, flaky outer layer of the baked strudel, the last third of the dough is left bare of filling and is buttered only instead.

There are two techniques for stretching the dough into the big, thin rectangle: both are implemented. One of the techniques explains how to stretch with palms turned down; the other explains how to stretch with palms turned up. In both techniques, it is crucial to pull the dough in a smooth motion and with a gentle touch.

MÜRBETEIGE

BAKING PAN
18 x 12-inch cookie sheet with rim, lightly buttered and lined with parchment paper

BAKING TEMPERATURE
375°F

BAKE TIME
45 to 50 minutes

RACK PLACEMENT
middle of oven

YIELD
one strudel (about 8 to 10 servings)

SPECIAL TOOLS
Large pot

Plastic dough scraper (if kneading the dough by hand)

Stiff plastic spatula (if using a stand mixer for the dough)

Smooth, tightly woven cotton dish towel (26 x 19 inches or larger)

APFELSTRUDEL (APPLE STRUDEL)

INGREDIENTS

FOR DOUGH

2 cups Italian pasta flour, plus extra ¼ cup for working dough

¼ teaspoon table salt

1 tablespoon sugar

1 egg

1 teaspoon vanilla paste or extract

⅔ cup water, lukewarm

1 teaspoon vinegar

FOR FILLING

¾ cup golden raisins, soaked in 3 tablespoons rum (prepare in step 1)

¾ cup breadcrumbs, roasted in 2 tablespoons butter (prepare in step 2)

3 ½ pounds Braeburn apples, not overripe

2 tablespoons lemon juice or lime juice

¾ cup sliced almonds

1 to 2 tablespoons cinnamon (according to taste; 2 tablespoons is for cinnamon lovers)

1 to 2 teaspoons vanilla paste or extract

2 tablespoons almond liqueur (for example, amaretto), or 2 teaspoons almond extract (see *note* at end of recipe)

2 tablespoons cornstarch

⅔ cup sugar

4 tablespoons butter, melted (for brushing on stretched-out dough in step 9)

1 egg, beaten (for egg wash, needed for steps 10 and 12)

OPTIONS FOR GARNISHING
(choose one)

Dust with powdered sugar

Make a sugar glaze (see step 13)

Make Vanilla Sauce (see page 242)

DIRECTIONS

1. Soak the raisins for the filling in rum. This can be done several hours beforehand.

2. In a skillet over medium heat, roast the breadcrumbs in the butter to golden brown and set aside until it is time to fill the dough in step 9.

3. Prepare to make the dough: Fill a large pot one-third full of water, cover, and bring to a boil. Turn off the burner but leave the hot water in the pot to keep it heated until the pot is needed in step 4 when the dough rests.

4. Make the strudel dough, either working by hand or with a stand mixer.

   Directions for working by hand: Set aside ¼ cup of the measured flour for use as needed while working the dough. Sift the remaining flour onto a large marble or wooden board.

MÜRBETEIGE

Form a well in the middle and sprinkle the salt around the edge. Sprinkle the sugar over the flour. Add the egg and vanilla into the well. Heat the water for 20 to 25 seconds in the microwave to lukewarm and then add the vinegar to the water. Using the tip of a plastic dough scraper, stir the egg in the well as if gently scrambling. With the dough scraper in one hand and the water mixture in the other, slowly and at a pace the flour can absorb, work the water mixture and the egg and vanilla into the flour; pour a little water into the well, collapse in some of the flour, and mix. Continue mixing and adding water until the dough starts to stick together. Then begin to knead by hand.

Dust hands and the kneading surface with flour. Brush off excess flour with your hand so the board is sparsely covered. Knead the dough until it becomes smooth, about 10 to 15 minutes. If the dough is too sticky, switch back to the dough scraper, then use hands again. Work the dough with the heel of your hands as well as with a flat hand. Flour hands as needed to keep dough from sticking, but only sparingly. The goal is to get a smooth, elastic dough that doesn't stick but still looks wet and is pliable. As the dough gets worked, it will become more pliable as the gluten is activated. Test the dough by pulling it gently and slowly with your thumb and two fingers. If the dough stretches easily without tearing, it is time to form it into a ball. Then fetch the heated pot, pour out the hot water, and dry it. Place the pot upside down over the ball of dough and let rest for 30 minutes.

Directions for using a stand mixer fitted with the dough hook: Add the dry ingredients into the bowl. Heat the water for 20 to 25 seconds in the microwave to lukewarm and then add the vinegar to the water. To begin mixing, first work in the bowl by hand; a strong mixer may spill flour out. Make a well in the dry ingredients and add the egg and vanilla and begin to add the water mixture slowly in increments. With a stiff plastic spatula in one hand and the water mixture in the other, slowly and at a pace the flour can absorb, work in the water mixture and the egg and vanilla; pour a little water into the well, collapse in some of the flour, and mix. Continue mixing and adding water until the dough starts to stick together. Once almost all water is incorporated, switch to mixing with the stand mixer on medium speed for 8 minutes, then form the dough into a ball. Fetch the heated pot, pour out the hot water, and dry it. Place the pot upside down over the ball of dough and let rest for 30 minutes.

5. Make the filling: Peel, core, and quarter the apples. If chopping by hand, slice each apple quarter in half lengthwise, gather a couple of slices together, and start chopping down the length of the slices, cutting pieces about ⅜ to ¼ inch thick; the width comes out to be about 1 inch. If using a stand mixer, fit the mixer with a large-size slicer or julienne disc. Cut the apple quarters crosswise to achieve smaller chunks; that way, after slicing, the pieces will be about 1 inch wide by ⅜ to ¼ inch thick. (Smaller shredding discs will make the apple pieces too small, and the apples will cook down too much.)

APFELSTRUDEL (APPLE STRUDEL)

Place the apple pieces into a large mixing bowl. Add the lemon or lime juice and stir to coat. Add the sliced almonds, cinnamon, golden raisins (drain away the rum before adding, see *note* at end of recipe), vanilla, and almond liqueur or almond extract. Mix thoroughly. Dust the cornstarch over the apple mixture. Mix again and set aside.

To avoid juice collection, wait to add the sugar until just before the filling is spread onto the stretched dough in step 9.

6. Prepare a towel for rolling and stretching the dough: On a large table or counter, place a smooth, tightly woven cotton dish towel, 26 x 19 inches or larger, and dust with flour. Cover the entire towel and spread evenly. Wipe off excess.

7. Roll and stretch the dough: Place the dough in the middle of the towel, and with a rolling pin, starting from the middle, push out and away in both directions, aiming for the sides of the towel. Push the dough longer and wider rather than pressing down when rolling. The dough only needs to resemble a smaller rectangle in the shape of the towel at this stage. Next, you will stretch the dough by hand until it is approximately 24 x 17 inches in size.

There are two techniques to stretch the dough; each starts by gently lifting the dough and sliding both hands underneath, beginning from the middle. With the palms-down technique, slightly close your hands, fingertips pointing down and away from the dough so as not to tear it. With the palms-up technique, turn

MÜRBETEIGE

thumbs in so they won't poke holes in the dough. Let dough rest lightly on relaxed fingertips. Be sure all fingers touch equally and softly, working as one. If more tension is on one finger, it is easier to tear the dough. Using either or both methods, gently stretch the dough, always pulling toward yourself and outward. Turn the towel and repeat on the other sides. Keep turning as necessary and gently pull the dough longer and wider, stretching it as thin as possible. This requires some patience (see tip).

~ TIP ~

Often you will hear that the strudel dough needs to be so thin that a newspaper can be read through it. This is very hard to do without tearing the dough. If you can see the pattern of the dish towel, you did well.

Continue to repeat sliding your hands under the dough, slightly lifting, pulling carefully toward your body and out to the sides. Work on all sides to get an even rectangle. Thin spots will start to form, and it is best to leave those alone and move on to the thicker areas. Should the dough tear, repair the hole immediately using dough from the edges, then continue stretching gently. Thin out edges by pulling on them carefully; the edges tend to roll up on their own. In step 9, when finished spreading the filling, there is a reminder simply to cut away thick parts along the edges. These strands can be cut up and used in soup as noodles.

8. Position a rack in the middle of the oven and preheat to 375°F. Lightly butter and line the cookie sheet with parchment paper in preparation for baking. Set aside.

9. Fill the dough: Mix the sugar into the apple filling. In a separate bowl, melt the butter.

    Before spreading the filling, keep in mind that one-third of the strudel dough is buttered only and not filled. This third will be rolled last and become the strudel's outer layer. On the two long sides, keep filling away from the edge by about ½ inch. On one short side, which will become the center of the rolled strudel, the filling can be spread almost to the edge.

    Start by brushing the entire dough with the melted butter, leaving ¼ inch to ½ inch bare on the edges. Beginning from the short end that will be the center of the roll, sprinkle the roasted breadcrumbs onto two-thirds of the buttered dough, keeping away from the long edges by about ½ inch. Spread the apple mixture on top of the breadcrumbs. On each long side, cut away any remaining thick edges, then lift the edge and stretch and fold over the filling by about ½ inch. This seal will keep filling from squeezing out when rolling up the strudel. Also fold the dough over the filling by about ½ inch on the short end that will be rolled up first and become the center of the strudel.

10. Roll up the strudel: First, beat 1 egg in a small bowl to use as an egg wash in this step and step 12; keep the egg wash on hand.

APFELSTRUDEL (APPLE STRUDEL)

Beginning from the short end covered with filling, the end that will become the center, start rolling up the strudel by lifting the towel and pulling slightly up and forward. Similar to a rug, the strudel will seemingly roll itself up. Stop when you reach the third without filling. Brush the remaining short edge with a little of the egg wash to help seal the seam. Pull this third of the dough up and over the roll. Gently press and make a seal. The strudel will seem huge after rolling up, but when it is baked, the apple filling will shrink considerably.

11. Transfer to the prepared cookie sheet: Take the parchment paper off the prepared cookie sheet and slide the parchment's long edge partially under the towel the rolled strudel is resting on. Pick up the towel on both sides and let the strudel roll from the towel onto the parchment's center, with the strudel lying seam down. If the strudel is too long for the cookie sheet, use the palms of your hands to shape the strudel into a slight crescent. Using the cookie sheet like a large spatula, hold onto a narrow side and lift at a 30-degree angle. Grip the parchment with the strudel on a narrow side and swiftly pull it onto the cookie sheet while simultaneously sliding the sheet under.

12. Brush the strudel with the remaining egg wash.

13. Bake for 45 to 50 minutes, until the outside of the strudel has deepened in color to light golden brown. To check doneness, insert a wooden skewer through the strudel. The apples should be soft but not mushy; carefully feel the skewer to ensure the filling is hot. Place sheet on a wire rack and let cool for 15 minutes, then slide the parchment with the strudel off the sheet and onto the cooling rack.

Serve the strudel after letting it cool but while still warm, and drizzle with Vanilla Sauce. Or let the strudel cool completely and then dust with powdered sugar or brush with sugar glaze before serving.

FOR SUGAR GLAZE

1 cup powdered sugar

2 ⅛ teaspoons lemon juice

1 teaspoon rum

1 teaspoon water

Directions for Sugar Glaze

Whisk together the powdered sugar, lemon juice, rum, and water to a thick but still fluid consistency. Add more powdered sugar if too thin. If too thick, add more liquid, just a few drops at a time. The consistency should be thicker than maple syrup but not as thick as molasses.

Note: Instead of almond liqueur or almond extract, the rum from soaking the raisins can be used. Drain the rum from the raisins into a bowl; measure out 2 tablespoons to use as a substitution and discard the rest.

ALMOND OR HAZELNUT CRUST

This recipe is a standby for basic almond and hazelnut crusts. Unblanched nut meal is used in this crust for a rustic, wholesome flavor. In a pinch, blanched almond flour can be used, but due to the absorption capacity of finely milled nuts, the amount must be reduced. The ingredient lists include the different measurements. Use the crust for no-bake fillings and fillings cooked on the stovetop rather than in the oven. For example, it is a great shell for chocolate mousse, key lime pie, or cream pies. This crust is also useful for oven-baked pies that recommend pre-baking before adding filling.

The recipe has options for both rimmed and rimless crusts. The baking pan size and the ingredient ratios will differ, but the preparation technique is the same. Rimmed crusts produce a traditional pie shell, while rimless crusts provide a sturdy base to go underneath layer cakes.

This crust can be made ahead and frozen. If freezing a rimmed crust, store on a freezer shelf where the crust will not be bumped or jostled so that the rim does not break off.

109

ALMOND OR HAZELNUT CRUST

BAKING PAN FOR RIMMED CRUST
9- or 10-inch nonstick tart pan with removable bottom or springform pan, buttered and floured

BAKING PAN FOR RIMLESS CRUST
10-inch springform pan, buttered and floured

BAKING TEMPERATURE
325°F

BAKE TIME
20 to 22 minutes

RACK PLACEMENT
middle of oven

YIELD
one 9- or 10-inch crust

INGREDIENTS

FOR 9-INCH RIMMED CRUST OR 10-INCH RIMLESS CRUST

1 cup unbleached all-purpose flour (protein 3 grams per ¼ cup; see page 7), plus extra for working dough

⅓ cup lightly packed unblanched almond meal or hazelnut meal (finely milled blanched almond flour can be substituted but reduce to ¼ cup; see *note* at end of recipe)

½ cup powdered sugar

⅛ teaspoon salt

1 egg

5 tablespoons unsalted butter, cold

FOR 10-INCH RIMMED CRUST

1 ⅛ cups unbleached all-purpose flour (protein 3 grams per ¼ cup; see page 7), plus extra for working dough

½ cup unblanched almond meal or hazelnut meal (finely milled blanched almond flour can be substituted but reduce to ⅓ cup; see *note* at end of recipe)

⅔ cup powdered sugar

⅛ teaspoon salt

1 egg

7 tablespoons unsalted butter, cold

DIRECTIONS

1. Prepare the crust: Set aside ¼ cup of the measured flour to use as needed while working the dough and pressing it into the form. Sift the remaining flour, nut meal, and powdered sugar onto a large marble or wooden board. Form a well in the middle and sprinkle the salt around the edge. Add the egg into the well. Cut the butter into small pieces, approximately ¼ to ½ inch (see page 21, "How to Cut Butter," in "Technique to Prepare Mürbeteig Dough"). Distribute the pieces over and around the flour. Using the tip of a metal dough scraper, stir

MÜRBETEIGE

the egg as if gently scrambling. Begin carefully pushing the dry ingredients into the well's center. Work to combine all ingredients, first with the dough scraper and then with your hands, until a ball of dough forms. It may seem a bit dry at first because of the powdered sugar but keep working the dough. Add flour sparingly or chill as necessary if the dough becomes too sticky.

2. Refrigerate the dough for 30 minutes. About 15 minutes into the refrigeration time, position a rack in the middle of the oven and preheat to 325°F. Butter and flour the pan in preparation for baking.

3. Mold dough into pan: Remove the dough from the refrigerator. Slice horizontally into four discs. Lay the discs into the prepared pan. They may overlap. With flour-dipped fingers, push the dough out, rather than pressing it down, to cover the pan evenly. If creating a rim, pull the dough up the pan's sides to the desired height. Even out any thin spots to get the dough to a fairly consistent thickness. If baking a rimless crust, do not pull the dough up the sides.

4. To prevent the pie from bubbling up during baking, weigh down the crust. Place parchment paper over the crust, then spread dried beans or pie weights over the paper (see tip 1). As an alternative to the parchment and weights, use a fork to poke the bottom of the crust in a few places to create air vents (see tip 2).

~ TIP 1 ~

Pie weights of different designs are available from baking stores.

~ TIP 2 ~

If bubbles should form, it is easy to open the oven door and give the bubble a quick poke with a wooden skewer; the crust will fall right back into place.

5. Bake for 20 to 22 minutes, until the crust is light golden brown in color and firm. Cool on a wire rack. Use as desired or wrap and store in freezer.

Note: Home-ground almond or hazelnut meal works best for this crust (see page 14 for grinding technique). Store-bought finely milled blanched almond flour can be substituted but the amount must be reduced; measure the store-bought almond flour loosely and do not pack.

CHERRY TURNOVERS
(made with puff pastry)

These easy Cherry Turnovers are made from frozen puff pastry sheets, available in stores in the freezer section. Though the turnovers do not use a Mürbeteig dough, I have included them in this chapter because they are an excellent way to use leftover filling from pies. This recipe contains one filling option made of organic cherry juice combined with sour pitted cherries. Tart or sour pitted cherries packed in water are the next best thing to fresh cherries. Forgo the filling in this recipe entirely and instead customize to ingredients or prepared extra filling already on hand. The puff pastry bakes up into airy layers and can accommodate any filling flavors the baker dreams up. Enjoy this easy-to-make snack with a cup of hot cocoa. Brush turnovers with the optional sugar glaze for extra sweetness.

MÜRBETEIGE

BAKING PAN cookie sheet, buttered and lined with parchment paper	**BAKING TEMPERATURE** 400°F **BAKE TIME** 10 to 15 minutes	**RACK PLACEMENT** middle of oven	**YIELD** nine turnovers

INGREDIENTS

FOR CHERRY FILLING

1 cup cherry juice, unsweetened organic

1 teaspoon lemon juice

2 tablespoons cornstarch (for an opaque glaze), or 2 ½ tablespoons potato starch (for a translucent glaze)

1 ½ tablespoons *kirschwasser* (cherry brandy), optional

⅓ cup sugar

10 ounces (1 very full cup) canned pitted tart or sour cherries, packed in water and drained (for example, Oregon brand)

FOR PASTRY

1 package frozen puff pastry sheets (not puff pastry shells)

FOR EGG WHITE WASH

2 egg whites

1 teaspoon water

FOR EGG YOLK WASH

2 egg yolks

1 tablespoon milk

FOR OPTIONAL SUGAR GLAZE

1 cup sifted powdered sugar

2 teaspoons water mixed with 2 teaspoons either lemon juice or rum (4 teaspoons liquid total)

CHERRY TURNOVERS

DIRECTIONS

For Making Filling

1. In a small bowl, whisk ¼ cup of the cherry juice and the lemon juice with the cornstarch or potato starch until dissolved.

2. Pour the remaining cherry juice and the kirschwasser into a medium-sized saucepan and cook over medium-high heat. Add the starch mixture and the sugar. Whisking constantly, bring to a boil. Once the mixture boils, turn down the heat and continue with a wooden spoon, stirring vigorously until it thickens to the consistency of jelly (see tip). Add the cherries and stir to coat; the cherries will release some liquid and thin the filling to a spreadable consistency. If the mixture is still too thick, add 1 or 2 tablespoons of juice and let cook briefly once more. Transfer to a bowl and refrigerate to cool.

~ TIP ~

The juice mixture can bubble over or stick to the saucepan's bottom very quickly, so do not leave unattended at any time. Once the mixture boils, stir rapidly, making sure to scrape the bottom of the saucepan to avoid sticking and burning. A flat wooden spoon works best for this task. The mixture is nearly ready when it starts to bubble, which means that it has begun to gel up. At this point, turn off the heat or reduce it to low. Stir and scrape a few more times to prevent burning, and the mixture is ready. If the mixture boils too rapidly too early, remove from heat for a moment to prevent a spillover, then turn down heat before replacing the saucepan.

For Preparing Puff Pastry

1. Position a rack in the middle of the oven and preheat to 400°F. Butter the pan and line with parchment paper in preparation for baking. Set aside.

2. Frozen puff pastry comes in folded sheets. For nine turnovers, defrost one sheet. Lay the folded sheet flat on the counter to defrost. Once defrosted, unfold the sheet on a large wooden or marble board, sprinkled with flour. Roll out the pastry to a 15 x 15-inch square. With a flour-dipped pastry cutter, cut into nine squares (each measuring 5 x 5 inches). These squares will be filled and folded into triangles in step 4.

3. Whisk the egg whites and the water with a fork until slightly foamy and set aside.

4. To form the turnovers, imagine a diagonal line running through each pastry square, creating two equal-sized triangles. Place a small amount (1 to 2 tablespoons) of cherry filling near, but slightly offset from, that imaginary center line. Brush each edge of the square with the egg white wash and fold over the filling to form a triangle. Press the edges together to seal, either with fingers or the end of a spoon. Transfer to the prepared cookie sheet.

MÜRBETEIGE

5. Whisk the egg yolks and milk with a fork until blended and brush onto the turnovers. Wipe away any egg yolk that drips onto the cookie sheet.

6. Bake for 10 to 15 minutes, until tops are golden brown. Some filling may run out while baking; it is easy to push filling back into the turnovers after they have cooled. If using optional sugar glaze, brush onto the turnovers when they have cooled completely.

For the Optional Sugar Glaze

Whisk together the powdered sugar and the liquid to a thick but still fluid consistency. If a thicker glaze is desired, add more powdered sugar. If too thick, add more liquid, just a few drops at a time.

**Christmas Cookies (Left to Right)
Coconut Macaroons, Spekulatius,
Hazelnut Macaroons**

COOKIES 2

In Germany, where there is so much delicious baking, cookies bring a wide variety of flavors such as lemon, raspberry, hazelnut, subtle liqueur, sweet almond paste, and chocolate. There are many textures, too, and the recipes in this chapter show the range of goods that fall under the classification of cookie. There are, for example, simple Butter Cookies, and then there are the more involved rolled Apricot Nut Cookies, chocolate-dipped Almond Paste Crescents, and two-layer Hazelnut and Jelly Sandwich Cookies. There is even a Gingerbread House recipe that will bring out one's inner baker and inner builder. When my children were young, I baked a gingerbread house every year for Christmas. The kids, always eager to decorate, were ready as soon as the frosting was dry and the house was stable. The kids had free rein in how they wanted to decorate, and it was nice to see the ideas changing year by year, as they grew older. There are also three brownie recipes: Candied Ginger Brownies (with dairy-free option), Coffee Liqueur Brownies, and Nut Brownies.

Any of these cookie recipes are delicious year-round, but come Christmastime, it is customary to bake batches of different cookies. Several of the recipes are rooted in the traditions of the winter

Almond Paste Crescents 121	**Butter Cookies**. 140
Vanillekipferl	**Candied Ginger Brownies** 143
(Vanilla Almond Crescents) 125	**Coffee Liqueur Brownies** 146
Cinnamon Stars 128	**Nut Brownies**. 149
Coconut Macaroons 132	**Hazelnut and Jelly Sandwich Cookies** 152
Hazelnut Macaroons. 134	**Apricot Nut Cookies** 157
Spekulatius Cookies 136	**Gingerbread House** 160

CHAPTER 2

holidays with deep nut flours, cinnamon, candied ginger, toasted coconut, and powdered sugar spiced with vanilla. At Christmastime in Germany, everyone feels they have to make a variety of cookies. Tins and jars are stacked with rich-smelling treats, so when guests stop by with wishes for a Merry Christmas or to deliver a present, the host is ready to serve tea or coffee with festive cookies. It is one of the sweetest customs, literally. And if bakers crave cookies during the rest of the year, these recipes can be enjoyed year-round.

PREPARATION TIME

Most recipes in this chapter involve few ingredients and very little preparation time. Allotting an hour of preparation time will suffice for many of these recipes. The cookies that require special shaping, kneading, or rolling, such as the Cinnamon Stars and Almond Paste Crescents, may take up to two hours, especially on the first try. For the small time investment, the baker will have a store of sweet gems on hand to offer when occasion calls. Cookies are not temperamental about their serving time. In fact, they get better a few days later because the flavors have an opportunity to blend, absorb, and harmonize.

There are some notable exceptions when it comes to preparation time. The *Vanillekipferl* (Vanilla Almond Crescents), the Hazelnut and Jelly Sandwich Cookies, and the Apricot Nut Cookies need chilling time before baking. The Gingerbread House requires several hours of time for each stage of preparation, assembly, and decorating. Spreading these stages over three days is recommended in the recipe.

GENERAL TIPS AND TRICKS

A Reminder about Flour and Nut Meal

Remember to observe the absorbency of flour and nut meal in the dough. Take note of the unbaked dough's consistency and the texture of the baked cookies. If cookies are consistently too dense or tough, cut back on the flour or nut meal amounts, a little at a time as needed. If dough is consistently too loose, increase flour or nut meal amounts, a little at a time as needed.

For cookie recipes, measure the flour un-sifted and fill the cup scantly. To get the scant measure, dip out a cup of flour and then shake off some of the flour so the cup measures somewhere between three-fourths full and full to the rim. Before getting started with cookie recipes, please read "Four Crucial Variables in Baking" starting on page 7, with special attention to "How to Measure Flour" (see page 7) and "Guidelines to Adjust Flour Amounts" (see page 9).

Baking Times and Temperatures

The most daunting task with cookies is determining when to pull them from the oven. Take the recipe bake times into account, but bakers should also make use of their senses to determine when cookies are just right to pull from the oven. The smell of ready-to-eat cookies will float through the air, and the cookies will feel firmer to the touch and easier to lift away from the sheet. Once senses are attuned to the smell and texture of cookies that are done, these recipes will be among the simplest treats in a baker's repertoire.

In this cookie chapter, some recipes have lower baking temperatures than recipes in other chapters.

COOKIES

This is especially true for cookies made with beaten egg whites or very little wheat flour (or none at all). My aunt—and many other German bakers I know—have a saying for these kinds of cookies: *They need to dry in the oven more than bake*. They bake at low temperatures, often on the convection setting to spread the heat evenly. This process will help achieve a cookie that stays moist. It is typically better to pull cookies earlier rather than later. Residual heat lingers in the dough, and the cookies will continue to bake as they cool on their racks. The individual recipes indicate cookies for which the "more drying than baking" concept is particularly important.

About Cookie Sheets and Baking in Batches

Cookie sheets come in a wide variety of sizes. Many of these cookie recipes produce enough dough to fill more than one large cookie sheet (about 16 x 12 inches) and definitely more than one smaller cookie sheet. Never crowd cookies to try to fit them all on one sheet. Restraint in spacing is especially important for cookies that expand while baking. The space will prevent cookies from melding into one large mass. For dough that expands, the recipes alert bakers to leave about two inches of space between cookies. Even those that do not expand much need a little space from their neighbors to bake evenly all around.

When the recipe produces enough dough for more than one cookie sheet, bake only one sheet at a time and keep the waiting batch in the refrigerator. Never cram multiple sheets onto the same rack too tightly. Heat needs to move between the sides of the sheet and the oven walls. Baking multiple sheets at once on different rack levels will also block heat. The cookies on the higher rack will have pale bottoms and dark tops. The cookies on the lower rack will have pale tops and dark bottoms. If there is a sheet sandwiched on a rack between two others, those cookies will have both pale tops and pale bottoms. If baking multiple sheets on different rack levels at one time is unavoidable, use convection to help evenly distribute the oven's heat.

Preparing Cookie Sheets for Baking

Another key to success for most cookies is lining the cookie sheet. Lining the sheet will prevent cookie bottoms from sticking, thus protecting both the cookies and the sheet from a charred mess. Use either a silicone mat or parchment paper for lining. If using parchment paper, butter the sheet first to help the parchment lie flat. Cookies with a loose dough containing beaten egg white, like Coconut or Hazelnut Macaroons, benefit from a base to help keep their shape during baking. For these cookies, German bakers commonly use *Back Oblaten*, edible paper-thin wafers placed under each individual cookie. The wafers come in different sizes for different types of cookies: forty, fifty, seventy, and ninety millimeters. Back Oblaten are made of flour and water, and they help to keep the cookie from sticking to the baking sheet and also provide a base so the cookie doesn't run too flat while baking. Back Oblaten keep their integrity as they bake into the cookie and are tasteless. They can be placed directly onto the silicone baking mat or the parchment paper that lines the cookie sheet. Back Oblaten are obtainable through online German specialty stores.

CHAPTER 2

About Yield

Cookie yields can be difficult to estimate. For consistent baking, cookies should be generally uniform in size, but there is no need to become preoccupied with the size or shaping. Do the best you can. Use the recipe yields, along with the directions for shaping and dropping cookies, as guides. If there is a little range in the final products, the lucky taster who gets the biggest cookie will be happy. The unlucky taster who gets the smallest can seize the excuse to go in for seconds.

A showcase of cookie videos for inspiration and helpful technique demonstrations is available at vimeo.com/showcase/10471279.

VIDEO SHOWCASE
Cookies
vimeo.com/showcase/10471279

RECOMMENDED TOOLS

- **Silicone baking mat, or a good supply of parchment paper**
- *Back Oblaten* **(paper-thin wafers made from flour and water to place under individual cookies)**
- **Cookie sheets**
- **Coffee mill or nut mill, if grinding fresh nuts to use instead of purchased nut meal**
- **Cookie scoop, or two teaspoons for shaping cookies and dropping onto sheet**

ALMOND PASTE CRESCENTS

These delicious almond paste cookies are one of my favorites. They are soft and slightly gooey, with a candy-like crunch around the edges. The chocolate-dipped ends make a heavenly finish. Choose one of the two options included in this recipe for the dipping chocolate. The easy dipping chocolate is simpler, and a good place to begin for new bakers. The tempered dipping chocolate requires more steps, but it produces a smoother covering.

ALMOND PASTE CRESCENTS

BAKING PAN
cookie sheet, lined with silicone baking mat, or buttered and lined with parchment paper

BAKING TEMPERATURE
325°F, convection

BAKE TIME
about 20 to 23 minutes, depending on the cookie sheet

RACK PLACEMENT
top third of oven, one rung above middle

YIELD
twenty crescent cookies

INGREDIENTS

FOR DOUGH

3 egg whites

7 ounces almond paste (see page 11)

1 tablespoon water, hot

1 tablespoon almond liqueur or almond extract

2 tablespoons lemon juice

1 ½ cups sugar

Pinch of salt (about ⅛ teaspoon)

1 ½ cups almond flour, plus ½ to ¾ cup reserved for kneading dough and shaping crescents

7 ounces sliced almonds (to roll the dough in when shaping the cookies in step 4)

FOR EASY DIPPING CHOCOLATE

1 cup semi-sweet chocolate chips

2 tablespoons coconut oil

FOR TEMPERED DIPPING CHOCOLATE

9 ounces Belgian 54% to 55% dark couverture chocolate (about 1 ¾ cups), high-quality brand recommended (see page 11)

1 ounce organic cocoa butter wafers or chunks

COOKIES

DIRECTIONS

1. Position a rack in the top third of the oven (one rung above middle) and preheat to 325°F (convection bake setting). Line a cookie sheet with a silicone mat, or butter and line with parchment. Set aside.

2. Whip the egg whites to stiff peaks in a large bowl, preferably copper.

3. Make the dough: Break the almond paste into small pieces and place in a standing mixer or a large mixing bowl if using a handheld mixer (see tip 1). Add the hot water, almond liqueur or almond extract, and lemon juice. Mix to combine. The paste may be lumpy. Add in the sugar and salt and continue mixing for about 1 minute. Add 1½ cups of almond flour. Reserve the remaining ½ to ¾ cup for rolling and shaping the crescents. Blend on medium-high until all the almond paste is incorporated smoothly and the dough is of a soft texture, about 2 to 3 minutes. Intermittently scrape down the bowl if necessary. At this point, the mixture can also be kneaded with gentle hands into a smooth, soft dough, making sure to break up any lumps. Add the egg whites and work by hand with a large spoon, spatula, or whisk to incorporate fully. Use a light, careful touch to preserve as much air in the egg whites as possible.

~ TIP 1 ~

Almond paste may occasionally harden in the packaging. If that occurs, remove from packaging and heat in the microwave for about 20 seconds to restore paste to a soft, workable consistency. Add a teaspoon of water if necessary.

4. Form the crescents: Sprinkle half of the remaining ½ to ¾ cup of almond flour onto a marble or wooden board. The other half is for working into the dough if it becomes too sticky to handle. With a light touch, roll the dough into a log, 19 to 20 inches long and about 1½ inches in diameter. Starting at one end, cut 1-inch pieces down the length of the log. Roll each piece into a 4-inch rope. Handle the dough gently and sprinkle more almond flour, a little at a time, onto the dough and/or work surface if the dough gets too sticky. Before the pieces lose all stickiness, roll them in the sliced almonds. Taper and bend the ends, shape into crescents, and place onto the prepared cookie sheet (see tip 2).

~ TIP 2 ~

To taper the ends, pinch the dough between your thumb and forefinger. Enjoy this part and don't worry if the tapering isn't always perfectly even.

ALMOND PASTE CRESCENTS

5. Arrange cookies 2 inches apart on cookie sheet to allow for spreading during baking.

6. Bake for about 20 to 23 minutes. Allow cookies to cool on the sheet for approximately 15 to 20 minutes so they do not break during transfer. Then move to a wire rack to continue cooling.

7. Prepare either the easy dipping chocolate (use the ingredient measurements listed at the beginning of this recipe and follow the directions for Easy Chocolate Glaze on page 261) or make the tempered dipping chocolate (use the ingredient measurements listed at the beginning of this recipe and follow the directions for Tempered Chocolate Glaze the Easy Way on page 265).

8. Dip the cookies: Once the cookies are completely cooled, lay parchment paper or a cookie sheet under the wire rack to catch drips. Dip one or both ends of each cookie into the chocolate. Place on rack to set. The chocolate will not harden completely, so move cookies carefully and store in a parchment-lined container.

VANILLEKIPFERL (VANILLA ALMOND CRESCENTS)

Vanillekipferl are one of the most recognizable Christmas cookies in Germany and other parts of Europe. These cookies are a particular favorite in my family. My mother uses the traditional ground almonds, which are listed in this recipe, but my aunt's specialty is to prepare them with ground hazelnuts instead. Give the hazelnuts a try if that flavor is preferred over almonds or create a mixture of ground almonds and ground hazelnuts. This dough needs thirty minutes to rest in the refrigerator, so be sure to factor that time into your preparations. Often, Vanillekipferl are made in conjunction with Coconut Macaroons or Hazelnut Macaroons to use up the egg whites, since the Vanillekipferl need only the yolks.

VANILLEKIPFERL (VANILLA ALMOND CRESCENTS)

BAKING PAN
two 16 x 12-inch cookie sheets, lined with silicone baking mats, or buttered and lined with parchment paper

BAKING TEMPERATURE
350°F

BAKE TIME
10 to 15 minutes

RACK PLACEMENT
middle of oven

YIELD
twenty-four to thirty 2 ½-inch cookies

INGREDIENTS

FOR DOUGH

1 ¼ cups unbleached all-purpose flour (protein 3 grams per ¼ cup; see page 7)

½ teaspoon baking powder

1 cup ground almonds, plus ¼ to ½ cup extra for sprinkling during rolling (see page 14 for technique if grinding yourself)

½ cup sugar

¼ teaspoon salt

1 teaspoon vanilla extract

1 teaspoon almond extract

1 egg yolk

10 tablespoons (1 ¼ sticks) unsalted butter, at room temperature

FOR COATING

½ cup powdered sugar

2 teaspoons vanilla sugar, or ½ of a vanilla bean (to scrape pulp and sift with the powdered sugar—see *note* at end of recipe)

DIRECTIONS

1. Position a rack in the middle of the oven and preheat to 350°F. Line each cookie sheet with a silicone mat, or butter and line with parchment. Set aside.

2. Make the dough: Sift 1 cup of the flour and the baking powder onto a marble or wooden board. Keep the remaining ¼ cup flour on the side. Distribute the ground almonds over the flour. Make a well in the center of the flour and add the sugar, salt, vanilla extract, almond extract, and egg yolk. Cut the butter into small pieces, approximately ¼ to ½ inch (see page 21, "How to Cut Butter," in "Technique to Prepare Mürbeteig Dough"). Distribute the butter around the well. Begin carefully pushing the dry ingredients into the well's center. Work to combine all ingredients, first with a metal dough scraper and then with your hands, until a ball of dough forms. Add more flour from the reserved ¼ cup, a little at a time, if the dough becomes too sticky.

COOKIES

3. Let dough rest in the refrigerator for about 30 minutes.

4. Form the crescents: Sprinkle a marble or wooden board with almond meal. Divide the dough into three equal sections. Work with one section at a time, leaving the rest in the refrigerator. Roll the section of dough into a rope, about 2 inches in diameter. Starting at one end, cut the rope into approximately ½-inch-long pieces. Roll each piece into a 4-inch-long rope and shape into a crescent with tapered ends (see tip). Handle the dough gently and sprinkle more ground almonds, a little at a time, onto the work surface if dough gets too sticky.

~ TIP ~

To taper the ends, pinch the dough between your thumb and forefinger. Enjoy this part, and do not fret over a lack of perfect uniformity.

5. Place cookies 2 inches apart on cookie sheet to allow for spreading during baking. Fourteen to sixteen cookies will fit on one (16 x 12-inch) sheet. If there is still space on the cookie sheet, remove another section of dough from the refrigerator to roll and shape.

6. As the first batch bakes, roll and shape the next batch, placing the crescents onto the second prepared sheet. Repeat this process until all dough has been used.

7. Bake for 10 to 15 minutes. Allow to cool on cookie sheet for a few minutes so that cookies do not break when transferring to wire rack. Cool to room temperature on a wire rack. Allow cookie sheet to cool completely before adding new cookies for baking.

8. Coat with sugar: Sift the powdered sugar and vanilla sugar into a large bowl and mix. Roll each cookie in the sugar mixture. Alternatively, transfer cookies to a plate and sift the sugar mixture liberally and evenly over the tops. Store in a closed container. Cookie tins work well.

Note: For strong vanilla flavor, use the German vanilla sugar packages available online or in local stores in some U.S. areas. If no German vanilla sugar is on hand, make a quick homemade version by scraping the pulp from half a vanilla bean and mixing it with the powdered sugar. Sift the sugar to remove any lumps.

CINNAMON STARS

Called *Zimtsterne* in German, these cookies have a soft, chewy center, and the icing bakes into a lovely thin, crisp shell of meringue. As they bake and cool, they deliver an enveloping scent of warm spices—cinnamon, clove, and vanilla. Some extra time and patience in their preparation are required, more than some other cookie types, but they are worth the diligence.

Both the cookie dough and the meringue icing use egg white only. Save the yolks for Butter Cookies or *Vanillekipferl*. If you prefer not to make the homemade meringue icing, meringue powder is commercially available as an alternative. It consists of dried egg whites with added sugar and cornstarch and is whipped up with water. If using meringue powder, follow the instructions on the packaging. See *note 1* at the end of this recipe for icing ingredients using meringue powder.

COOKIES

BAKING PAN
two cookie sheets, lined with silicone baking mat, or buttered and lined with parchment paper

BAKING TEMPERATURE
325°F

BAKE TIME
16 to 17 minutes

RACK PLACEMENT
bottom third of oven, one rung below middle

YIELD
about fifty 3-inch cookies

SPECIAL TOOLS
3-inch, star-shaped cookie cutter

Bendable plastic dough scraper

INGREDIENTS

FOR DOUGH

3 egg whites

2 ½ cups powdered sugar (about 8 ounces)

3 teaspoons potato starch

1 tablespoon lemon juice to add into egg whites, plus ¾ tablespoon to add into dough

3 cups almond meal or ground almonds (about 2 ¼ cups whole almonds, or 12 ounces, if grinding yourself; see page 14 for technique) (see *note 2* at end of recipe)

2 ½ cups hazelnut meal or ground hazelnuts (about 2 cups whole, or 8 ounces, if grinding yourself; see page 14 for technique)

6 teaspoons cinnamon

⅛ teaspoon ground cloves

2 teaspoons vanilla sugar or vanilla extract

2 teaspoons almond extract, or 1 tablespoon almond liqueur

FOR MERINGUE ICING

1 egg white

1 cup powdered sugar (see page 12)

1 teaspoon cream of tartar

1 ¾ tablespoons lemon juice

FOR ROLLING THE DOUGH

¼ to ½ cup powdered sugar

¼ cup nut meal or ground almonds or hazelnuts

CINNAMON STARS

DIRECTIONS

1. Position a rack in the bottom third of the oven (one rung below middle) and preheat to 325°F. Line each cookie sheet with a silicone mat, or butter and line with parchment. Set aside.

2. Prepare the egg whites for the dough: In a large bowl, whip the egg whites just enough to be foamy. In a separate bowl, sift the powdered sugar and potato starch; mix to combine and then distribute over the egg whites. Mix with an electric mixer, slowly at first to prevent a cloud of dust from the sugar. Stop the mixer to add the lemon juice (1 tablespoon) and scrape down powdered sugar stuck on the sides, then continue beating until thick. Ripples from the beaters will be visible in the heavy mixture. It should be shiny and thick and flow slowly in a stream from a spoon or spatula. The mixture will not stand in peaks in the bowl, but a small, heavy peak will barely stand when scooped onto a whisk.

3. Make the dough: In a large bowl, combine the almond meal, hazelnut meal, cinnamon, and cloves. In a small bowl, combine the vanilla, almond extract or liqueur, and lemon juice (¾ tablespoon) and mix to combine. Pour the flavors over the nut mixture and stir. Add one half of the nut meal mixture to the egg white mixture; use a bendable dough scraper to mix carefully. Add the second half of the nut meal mixture; carefully mix with the dough scraper until fully incorporated.

4. Refrigerate the dough for 30 minutes. Meanwhile, prepare the meringue topping.

5. Prepare the meringue icing: Whip the egg whites just enough to be foamy. In a separate bowl, sift the powdered sugar and cream of tartar; mix to combine and then distribute over the egg whites. Mix with an electric mixer on low speed at first to prevent a cloud of dust from the sugar. Stop the mixer to add the lemon juice and scrape down powdered sugar stuck on the sides, then continue beating until thick (about 1 minute). If the icing turns out too thick for brushing onto cookies (step 7), add a few more drops of lemon juice. If the icing is too thin, add more powdered sugar. The consistency should be thick but spreadable to smooth over the cookies, with hardly any running down the sides. Set the icing aside.

6. Roll and cut the dough: Divide the dough in half and return one half to the refrigerator. Sprinkle a wooden or marble board with powdered sugar or nut meal. Rub some powdered sugar or nut meal onto a rolling pin. Roll the dough to about ¼-inch thickness. Sprinkle more powdered sugar or nut meal, a little at a time, over the work surface and dough if the dough sticks (see tip 1). Dip the cookie cutter into water or powdered sugar (either method works to prevent sticking) and cut out stars. Gather and reroll the cut away dough to cut out more stars.

~ TIP 1 ~

Do not be afraid to adjust for sticky dough. Sprinkle a little powdered sugar here and there or extra nut meal if need be. Scrape the dough back to center to work in the powdered sugar or nut meal. Take care not to go

COOKIES

too overboard with the powdered sugar or nut meal, which would produce a dry dough. Add just enough to help the dough reach a consistency that tolerates handling without clinging to fingers. Thick plastic wrap laid over the top of the dough also prevents the rolling pin from sticking, as does a pastry sock fitted onto the rolling pin.

7. Assemble for baking: Arrange the stars on one prepared sheet in three or four rows. With a brush or spoon, put a large dollop of icing onto each cookie's center and then draw out to the points of the star to cover the entire surface. Add more icing if necessary. Aim for good coverage; the dough should not show through (see tip 2).

~ TIP 2 ~

A #12 art brush or a pastry brush is ideal for this task. A teaspoon also works. Take a little icing in the spoon, drizzle it on the cookie, and smooth it with the back of the spoon.

8. Bake for 16 to 17 minutes. The icing should now be crisp, either white or with a light golden color like toasted marshmallow. The underside of the cookies should still be soft but not moist. The center of the cookies should be moist. Pull them earlier rather than later. If the cookies bake past 17 minutes, the risk for dryness in the middle is higher. They continue to dry as they cool. There is a saying that cinnamon stars need to dry in the oven rather than bake. Pull the parchment with the cookies onto a wire rack and cool before transferring to a serving plate or storage container.

9. Repeat steps 6 through 8 with the second half of the dough. Keep in mind that after the first batch, the oven will be thoroughly hot and the second batch might bake faster.

10. Store in a metal cookie tin or an airtight plastic container. In dry climates, the cookies may dry out a bit after a couple of days. Should this happen, adding a slice of apple in the cookie tin or container will soften them up right away.

Note 1: For icing with meringue powder rather than egg white, use:

  ⅛ cup meringue powder
  ¼ cup cold water
  ¼ teaspoon lemon juice
  1 cup sifted powdered sugar (see page 12)

Whip the meringue powder with the cold water and the lemon juice to stiff peaks. Sift the powdered sugar over the meringue mixture. Whip once more to incorporate. When beating the egg white powder with water, the icing gains volume. Follow the directions in step 7 to spread over the cookies before baking. There may be some icing left over. Note that different meringue powder brands yield different results, and powdered sugar amounts may need to be adjusted for desired consistency. I have used Wilton brand meringue powder with good results.

Note 2: Store-bought almond meal can be substituted, but avoid super finely milled almond flour.

COCONUT MACAROONS

Simple, moist, and delicious, these cookies are another treat seen in abundance in Germany around Christmastime. Often, they are made in conjunction with Butter Cookies or *Vanillekipferl* to use up the egg whites from those yolk-heavy recipes. When baked, the Coconut Macaroons are toasty light brown and airy. Because of their light texture, they serve as a splash of variety on a platter with richer butter and nut meal cookies. Using a thin wafer called *Back Oblaten* underneath each macaroon is common in Germany and helps maintain the cookie's shape. Back Oblaten are optional, but if you would like to use them, the fifty-millimeter size is best for these macaroons (more about Back Oblaten on page 119, "Preparing Cookie Sheets for Baking").

COOKIES

BAKING PAN
two cookie sheets, lined with silicone baking mats, or buttered and lined with parchment paper

BAKING TEMPERATURE
300°F, convection

BAKE TIME
20 to 22 minutes

RACK PLACEMENT
middle of oven

YIELD
about sixteen 2-inch cookies using two spoons to shape; fourteen cookies using a 2-inch cookie scoop

INGREDIENTS

2 egg whites

1 ¾ cups powdered sugar

2 cups unsweetened shredded coconut (see *note* at end of recipe)

1 teaspoon almond extract

1 tablespoon lemon juice

DIRECTIONS

1. Position a rack in the middle of the oven and preheat to 300°F (convection bake setting). Line two cookie sheets with silicone mats, or butter and line with parchment. Set aside.

2. Make the dough: Beat the egg whites to stiff peaks. Sift the powdered sugar over the egg whites and sprinkle the shredded coconut onto the powdered sugar. Combine the almond extract with the lemon juice and drizzle over the coconut. With a wire whisk, use a slow, careful folding motion to pull the sugar, coconut, and lemon juice mixture through the egg whites. Finish folding with a large wooden spoon or spatula to incorporate fully, but do not overmix. Overmixing will deflate the egg whites.

3. If using Back Oblaten, place wafers onto lined cookie sheets.

4. Form the macaroons: Use a 2-inch cookie scoop or two teaspoons to achieve the mound shape. If using teaspoons, scoop up a spoonful of dough on one spoon, but do not overload it. With the other spoon, carefully scrape the mound onto the Back Oblaten, if using, or directly onto the lined cookie sheet. Space the cookies about 2 inches apart.

5. Bake for 20 to 22 minutes, until tips are lightly toasted. These cookies need to dry slowly as they bake, so it works well to use a low temperature and convection setting. Cool on a wire rack.

. . . .

Note: For best results, look for shredded coconut, not too finely ground but not large flakes. Health food stores and quality grocers often have an array of options.

HAZELNUT MACAROONS

This recipe is the nutty twin of the Coconut Macaroons. The preparation is identical, and the only difference in the ingredients is the swap of ground hazelnuts for the ground coconut. Because of the hazelnut, these cookies have a richer, almost buttery taste compared to the lighter Coconut Macaroons. The Hazelnut Macaroons may also need one to three more minutes of bake time than the Coconut Macaroons. When done, they are soft, moist, and perfect for dunking into steaming coffee or hot chocolate. Using a thin wafer called *Back Oblaten* underneath each macaroon is common in Germany and helps maintain the cookie's shape. Back Oblaten are optional, but if you would like to use them, the fifty-millimeter size is best for these macaroons (more about Back Oblaten on page 119, "Preparing Cookie Sheets for Baking").

COOKIES

BAKING PAN
two cookie sheets, lined with silicone baking mats, or buttered and lined with parchment paper

BAKING TEMPERATURE
300°F, convection

BAKE TIME
22 to 25 minutes

RACK PLACEMENT
middle of oven

YIELD
about twenty-two 2-inch cookies using two spoons to shape; twelve cookies using a 2-inch cookie scoop

INGREDIENTS

2 egg whites

1 ⅔ cups powdered sugar

1 ¾ cups hazelnut meal or ground hazelnuts (see page 14 for technique if grinding yourself)

1 tablespoon lemon juice

DIRECTIONS

1. Position a rack in the middle of the oven and preheat to 300°F (convection bake setting). Line two cookie sheets with silicone mats, or butter and line with parchment. Set aside.

2. Make the dough: Beat the egg whites to stiff peaks. Sift the powdered sugar over the egg whites and sprinkle the hazelnut meal onto the sugar. Drizzle the lemon juice over the hazelnut meal. With a wire whisk, use a slow, careful folding motion to pull the sugar, hazelnut meal, and lemon juice through the egg whites. Finish folding with a large wooden spoon or spatula to incorporate fully, but do not overmix. Overmixing will deflate the egg whites.

3. If using Back Oblaten, place wafers onto lined cookie sheets.

4. Form the macaroons: Use a 2-inch cookie scoop or two teaspoons to achieve the mound shape. If using teaspoons, scoop up a spoonful of dough on one spoon, but do not overload it. With the other spoon, carefully scrape the mound onto the Back Oblaten, if using, or directly onto the lined cookie sheet. Space the cookies about 2 inches apart.

5. Bake for 22 to 25 minutes. These cookies need to dry slowly as they bake, so it works well to use a low temperature and convection setting. Cool on a wire rack before transferring cookies.

SPEKULATIUS COOKIES

Spekulatius are a crunchy spiced cookie with spices like cinnamon, cloves, ginger, cardamom, and lemon zest. It is worth baking these cookies for the aroma enveloping the kitchen, alone, not to mention the well-rounded mixture of spices that inevitably lead to not eating just one. Even though similar to American gingersnaps, the unique blend of spices creates a different flavor. Ready-made spekulatius spice is available through online German specialty stores (I have used Ostmann brand, available at Germanshop24.com, and find it to be a well-rounded spice). This recipe enhances the ready-made spice blend with extra individual spices for the delicate taste I remember from my years living in Germany. Spekulatius have a preparation like Butter Cookies, and then bakers use wooden molds or carved rolling pins to imprint them with patterns. Because spekulatius are traditional around Saint Nicholas Day and Christmastime, imprints often feature Saint Nicholas or Christmas designs. Other common imprints are windmills and ships, influenced by the Dutch, who call these cookies *speculaas*.

The old-fashioned wooden carved or stenciled molds are still available on eBay. Newly carved molds by talented craftsmen are available online.

COOKIES

For an old-world feel, try the carved molds. For an easier option, carved rolling pins are available in online baking and cooking shops. The small rolling pins, with a five-inch carved surface (measured without the handles), have three rows of cookie molds. To use them, first roll out the dough with a regular rolling pin, and then for the last roll, run the carved rolling pin over the dough with light to medium pressure. Separate the cookies easily with a knife and transfer them onto a sheet for baking. Brushed with an egg white wash, they sport a shiny coating when baked. As with all cookies, they can be baked and enjoyed year-round, even if traditionally associated with Christmas.

BAKING PAN
cookie sheet, buttered and lined with parchment paper

BAKING TEMPERATURE
350°F

BAKE TIME
12 to 14 minutes

RACK PLACEMENT
middle of oven

YIELD
about thirty-two cookies of various sizes, from 2 x 1-inch cookies made with a carved rolling pin to 3 x 3-inch hearts or 3 ½ x 2-inch windmill cookies made with wooden molds

SPECIAL TOOLS
1 regular rolling pin

1 carved rolling pin (the small 5-inch size—10 inches when including the handles—is easiest to work with), or carved wooden mold

INGREDIENTS

1 ¾ cups unbleached all-purpose flour (protein 3 grams per ¼ cup; see page 7), plus ¼ cup for working and rolling dough

¾ cup ground almonds (about 1 cup whole almonds if grinding yourself, see page 14 for technique; use leftover for rolling dough)

½ cup packed brown sugar

¼ cup granulated white sugar

¼ teaspoon salt

2 teaspoons spekulatius spice

1 teaspoon cinnamon

⅛ teaspoon cloves

¼ teaspoon ginger

½ teaspoon cardamom

1 teaspoon lemon zest

1 egg

2 tablespoons milk

10 tablespoons (1 ¼ sticks) unsalted butter, cold

FOR EGG WHITE WASH

2 egg whites

1 teaspoon water

SPEKULATIUS COOKIES

DIRECTIONS

1. Position a rack in the middle of the oven and preheat to 350°F. Butter a cookie sheet and line with parchment. Set aside.

2. Make the dough: Sift the flour and ground almonds into a large bowl. Add the brown and white sugars to the flour mixture and mix thoroughly with a wire whisk or by hand. In a separate small bowl, mix the salt, spices, and lemon zest. Add the spice mixture to the flour mixture and mix with a wire whisk or by hand. Turn the dry ingredients out onto a large marble or wooden board. Form a well in the middle. Add the egg and milk into the well. Cut the butter into small pieces, approximately ¼ to ½ inch (see page 21, "How to Cut Butter," in "Technique to Prepare Mürbeteig Dough"). Distribute the pieces over and around the flour. Using the tip of a metal dough scraper, stir the egg with the milk as if gently scrambling. Begin carefully pushing the dry ingredients into the well's center. Work to combine all ingredients, first with the dough scraper and then with your hands, until a ball of dough forms. Add flour or chill as necessary if the dough becomes too sticky. When the dough forms a smooth, non-sticky ball, place on a plate and cover the dough with plastic wrap. Refrigerate the dough for 1 hour (see tip 1).

~ TIP 1 ~

Chilling the dough for 1 hour before rolling works well to fend off stickiness with this dough. After 1 hour, take off a chunk to begin rolling and cutting the cookies while the rest of the dough remains in the refrigerator.

3. Roll and imprint the dough: Use one of the following methods to imprint the cookies with either a carved rolling pin or with a carved mold.

Using a carved rolling pin: Take out half the dough and leave the other half in the refrigerator. Sprinkle the work surface and top of the dough with leftover ground almonds or with flour. Roll out the dough with a regular, non-carved rolling pin to about 3⁄16-inch thickness. If using a 5-inch carved rolling pin to imprint the cookies, the dough should be rolled into a rectangular shape that is 5½ inches wide. If the dough sticks during rolling, sprinkle more flour, a little at a time, over the dough and onto the rolling pin. After rolling out the dough with a non-carved, regular rolling pin, the carved rolling pin is used for one last roll to imprint the cookie design. Lightly dust the carved rolling pin, shake off extra flour, and with light to medium pressure, roll over the dough so the outlines of the carvings are clearly visible. For even pressure, it helps to lay both palms over the carved part of the pin, not the handles, when rolling. To transfer the cookies, pay attention to the imprint outlines. With a sharp knife

COOKIES

dipped in flour, cut the marked lines outlining each cookie and transfer the cookies onto the prepared baking sheet. Gather remnants of dough and place in refrigerator for cooling to roll out with the next batch. Repeat the rolling process to use up all dough.

Using the carved molds: Take out half the dough and leave the other half in the refrigerator. Sprinkle the work surface and top of the dough with leftover ground almonds or with flour. Roll out the dough with a regular, non-carved rolling pin to about ½- to ¾-inch thickness. Flour the molds and knock out extra flour. Cut a piece of dough approximately the size of the mold and push the dough into the mold, covering the design. Turn the mold over and press down onto the work surface to compress the dough into the mold. Dip a sharp knife in flour and, holding it horizontal to the carving, slice off extra dough. Now only the carved shape should be clearly visible. If there is dough spread thinly over the edge of the carving, use a butter knife or small cake spatula to scrape it gently back into the carving. This will give the dough a clear edge lining out the shape, and it will allow dough to fall easier from the mold. To remove the shaped dough, turn the mold over and knock the edge onto the work surface to loosen one end. Turn the mold 80 degrees and repeat on the other side. With a little help, the cookie will fall out of the mold into the hand. Repeat the process to use up all the dough.

4. Assemble for baking: Arrange cookies on the prepared sheet. Some carvings make shallower cookies than others; place cookies of the same thickness together for even baking.

5. Prepare the egg white wash: Whisk the egg white with the water in a small bowl and brush over cookies for a shiny glaze (see tip 2).

~ TIP 2 ~

A pastry brush is ideal for this task, but if one is not available, dip the edge of a balled paper towel into the whisked egg white and use that for brushing.

6. Bake for 12 to 14 minutes. Transfer cookies to a wire rack to cool.

BUTTER COOKIES

These are a basic, delicious cookie similar in flavor and texture to a shortbread. They offer a satisfying crunch on first bite and then melt in your mouth. Their simplicity makes them ideal to have on hand as a quick accompaniment for coffee, tea, snacks, or desserts. They also present a blank slate for decoration. Take free rein should creativity strike. Experiment with the shapes of cookie cutters. Consider adding colored sprinkles or sugar pearls—both will adhere well to the egg yolk brushed over the top of the cookies. You can also make a powdered sugar icing, colored as you like to accent any occasion or season. They take on Christmas shapes and colors beautifully. Sprinkles or pearls should be applied before baking so that they stick properly. Icing should be applied after baking.

COOKIES

BAKING PAN
cookie sheet, lined with silicone baking mat, or buttered and lined with parchment paper

BAKING TEMPERATURE
350°F, regular setting; 325°F, convection

BAKE TIME
10 to 12 minutes

RACK PLACEMENT
middle of oven

YIELD
about forty 2-inch cookies

SPECIAL TOOLS
Cookie cutters of different shapes, such as star, moon, and heart, about 2 inches in size

INGREDIENTS

1 ¾ cups unbleached all-purpose flour (protein 3 grams per ¼ cup; see page 7), plus ¼ cup for working and rolling dough

½ cup cornstarch

1 teaspoon baking powder

½ cup sugar

1 egg

9 tablespoons (1 ⅛ sticks) unsalted butter, cold

1 to 2 egg yolks (for brushing—see *note* at end of recipe)

DIRECTIONS

1. Position a rack in the middle of the oven and preheat to 350°F (regular setting) or to 325°F (convection bake setting). Line a cookie sheet with a silicone mat, or butter and line with parchment. Set aside.

2. Make the dough: Sift the flour, cornstarch, and baking powder onto a large marble or wooden board. Form a well in the middle. Add the sugar and egg into the well. Cut the butter into small pieces, approximately ¼ to ½ inch (see page 21, "How to Cut Butter," in "Technique to Prepare Mürbeteig Dough"). Distribute the pieces over and around the flour. Using the tip of a metal dough scraper, stir the egg as if gently scrambling. Begin carefully pushing the dry ingredients into the well's center. Work to combine all ingredients, first with the dough scraper and then with your hands, until a ball of dough forms. Add flour or chill as necessary if the dough becomes too sticky. When the dough forms a smooth ball, place on a plate and cover the dough with plastic wrap. Refrigerate for 30 minutes.

3. Roll and cut the dough: Sprinkle a work surface and rolling pin with flour. Roll the dough to about ¼-inch thickness. If the dough sticks,

BUTTER COOKIES

sprinkle more flour, a little at a time, over the dough and onto the rolling pin (see tip 1). Dip cookie cutters into flour and cut out shapes. If there is extra dough, gather it back to center and reroll to cut out more cookies.

~ TIP 1 ~

Chilling the dough for 30 minutes before rolling works well to fend off stickiness with this dough. Take off a chunk to begin rolling and cutting the cookies while the rest of the dough remains in the refrigerator. A pastry sock over the rolling pin also prevents sticking.

4. Whisk the egg yolk (or yolks) in a small bowl.

5. Assemble for baking: Arrange cookies on the prepared sheet and brush with the egg yolk. Do not allow the yolk to drip onto the sheet (see tip 2).

....

Note: To stretch one egg yolk, add a little milk. The tops of the cookies will be less vibrant in color, but the flavor will not be affected.

~ TIP 2 ~

A pastry brush is ideal for this task, but if one is not available, dip the edge of a balled paper towel into the whisked yolk and use that for brushing. A teaspoon also works. Take a little yolk in the spoon, drizzle it on the cookie, and smooth with the back of the spoon. With a little care, it is easy to keep the yolk atop the cookie and avoid drips onto the sheet. Drips on the sheet will turn dark and bitter during baking.

6. Bake for 10 to 12 minutes. The yolk topping should be bright lemon yellow in color. Place the sheet on a wire rack to cool before transferring cookies. Decorate as desired.

CANDIED GINGER BROWNIES
(with dairy-free option)

This recipe is a combination of a German chocolate cookie and an American brownie. The candied ginger brings a deep, spicy layer to the chocolate, and the sweet, plump raisins help to preserve moisture. These fudgy brownies are even better the next day, after the nectar of the candied ginger and raisins have had time to soak into the cake.

CANDIED GINGER BROWNIES

BAKING PAN
9 x 12-inch brownie or sheet cake pan, buttered and lined with parchment paper

BAKING TEMPERATURE
350°F

BAKE TIME
25 to 30 minutes

RACK PLACEMENT
middle of oven

YIELD
about twenty-four 2-inch-square brownies

INGREDIENTS

⅓ cup raisins

¾ cup candied ginger (see *note* at end of recipe)

3 eggs

1 ½ cups sugar

1 teaspoon vanilla extract or vanilla paste

1 cup chocolate chips

8 tablespoons (1 stick) unsalted butter, at room temperature and very soft; or, for dairy-free, ½ cup plus 1 tablespoon safflower oil, sunflower oil, or canola oil

1 cup unbleached all-purpose flour (protein 3 grams per ¼ cup; see page 7)

½ cup ground hazelnuts or hazelnut meal (see page 14 for technique if grinding yourself)

DIRECTIONS

1. Position a rack in the middle of the oven and preheat to 350°F. Butter the pan and line with parchment paper in preparation for baking. Set aside.

2. Have the raisins on hand and chop the ginger into raisin-sized pieces.

3. Make the batter: For this recipe, a blender is preferred, but a standing mixer can also be used if a blender is not available. In a blender, beat the eggs on almost high for 2 minutes, until slightly frothy. Add the sugar and vanilla and blend for 1 minute more, until fluffy, creamy, and light yellow in color. Pour into a large bowl. From here on, continue mixing by hand.

4. Melt the chocolate in a microwave or double boiler (see page 15 for technique). Off the heat, stir in half of the soft butter or oil. Repeat with the remaining butter or oil until blended with the chocolate. Soften butter for 20 seconds (or less) in microwave, if necessary.

5. Take about ½ cup of the egg mixture and stir into the chocolate and butter mixture to help cool. Pour in the rest of the egg mixture and

COOKIES

stir to combine. Mix carefully and briefly and stop as soon as the egg mixture and chocolate are blended. Do not overmix.

6. Sift the flour into a large bowl, add the ground hazelnuts, and combine with a wire whisk. Add in the raisins and candied ginger. Fold the flour mixture into the egg mixture. Mix, then stop as soon as the flour is incorporated. Do not overmix. Spread the batter evenly into the prepared pan.

7. Bake for 25 to 30 minutes. Insert a wooden skewer into the center to check doneness. The skewer will come out a bit sticky, but there should be no runny batter. The rim, when tested with the skewer, should come out clean. Let cool in pan on a wire rack before cutting into individual pieces.

. . . .

Note: Candied ginger is available at many grocery stores as well as specialty markets and traditional candy shops. Take note of the size and shape of the candied ginger, as there is some variety across brands. The pieces will diffuse throughout the batter more easily and consistently if cut small. If you cannot find candied ginger already cut into small pieces, run a knife through the bigger pieces until they are about the same size as the raisins. Taste also varies across brands. Brands that offer larger cubes (¾ inch x ½ inch) of candied ginger have more of a punch than brands that offer candied ginger in the shape of flat discs. Perhaps use slightly less of the cubed candied ginger. A good way to decide on candied ginger is tasting it first. If it is too strong, it will overpower the brownies.

COFFEE LIQUEUR BROWNIES

These are delicious, full-bodied chocolate brownies. The ingredients suggest either coffee or chocolate liqueur, each liqueur giving a slightly different flavor. It is definitely worth trying out both variations. Always a favorite, this recipe can be made quickly, perfect for guests on short notice. Serve the brownies as is, with a dusting of powdered sugar, or with a chocolate glaze.

COOKIES

BAKING PAN
9 x 12 x 2-inch brownie or sheet cake pan, buttered and floured or buttered and lined with parchment paper

BAKING TEMPERATURE
350°F

BAKE TIME
25 to 30 minutes

RACK PLACEMENT
middle of oven

YIELD
about twenty-four 2-inch-square brownies

INGREDIENTS

4 eggs

1 ¾ cups sugar

Pulp of 1 vanilla bean, or 2 teaspoons vanilla extract

2 tablespoons coffee liqueur or chocolate liqueur

¾ cup dark chocolate bar (broken into pieces) or chips (5 ounces), at least 55% and up to 70% cocoa

8 tablespoons (1 stick) unsalted butter, at room temperature and soft

1 cup unbleached all-purpose flour (protein 3 grams per ¼ cup; see page 7)

¾ cup pecan pieces

¼ cup finely ground pecans, optional (see page 14 for technique if grinding yourself)

OPTIONS FOR GARNISHING

Easy Chocolate Glaze (see page 261)

⅓ cup powdered sugar (for dusting)

DIRECTIONS

1. Position a rack in the middle of the oven and preheat to 350°F. Butter and flour the pan, or butter and line with parchment paper in preparation for baking. Set aside.

2. Make the batter: For this recipe, a blender is preferred, but a standing mixer can also be used if a blender is not available. In a blender, beat the eggs on almost high for 2 minutes, until slightly frothy. Add the sugar and vanilla and blend for 1 minute more, until fluffy, creamy, and light yellow in color. Add the liqueur and blend an additional 10 to 15 seconds. Pour into a large bowl. From here on, continue mixing by hand.

COFFEE LIQUEUR BROWNIES

3. Melt the chocolate in a microwave or double boiler (see page 15 for technique). Off the heat, stir in half of the soft butter. Repeat with the remaining butter until blended with the chocolate. Soften butter for 20 seconds (or less) in microwave, if necessary.

4. Take ½ cup of the egg mixture and stir into the chocolate and butter mixture to help cool. Pour into the rest of the egg mixture and stir to combine. Mix carefully and briefly and stop as soon as the egg mixture and chocolate are blended. Do not overmix.

5. Sift the flour into a large bowl, add the pecan pieces and optional ground pecans, and combine with a wire whisk. Fold the flour mixture into the egg mixture. Mix, then stop as soon as the flour is incorporated. Do not overmix. Spread the batter evenly into the prepared pan.

6. Bake for 25 to 30 minutes. Insert a wooden skewer into the center to check doneness. The skewer will come out a bit sticky, but there should be no runny batter. The rim, when tested with the skewer, should come out clean. Let cool in pan on a wire rack before cutting into individual pieces.

NUT BROWNIES

This recipe creates the texture of a brownie, but the dominant flavor comes from the nut meal, with the chocolate working subtly in the background. It is worth taking the time to toast the nut meal to infuse the batter with buttery depth. Toasting the nut meal takes very little time, but it is also fine to omit that task if you are in a rush and need simplicity. The ingredients suggest several options for the nut meals, with almond liqueur, almond extract, or chocolate liqueur rounding off the rich nut flavor. Explore the pairings as you like. Serve the brownies with powdered sugar, Easy Chocolate Glaze, or deliciously plain.

NUT BROWNIES

BAKING PAN
9 x 12-inch brownie or sheet cake pan, buttered and floured, or buttered and lined with parchment paper

BAKING TEMPERATURE
350°F

BAKE TIME
25 to 30 minutes

RACK PLACEMENT
middle of oven

YIELD
about twenty-four 2-inch-square brownies

INGREDIENTS

⅓ cup hazelnut meal, macadamia nut meal, or almond meal

4 eggs

1 ¾ cups sugar

⅛ teaspoon salt

¾ cup chocolate chips

8 tablespoons (1 stick) unsalted butter, at room temperature

2 tablespoons almond liqueur or chocolate liqueur, or 1 tablespoon almond extract

¾ cup unbleached all-purpose flour (protein 3 grams per ¼ cup; see page 7)

¾ cup chopped pecans

OPTIONS FOR GARNISHING

Easy Chocolate Glaze (see page 261)

⅓ cup powdered sugar

DIRECTIONS

1. Position a rack in the middle of the oven and preheat to 350°F. Butter and flour the pan, or butter and line with parchment paper in preparation for baking. Set aside.

2. Toast the nut meal (this is an optional step and can be omitted): Heat a skillet over medium to medium-high. Add the nut meal into the skillet and flatten it down with a spatula. Toast the nut meal for about 5 minutes, until a light brown color, then stir and flip regularly to brown evenly. If smoke starts to develop, the skillet is too hot. If that happens, remove from heat for a brief time and continue stirring, then return to heat as needed, with the temperature reduced as needed. Aim for golden brown, not dark brown. If the nut meal darkens too much, it will become bitter. Spread out nut meal on a plate to cool.

3. Make the batter: Beat the eggs with an electric mixer on almost high for 2 minutes. Add the sugar and salt and blend for 1 minute more, until very fluffy and creamy. Pour into a large bowl. From here on, continue mixing by hand.

COOKIES

4. Melt the chocolate in a microwave or double boiler (see page 15 for technique). Remove from heat and stir in half of the soft butter. Repeat with the remaining butter until blended with the chocolate. Soften butter for 20 seconds (or less) in microwave, if necessary.

5. Take ½ cup of the egg mixture and stir into the chocolate and butter mixture to help cool. Pour into the rest of the egg mixture and stir to combine. Just before uniformly mixed, stir in the almond or chocolate liqueur or the almond extract.

6. Sift the flour into a large bowl, add the nut meal and chopped pecans, and combine with a wire whisk. Add the flour mixture over the egg mixture and fold the flour into the batter. Stop as soon as the flour is incorporated. Do not overmix.

7. Spread the batter evenly into the prepared pan.

8. Bake for 25 to 30 minutes. Insert a wooden skewer into the center to check doneness. The skewer will come out a bit sticky, but there should be no runny batter. The rim, when tested with the skewer, should come out clean. Let cool in pan on a wire rack before cutting into individual pieces.

HAZELNUT AND JELLY SANDWICH COOKIES

These are some of my favorite cookies, cherished because the hazelnut reminds me of my teenage years. Back then, we visited the countryside quite often as a family. My dad had a place in a mountain region called Odenwald. One morning, I got up at dawn and went for a hike looking for wildlife—deer, rabbits, falcons, hawks, pheasants. I loved to watch them all. Even the sheep out in the fruit orchards still sleeping all curled up were a delight to see in the glow of the morning. As I walked, I circled around a large meadow, where lupines grew along the edges, and in the middle was a hazelnut bush, standing all by itself with loads of fruit. I took a bunch home, cracked them, and ate them plain. The taste was rich, woodsy, and much more intense than the store-bought nuts I'd had. The taste has not dulled in my memory over all these years. I've tried to draw forth that flavor in these cookies. Buying whole hazelnuts and grinding them to a fine meal in a food processor, nut mill, or coffee mill will give more flavor than using purchased hazelnut meal.

I once brought these cookies to a party attended by both children and adults. Not a crumb was left by the end. One busy mother asked me about the recipe, but then worried that she would never have time to make them because the tops and bottoms must bake separately, before assembly. These cookies involve more time and attention than some other types of cookies. That is undeniable. But they also deliver extra delight with the sweet hazelnut, vibrant lemon, and tart jelly. Children are usually happy to help with spreading the jelly and sandwiching the cookies, which makes preparation a fun family activity. And, if the cookies last to the next day, they are even better then. The flavors will have had time to soak and settle, and the texture will have softened. I use four-inch butterfly and heart cookie cutters in this recipe, with smaller two-inch cutters to stamp out the middle of each top cookie. But any shape cookie cutter will serve, provided a small enough cutter is available to stamp out the top middles. One of the easiest shapes to find in several cookie cutter sizes is the circle. Also note this dough needs one hour refrigeration time to make handling easier. Plan preparation time accordingly.

COOKIES

BAKING PAN
2 cookie sheets, lined with silicone baking mats, or buttered and lined with parchment paper

BAKING TEMPERATURE
350°F

BAKE TIME
top cookies (middle cut out) 10 to 12 minutes; bottom cookies 12 to 14 minutes

RACK PLACEMENT
top third of oven

YIELD
twelve 4-inch sandwich cookies

SPECIAL TOOLS
Nested cookie cutters, or Linzer cookie cutter set

HAZELNUT AND JELLY SANDWICH COOKIES

INGREDIENTS

FOR DOUGH

2 cups unbleached all-purpose flour (protein 3 grams per ¼ cup; see page 7), plus ¼ to ⅓ cup extra for rolling dough

½ cup unblanched hazelnut meal, loosely measured (a full ⅓ cup whole nuts if grinding yourself, see page 14 for technique)

1 ⅛ cups powdered sugar

⅛ teaspoon salt

Zest of 1 small lemon (about 2 teaspoons)

1 egg yolk

2 tablespoons almond liqueur, or 1 tablespoon almond extract

14 tablespoons (1 ¾ sticks) unsalted butter, cold

FOR FILLING

½ cup seedless jelly, such as apricot, raspberry, or red currant (if straining out seeds, start with 1 cup; about ½ cup will be left)

2 teaspoons lemon juice

1 teaspoon orange liqueur or *kirschwasser*, optional

FOR DUSTING

⅓ cup powdered sugar

DIRECTIONS

1. Prepare the dough: Sift the flour, hazelnut meal, and powdered sugar onto a large marble or wooden board. Form a well in the middle and sprinkle the salt and lemon zest around the edge (see tip 1). Add the egg yolk and almond liqueur or almond extract into the well. Cut the butter into small pieces, approximately ¼ to ½ inch (see page 21, "How to Cut Butter," in "Technique to Prepare Mürbeteig Dough"). Distribute the pieces over and around the flour. Using the tip of a metal dough scraper, stir the egg yolk as if gently scrambling. Begin carefully pushing the dry ingredients into the well's center. Work to combine all ingredients, first with the dough scraper and then with your hands, until a ball of dough forms. Add flour, a little at a time, or chill as necessary if dough becomes too sticky.

~ TIP 1 ~

Toss the lemon zest in 1 to 2 tablespoons of flour. The flour coating makes it easier to distribute without sticking.

2. Refrigerate for 1 hour. The dough is easier to roll and cut when chilled.

3. Position a rack in the top third of the oven and preheat to 350°F. Line the cookie sheets with silicone mats, or butter and line with parchment. Set aside.

COOKIES

4. Roll the dough for the top of the cookies: Sparsely rub flour on a work surface and rolling pin. Remove half of the dough from the refrigerator and roll out to ⅛-inch thickness. Cut out the cookies using the large cookie cutter. Use the smaller cookie cutter to stamp a hole in the middle of each cookie. This hole will allow the jam to show when the cookies are assembled. Scrape together leftover dough (including the pieces stamped from the middles), form into a ball, and place back with the dough resting in the refrigerator.

5. Use a large spatula or pastry scraper, dipped in flour if needed, to transfer the top cookies to one of the prepared sheets. Transfer carefully so the cookies do not lose their shape.

6. Bake the top cookies for 10 to 12 minutes, until lightly toasted. Cool on the sheet for 5 minutes before transferring to a cooling rack with a spatula. While the tops are baking and cooling, work on the bottoms.

7. Roll the dough for the bottom cookies: Remove all remaining dough from the refrigerator and roll out to ⅛-inch thickness. Cut out the bottom cookies using the large cookie cutter. Do not stamp a hole in these. Make sure to cut out the same number of bottom cookies as tops. Form leftover dough into a disc and place into the refrigerator to chill for a second batch (see tip 2).

~ TIP 2 ~

If there is leftover dough, scrape it together, roll into a ball, and chill again. When the leftover dough is chilled enough to work with, cut out more cookies, making sure to create an even number of tops and bottoms. Follow the baking instructions in steps 6 and 9.

8. Use a large spatula or pastry scraper, dipped in flour if needed, to transfer the bottom cookies to the other prepared sheet. Transfer carefully so the cookies do not lose their shape. Push back into shape if they get scrunched during transfer.

155

HAZELNUT AND JELLY SANDWICH COOKIES

9. Bake the bottom cookies for 12 to 14 minutes, until lightly toasted. They require more baking time than the tops. Place cookie sheet onto a cooling rack and cool cookies on the sheet for 5 to 10 minutes before transferring to a cooling rack with a spatula. They also require slightly longer cooling time than the tops.

10. Assemble cookies: While top and bottom cookies are cooling, vigorously mix the jelly, lemon juice, and optional orange liqueur or kirschwasser until smooth (see tip 3). Brush the jelly mixture onto the bottom cookies. Place the tops on and press down lightly (see tip 4). Dust with powdered sugar.

~ TIP 3 ~

If omitting alcohol, use 1 teaspoon of water to thin the jelly mixture if it seems too thick.

~ TIP 4 ~

It may take a minute or two for the tops to stick fully. Try not to move the cookies for a few minutes after assembling to prevent sliding tops. If you do need to move them immediately, grasp by the bottom cookie and keep them level while moving.

APRICOT NUT COOKIES

These hearty cookies are crunchy and gooey at the same time, making them hard to stay away from. Tasting one will inevitably lead to cravings for another. They are especially enjoyable on cold winter days by the fire hearth or as a wholesome snack to take on a hike instead of an energy bar. During preparation, this dough requires two chill times, which together total an hour to an hour and a half. Plan accordingly.

BAKING PAN
16 x 12-inch cookie sheet, lined with silicone baking mat, or buttered and lined with parchment paper

BAKING TEMPERATURE
375°F

BAKE TIME
15 minutes

RACK PLACEMENT
top third of oven

YIELD
about thirty-two 2 ½-inch cookies

SPECIAL TOOLS
1 or 2 extra cookie sheets, lined with silicone baking mats or parchment, for chilling rolled dough

APRICOT NUT COOKIES

INGREDIENTS

FOR DOUGH

3 cups unbleached all-purpose flour (protein 3 grams per ¼ cup; see page 7), plus ¼ cup extra for rolling dough

⅛ teaspoon salt

½ cup packed light brown sugar

1 egg

2 teaspoons vanilla extract, or 2 to 3 teaspoons vanilla sugar

8 tablespoons (1 stick) unsalted butter, cold

FOR APRICOT AND NUT FILLING

1 ½ cups chopped dried apricots (about 8 ounces), or 1 cup chopped dried apricots and ½ cup dried cranberries (for flavor contrast)

½ cup water

⅓ cup sugar

2 tablespoons honey

2 tablespoons orange liqueur

¾ cup pecans, chopped

DIRECTIONS

1. Prepare the dough: Sift the flour onto a large marble or wooden board. Form a well in the middle and sprinkle the salt around the edge. Add the light brown sugar, egg, and vanilla into the well. Cut the butter into small pieces, approximately ¼ to ½ inch (see page 21, "How to Cut Butter," in "Technique to Prepare Mürbeteig Dough"). Distribute the pieces over and around the flour. Using the tip of a metal dough scraper, stir the egg as if gently scrambling. Begin carefully pushing the dry ingredients into the well's center. Work to combine all ingredients, first with the dough scraper and then with your hands, until a ball of dough forms. Add flour, a little at a time, or chill as necessary if the dough becomes too sticky.

2. Refrigerate the dough for 30 minutes. Meanwhile, prepare the filling.

3. Prepare the apricot filling: Into a medium saucepan, add the apricots, water, sugar, honey, orange liqueur, and pecan pieces (chopped small) (see tip). While stirring constantly, cook over medium to high heat for 5 to 10 minutes, or until the filling thickens to a chutney-like consistency. Spread filling onto a plate to cool.

~ TIP ~

Easily break pecan halves into pieces by placing them into a plastic sandwich bag and smashing with a rolling pin.

COOKIES

4. Line one or two cookie sheets with silicone baking mats or parchment paper (no butter necessary beneath the parchment). Set aside until needed for chilling the rolled dough in steps 7 and 8.

5. Roll half the dough: Sparsely rub flour on a work surface and rolling pin. Remove half of the dough from the refrigerator and roll out to a rectangular shape, 16 x 9 inches in size and ¼ inch in thickness. If the sides of the rectangle are not straight, cut away uneven edges and add them on where needed. Push the added dough into place and smooth over with another roll of the rolling pin.

6. Assemble: Spread half the filling over the rolled-out dough. Stay away from the edges by ¼ inch along the two shorter sides and one of the long sides. This will leave room for the filling to spread, without squeezing out, when rolling up the dough. On the other long side, leave ¾ inch of space.

7. Starting at the long side with ¼ inch of space between the edge and the filling, gently roll up the dough fairly tightly. If needed, use a pastry cutter for assistance. Dip the pastry cutter in flour and slide it under the dough. Move it along the length of the dough, carefully lifting, rolling, and pressing. When getting near the end, stop and, instead of rolling more, lift the part that remains and connect it with the rolled-up dough. Press to form a seal. The dough will look like a log or a tube. Gently roll it, seam-side down, onto the lined cookie sheet. Refrigerate for 30 minutes to 1 hour.

8. While the first batch is chilling, repeat the rolling process with the remaining dough and filling. Place the second batch into the refrigerator to chill for 30 minutes to 1 hour.

9. Position a rack in the top third of the oven and preheat to 375°F. Line a cookie sheet with a silicone mat, or butter and line with parchment in preparation for baking.

10. Cut the cookies: Once the chilling time is complete for the first batch, remove from the refrigerator. Slice the roll into discs, 1 to 1½ inches thick. Transfer to the prepared cookie sheet. Lay cookies flat so that the snail (spiral) pattern is visible. Space evenly apart. Sixteen cookies will fit onto a 16 x 12-inch sheet if placed in three rows, with a few cookies being offset.

11. Bake for 15 minutes. Transfer to a wire rack to cool.

12. Repeat cutting and baking for the second batch. Cool the second batch on a wire rack as well.

GINGERBREAD HOUSE

The Gingerbread House is both a recipe and an activity. It is great fun for a crafty baker, but if you don't enjoy crafting, it may get frustrating. The recipe, assembly, and decoration all require investments of time—several hours of it. But the work is enjoyable; you will feel like a baker, a master carpenter, and a great artist all in one. And when finished, the wonder makes it worth the while. The Gingerbread House can stand for a month, so you can make it after Thanksgiving and keep it pristine through Christmas. Or allow the kids (and adults) to break off little pieces and nibble. Just warn them to be careful. The witch might come out, or at least that is how the tradition goes. In Germany, gingerbread houses have a connection to Christmas and the fairytale of Hänsel and Gretel. The witch lives in the forest in her witch-house (or *Hexen-Haus*); the windows are made of sugar, and the house is decorated with cake and gingerbread (*lebkuchen*). Hänsel and Gretel, lost in the woods, are so hungry they start nibbling on the gingerbread, then the witch appears. She croaks, "Crunch, crunch, crunch, who is nibbling on my little house?"

The work of baking, constructing, and decorating a gingerbread house can be spread over three (or more) days to be more manageable. This recipe divides the ingredients and the directions by day.

VIDEO SHOWCASE
Gingerbread House
vimeo.com/1001786145

On the first day, make the dough and bake the gingerbread pieces. If using the German ingredients *hirschhornsalz* and *potash* as the leavening in the dough, an extra day is needed so that the dough can rest (see *note 1* at end of day one's directions). In the morning of the second day, assemble the house's walls and decorate the pieces that are not part of the house's frame, such as the figures, trees, fence, and shutters. In the evening of the second day, glue on the roof. On the third day, decorate the house and add the pieces decorated on day two. These days do not necessarily need to be consecutive. For example, bakers could make the gingerbread pieces and assemble the house in two days over a weekend, and then wait until later in the week to have helpers come over to decorate.

Before the instructions for day one, there is an overview of all ingredients needed for the recipe. That way, bakers will have a complete list before beginning. The list of ingredients repeats within each particular day so that bakers know what is needed for that day's work. German leavenings (hirschhornsalz and potash) and gingerbread spices (*lebkuchengewürz*) listed in the ingredients can be ordered online.

For a video demonstration of constructing the Gingerbread House, see vimeo.com/1001786145.

COOKIES

BAKING PAN
several large cookie sheets (at least two or three), coated with oil and floured, or oiled and covered with parchment

BAKING TEMPERATURE
325°F, convection

BAKE TIME
12 to 15 minutes (per cookie sheet) (see *note 2* at end of day one's directions)

YIELD
makes one house (8 inches wide x 10 inches long x 14 inches tall) plus fence, two trees, and Hänsel and Gretel

RACK PLACEMENT
middle of oven

SPECIAL TOOLS AND MATERIALS
Fast-read kitchen thermometer

Cookie cutters (trees, gingerbread boy and girl, or other desired shapes) (see *note 3* at end of day one's directions)

Two large, wide mixing bowls (each 4 quarts, 10-inch diameter and 5-inch height)

18 x 20-inch or 14 x 23-inch board to assemble house (a large cutting board; plywood; or a large, sturdy cookie sheet covered with tinfoil works well)

GINGERBREAD HOUSE

INGREDIENTS OVERVIEW

FOR GINGERBREAD DOUGH

32 ounces honey

3 cups sugar

¼ teaspoon salt

8 tablespoons (1 stick) unsalted butter, at room temperature

12 to 13 cups unbleached all-purpose flour (protein 3 grams per ¼ cup; see page 7) (start with 1 cup less; add more as needed when working and rolling out the dough)

1 teaspoon (4.6 grams) hirschhornsalz (in English, called hartshorn or ammonium hydrogen carbonate)

1 ½ teaspoons (7 grams) potash (potassium carbonate)

> Hirschhornsalz and potash are both German leavenings for gingerbread; substitute 3 teaspoons baking powder if potash and hirschhornsalz are not available (see note 1 at end of day one's directions).

12 ounces ground almonds (see page 14 for technique if grinding yourself)

19 teaspoons (30 grams) lebkuchengewürz (German gingerbread spice) (two 15-gram packets are best)

> Or substitute a basic homemade mix of:
> ¼ teaspoon cloves
> ¼ teaspoon nutmeg
> 4 teaspoons cinnamon
> 2 teaspoons ground ginger

> Other ground spices like ground star anise, ground fennel, mace, and cardamom are also complementary in small amounts.

Zest of 1 big lemon (about 4 teaspoons)

Juice of 1 big lemon (about 6 tablespoons)

3 eggs

8 ounces whole blanched almonds (to press into dough for shutters and shingles before baking; see page 13 for blanching technique)

FOR ASSEMBLY AND DECORATION

DAY 1
For royal icing (to cover board):
    4 egg whites
    4 cups powdered sugar
    1 teaspoon lemon juice

DAY 2
For royal icing (to assemble and decorate):
    3 egg whites
    5 cups powdered sugar

DAY 3
For royal icing (to cover roof and decorate):
    3 egg whites
    5 cups powdered sugar

TOTAL AMOUNTS NEEDED FOR EGG WHITES AND POWDERED SUGAR

10 egg whites

4 pounds powdered sugar

SUGGESTIONS FOR DECORATIONS

Use colorful candy, small cookies, shredded coconut, sprinkles, dried fruit, and nuts. Good candy choices include candy corn, gummy bears, candy-coated chocolate, hard candies, licorice, and gumdrops. Chocolate nonpareils make nice shingles for covering or accenting the roof. Food coloring for the icing to decorate pine trees or to paint clothes on Hänsel and Gretel is a nice touch.

COOKIES

DIRECTIONS

Day 1: Prepare the Dough, Bake the Pieces, and Cover the Assembly Board

* If using hirschhornsalz and potash in the dough, an extra day is needed so that the dough can rest (see *note 1* at end of day one's directions).

INGREDIENTS FOR GINGERBREAD

32 ounces honey

3 cups sugar

¼ teaspoon salt

8 tablespoons (1 stick) unsalted butter, at room temperature

12 to 13 cups unbleached all-purpose flour (protein 3 grams per ¼ cup; see page 7) (start with 1 cup less; add more as needed when working the dough in step 3 and rolling the dough in step 6)

1 teaspoon (4.6 grams) hirschhornsalz (in English, called hartshorn or ammonium hydrogen carbonate)

1 ½ teaspoons (7 grams) potash (potassium carbonate)

> Hirschhornsalz and potash are both German leavenings for gingerbread; substitute 3 teaspoons baking powder if potash and hirschhornsalz are not available (see *note 1* at end of day one's directions).

12 ounces ground almonds (see page 14 for technique if grinding yourself)

19 teaspoons (30 grams) lebkuchengewürz (German gingerbread spice) (two 15-gram packets are best)

> Or substitute a basic homemade mix of:
> ¼ teaspoon cloves
> ¼ teaspoon nutmeg
> 4 teaspoons cinnamon
> 2 teaspoons ground ginger

> Other ground spices like ground star anise, ground fennel, mace, and cardamom are also complementary in small amounts.

Zest of 1 big lemon (about 4 teaspoons)

Juice of 1 big lemon (about 6 tablespoons)

3 eggs

8 ounces whole blanched almonds (to press into dough for shutters and shingles before baking; see page 13 for blanching technique)

INGREDIENTS FOR ROYAL ICING
(to cover board)

4 egg whites

4 cups powdered sugar

1 teaspoon lemon juice

GINGERBREAD HOUSE

Gingerbread House Template

Printable PDF at heidrunmetzler.com/resources

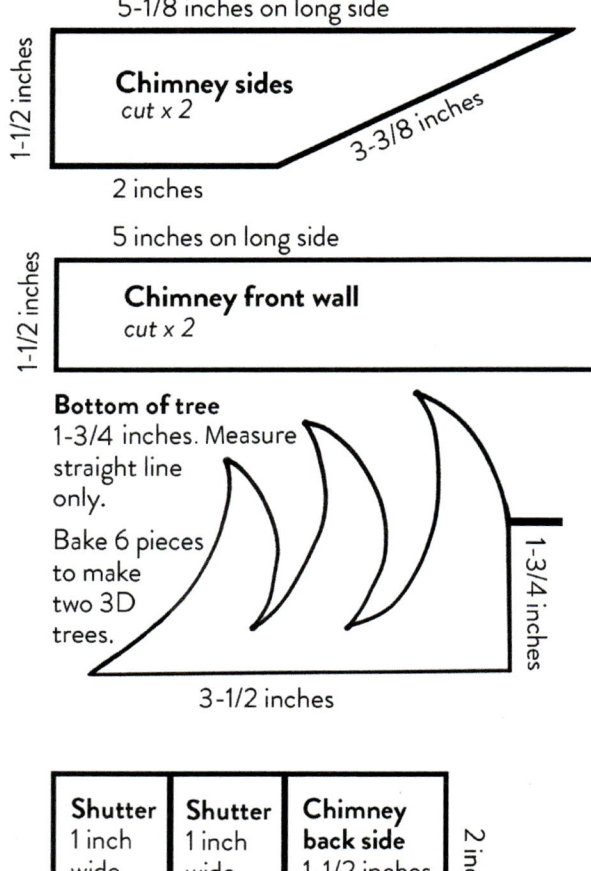

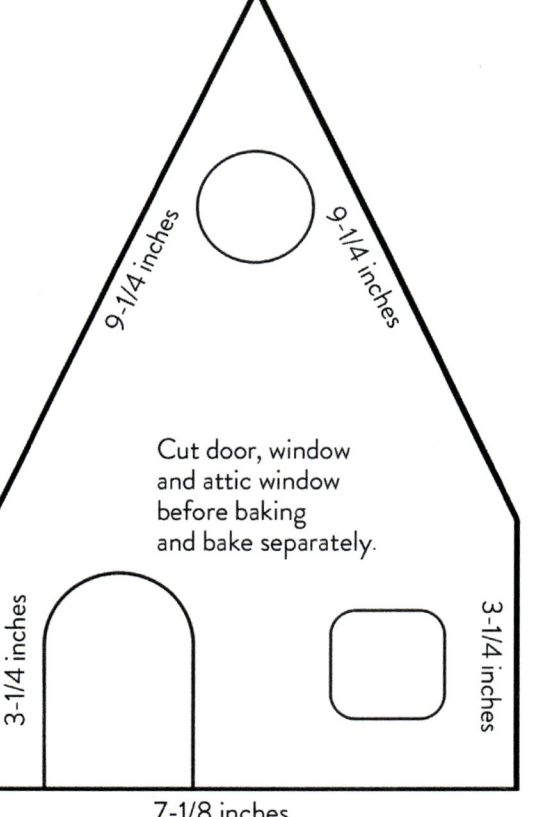

COOKIES

GINGERBREAD HOUSE

1. Start by drawing and cutting out the shapes for the house on drawing pad paper (11 x 14-inch size). If the cutouts are to be used next Christmas, make two sets: one in parchment paper and one in very sturdy drawing paper. Use the parchment set to lay on the dough when cutting out the parts. Save the sturdy paper set to use as a template year after year. Make sure to label each piece of this set. Include dimensions and whether a particular piece, such as a wall or chimney, must be used twice. See drawings and sizes at the beginning of this recipe (see page 164).

2. Begin with the dough: Combine the honey, sugar, salt, and butter into a medium saucepan over medium heat. Slowly heat and stir until smooth and incorporated. Monitor the temperature with a fast-read kitchen thermometer and do not heat the honey over 176°F/80°C; pour into a bowl and let cool to 104°F/40°C before adding to the flour in step 3.

3. Sift half the flour into a large bowl and the other into another large bowl. If using baking powder instead of hirschhornsalz and potash, sprinkle half into one bowl of flour and half into the other bowl of flour now. If using hirschhornsalz and potash, dissolve the hirschhornsalz and the potash in separate cups in 2 to 3 tablespoons of warm water and set aside.

   Add half of the ground almonds, lebkuchengewürz (or the homemade mix of cloves, nutmeg, cinnamon, ginger, and other spices), and lemon zest into one bowl of flour and half into the other bowl. In each bowl, slightly mix the dry ingredients and make a well in the center.

   Add the lemon juice to the honey mixture and stir, then add half into the well of each bowl. Briefly whisk the eggs to combine yolks and whites; add half to the honey mixture in each bowl. Gently mix the honey and eggs with a few strokes. If using hirschhornsalz and potash instead of baking powder, pour half of the dissolved hirschhornsalz and potash over the honey and egg mixture in one of the bowls (save the remaining half for when working with the second bowl at the end of this step). Begin pushing the dry ingredients into the wet ingredients with your hands. After most of the flour is incorporated, transfer onto a wooden or marble worksurface and continue kneading to form a smooth ball (see tip 1). The dough may stick to hands quite a bit. If that happens, keep adding flour, a little at a time, to hands and to the dough. Repeat adding the dissolved potash and hirschhornsalz to the second bowl and kneading the dough.

   ### ~ TIP 1 ~
   Because of the volume of ingredients, it will take several minutes of work before the dough forms into a ball. Be patient and keep at it.

4. Let the dough rest in the refrigerator for 45 minutes if baking powder is used. If hirschhornsalz and potash are used, let dough rest overnight in a cool room (60°F or less). If none is available, the dough can rest in the

refrigerator with the temperature raised to 42°F or higher (temperature range depends on the refrigerator).

5. Position a rack in the middle of the oven and preheat to 325°F (convection bake setting). Have ready two to three baking sheets, oiled and floured, or oiled and covered with parchment. Though only one filled sheet will bake at a time, it is helpful to lay cut-out dough onto the extra sheets. As soon as one sheet comes out of the oven, another is ready to go in.

6. To roll, cut, and bake the dough, you will need to work in batches. Move through the following process until all the dough has been used up.

Roll the dough: Roll the dough out to ¼-inch thickness before cutting it into shapes. It is best not to go thicker for the house. Depending on the size of the workspace, take as little as one quarter or as much as one half of the dough from the refrigerator. Refrigerate the dough not currently being rolled. Don't be afraid to be as generous with the flour as needed to prevent dough from sticking to the work surface and rolling pin.

Cut the dough: As batches of dough are rolled out, lay the cutouts on top of the dough and use them as guides to cut pieces of the house, roof, and fence. Pay close attention to the dimensions and instructions on the cutouts. Instructions on the cutouts indicate when a particular piece (such as a wall) must be used twice. Use cookie cutters to cut desired shapes, figures, decorations, trees, or features for the house (see *note 3* at end of day one's directions). Cut out shutters, if desired, to match the height of the window. Shingles can be cut to lay along the roof's ridge to cover gaps where the plates come together. For the shutters and shingles, press a whole blanched almond in the middle of the piece, as decoration, before baking.

Bake: Bake the pieces when they fill a cookie sheet while continuing to work on the other cutouts (see tip 2). Each batch should bake for about 12 to 15 minutes. Smaller pieces such as the fence and shingles may not need as long. Transfer the large pieces with a large cake spatula or *kuchenretter* (German cake lifter); if parchment paper is used, pull entire baked pieces with parchment onto the cooling rack. Lay house pieces flat on a straight cooling rack to cool. Brush more oil and dust more flour onto the baking sheet as needed between batches, or oil and cover with new parchment as needed.

~ TIP 2 ~

When laying the dough onto the cookie sheet, it may get distorted or stretched. Try to push the dough back into the correct shape. This attention is especially important for the pieces that make up the house. Assembly will be easier if the house pieces are the proper size. Similarly, the pieces may distort when cooling if they do not lie flat. If possible, transfer pieces only onto a straight (not bowed) cooling rack or leave the baked pieces on the cookie sheet and place it onto the cooling rack. Then transfer pieces when they are cool and hardened.

GINGERBREAD HOUSE

Preparations for Assembly

7. Prepare royal icing: Whip egg whites to stiff peaks. Add the powdered sugar and lemon juice and mix again. This icing will be used in the next step to spread over the covered board; to make spreading easy, this icing should be thinner than the icing that will be used in days two and three for gluing and decorating. If the icing is too thick to spread easily, add water or more lemon juice, in very small amounts, just a few drops at a time. It does not take much liquid to thin the icing. If the icing is too thin, add more powdered sugar, a little at a time (see tip 3).

8. Cover the board: Use aluminum foil to wrap the board that will serve as the house's base. Spread the royal icing over the foil so that the landscape looks snowy. Do not worry about drips or swirls. The icing does not need to be perfectly smooth. In fact, imperfections create the effect of snow drifts. Remember this note about the beauty of imperfections while working on other snowy parts of the house. Icing drips along the seams, corners, and roof only add to the wintry charm.

9. Allow the covered board to dry overnight. Also allow all gingerbread pieces to continue cooling and drying overnight.

~ TIP 3 ~

Be prepared and have extra eggs and powdered sugar on hand to make more icing, and adjust consistency of the icing throughout the various steps on various days. As a rule of thumb, the steeper the drying angle, the thicker the icing needs to be. It is best to make a batch of icing for the day you plan to use it. If there is leftover icing, store it in the refrigerator in an airtight container. Some whipping to fluff up the icing may be needed the next day. More powdered sugar may need to be added. You can also mix leftover icing in with freshly made icing.

COOKIES

Note 1: In traditional German baking, hirschhornsalz and potash are used in gingerbread-type dough and cookies around Christmastime. Baked with hirschhornsalz and potash, the gingerbread will last longer, and in old times, that was a good thing because ingredients were hard to come by. Churches distributed gingerbread in times of famine. When the gingerbread was longer lasting, the children and adults had a cookie now and then to add to their meals for several weeks after Christmas. If hirschhornsalz and potash are used, the dough will need to rest overnight in a cool place before baking. This will add an extra day to the work, so plan accordingly. Alternatively, baking powder can be substituted. With baking powder, the gingerbread will be softer, which is great for eating, but more care is needed when assembling the house. If baking powder is used, the dough will need to rest for 45 minutes only, not overnight.

Note 2: If there is leftover dough, make cookies to eat. Dough for cookies should be rolled out thicker and baked for less time than dough used for the house and its decorations; the thicker dough and shorter bake time make the cookies soft for eating, whereas gingerbread for the house is rolled thinner and bakes longer to be dry for a sturdy house. For cookies to eat, roll the dough to ⅜-inch thickness and cut into shapes such as circles or hearts to decorate. Bake cookies on a rack in the middle of the oven at 325°F (convection bake setting) for 10 to 12 minutes.

For circles, 3- or 4-inch round cookie cutters work well. Once baked and cooled, fancy up the cookies by dipping the bottoms in an Easy Chocolate Glaze (see page 261), then top with a thin Sugar Glaze (see page 260).

Alternatively, make heart-shaped cookies to decorate. Decorated heart-shaped gingerbread cookies are a tradition at the Christmas Market in Frankfurt. To make these cookies at home, cut the rolled-out dough with a 4-inch or larger heart-shaped cookie cutter. Brush an egg white wash onto each cookie before baking to bring out a shine; make the wash by using a fork to beat an egg white with a teaspoon of water until it foams. Once baked, decorate the hearts with icing made of meringue powder (follow directions on the container) mixed with food coloring of choice. Place the icing into a pastry bag fitted with the writing tip. At the Frankfurt Christmas Market, the gingerbread hearts have popular sayings written on them in icing: *I love you*; *My darling*; *I give you my heart*; *My heart beats for you*. Pipe one of these sayings onto the middle of each cookie. Next, pipe a trim around the edge of the heart with the decorating tip of your choice. Give to your favorite person.

Note 3: To create three-dimensional trees that can stand on their own, use the half-tree shape provided on page 164 and cut out three half shapes for each tree. Alternatively, stamp out tree shapes with a large pine-tree-shaped cookie cutter. Cut these trees in half, vertically, before baking. Later when assembling the house, use royal icing to glue three halves together to create a three-dimensional tree.

If wanting to make a skirt for the gingerbread girl before baking, cut a trapezoid-shaped piece of dough, about 2 inches wide at the top, 3½ inches wide at the bottom, and 2¼ inches tall. Place the trapezoid onto the cutout gingerbread figure before baking; tuck the shape in at the waist and let the rest of the skirt drape over the legs so only the feet show.

GINGERBREAD HOUSE

Day 2: Assembly

(Morning) assemble the house frame and decorate pieces not attached to the frame; (Evening) glue on the roof.

SPECIAL TOOLS AND MATERIALS

Items to support frame during assembly, such as coffee mugs, tea boxes, skewers, and toothpicks

INGREDIENTS FOR ROYAL ICING
(to assemble and decorate)

3 egg whites

5 cups powdered sugar

Food coloring, optional to dye icing as desired (liquid food coloring thins icing; adjust consistency as needed)

*Keep more icing ingredients on hand to make icing as needed during gluing and decorating.

Suggestions for edible decorations:
Nonpareils, candy corn, gummy bears, candy-coated chocolate, hard candies, licorice, gumdrops, small cookies, shredded coconut, sprinkles, dried fruit, nuts

Directions for Assembly

1. Prepare the icing "glue": Whip the egg whites to stiff peaks. Add the powdered sugar and mix again. The icing should be of a thick, paste-like consistency to glue the house together, about the consistency of toothpaste. Add more powdered sugar if needed to get the desired consistency. If the icing is too thick to smear and spread, add water or lemon juice in very small amounts, just a few drops at a time. It does not take much liquid to thin the icing.

2. Prepare to assemble the frame: Find a place on the countertop to push the prepared board against the wall so it does not slip during the work. Gather anything you can think of to use as support for the house while the icing glue sets. Options include coffee mugs, tea boxes, skewers, and toothpicks.

3. Assemble the frame: Start by placing tea boxes (or items of similar size) at the back of the board, where it is pushed against the wall. These will act as spacers for the house's back wall and provide support. Spacing is important to ensure that the house is offset on the board, which will leave plenty of room for decoration.

   Begin assembly with one gable wall (back wall), and then add the side walls. Use plenty of icing along the gable and side wall bases and along the corners where the pieces join. Continue to place items to support the side walls, as needed. At the corners where the gable and side walls meet, poke a skewer or toothpick diagonally through the pieces if necessary to keep the pieces together. You should see the skewer go through the corner on the inside. Add the front gable wall and glue and secure in the same manner. When the frame is complete, place more items, like tea mugs, for support all around, even on the inside, to help keep the house straight and to hold the pieces together as they dry.

COOKIES

Let the frame dry for the rest of the morning and the afternoon, about 8 hours, or overnight. In the meantime, complete step 4.

4. Decorate the roof in advance, allowing it to dry before placing on the house (see tip). For decoration, either cover with icing and a sprinkling of coconut flakes, or pipe shingles or other patterns with a decorating bag. Let dry 8 hours, or overnight; if drying overnight, glue roof to the walls on day three and wait an extra day to decorate the house. If planning to glue nonpareils, cookies, candy, or shingles to the roof, wait until it is assembled and dried.

~ TIP ~

Another option is icing the roof after placing it on the house. This option is trickier, but it creates an attractive snowdrift effect. Having the correct consistency of icing is the key. If icing is too thick to spread over the roof, scoop the amount needed into a smaller bowl and add water or lemon juice, one or two drops at a time, to reach the desired consistency. If icing is too thin, add more powdered sugar. With this option, still allow the frame to set for 8 hours, or overnight, before adding the roof. Allow roof to set on frame for another 8 hours, or overnight, before icing.

5. While the frame sets and the roof dries, decorate other pieces such as the figures, trees, fence, and shutters. Adjust icing consistency as needed for spreading and gluing.

6. Prepare to add the roof after the house frame and roof have dried. Remove any items placed inside the house as support during drying. Check icing amount and consistency; the icing should be a thick consistency, like toothpaste, for gluing. Add more sugar if needed to get the desired consistency. If the icing is too thick to smear and spread, add water or lemon juice in very small amounts, just a few drops at a time. Make more icing if needed.

7. Add the roof: The pieces will form an A-frame. Use whatever you can find to help prop up roof and wall pieces as they dry. Small cups the size of shot glasses work well. If necessary, use skewers to help stabilize. Poke the skewers through the connecting corners at the roof's peak. Let dry overnight.

Weihnachtsmarkt, the Frankfurt Christmas Market. Photo credit: my nephew Christian Metzler.

GINGERBREAD HOUSE

Day 3: Decorate the House

> **SPECIAL TOOLS AND MATERIALS**
> Toothpicks

INGREDIENTS FOR ROYAL ICING

3 egg whites

5 cups powdered sugar

Food coloring, optional to dye icing as desired (liquid food coloring thins icing; adjust consistency as needed by adding more powdered sugar)

*Keep more icing ingredients on hand to make icing as needed during decorating.

Suggestions for edible decorations: Nonpareils, candy corn, gummy bears, candy-coated chocolate, hard candies, licorice, gumdrops, small cookies, shredded coconut, sprinkles, dried fruit, nuts

Suggestion for non-edible decoration: Loose cotton to create chimney smoke (the cotton from the top of a medicine bottle works well)

Directions for Decoration

1. Make icing in the same manner as on days one and two. Adjust consistency as needed for gluing decorations to the house, trees, figures, and any other pieces.

2. Before removing any items used to prop house and roof, as well as any skewers, check that icing is dry and the house is sturdy.

3. Decorate: Invite helpers (especially kids) to decorate with candy, gummy bears, nonpareils, sprinkles, dried fruit, nuts, or whatever else they like. Use toothpicks as needed to keep decorations from sliding. Also use toothpicks, if needed, to help secure the three parts of the chimney to the roof while the icing glue dries. Use icing to secure cotton to the chimney so that it looks like smoke.

The fence goes on toward the end of decorating. Lean one edge of the fence onto the side of the house for stability. Gumdrops placed behind the fence can also help to

COOKIES

prop it up. Place Hänsel and Gretel and trees in the front yard. Gumdrops and other sticky candy make good props for people and trees.

The front and back of the roof look nice with icicles. To create icicles, use very thick icing. The consistency should be as thick or a bit thicker than that of the icing glue. Place a small amount of icing into a bowl and add powdered sugar to achieve the necessary thickness. Scoop some icing onto a teaspoon, touch the roof's edges with the icing where you want the icicle to go, and then draw the spoon down and away. The icing will form a tip resembling an icicle.

Use any leftover icing to patch up bare spots and create a snowy effect around the house.

4. Enjoy the sight, scent, and taste (when nibbling) of this Christmas masterpiece.

Weihnachtsmarkt, Frankfurt Gingerbread Hearts. Photo credit: my nephew Christian Metzler.

SPONGE CAKE-BASED TORTES   3

Sponge cakes are light and airy, gaining their moisture and texture from whipped egg whites in the batter rather than from butter, oil, or dairy. They lend themselves to layering or rolling with cream fillings, jellies, and fruits. Several of these recipes feature cool fillings and fruit flavors reminiscent of summertime, especially the Strawberry Yogurt Cream Torte and the Quark Cream Torte with Mandarins. But they are delicious in any other season, too, and there are also cakes with deep, year-round flavors of coffee, espresso, and chocolate such as the Tiramisu, the Mocha Sponge Cake Roll, and the minty Chocolate Mousse Cake.

Sponge Cake Roll with Lemon Buttercream	180
Mocha Sponge Cake Roll	184
Chocolate Mousse Cake	190
Hazelnut Sponge Cake	198
Strawberry Yogurt Cream Torte	208
Quark Cream Torte with Mandarins	213
Tiramisu	218
Black Forest Torte	225
Chocolate Irish Cream Cake	233

CHAPTER 3

PREPARATION TIME

Sponge cakes bake quickly, in about ten to just over twenty minutes depending on the thickness of the cake, and they need about forty-five minutes of preparation time. Preparing the fillings and assembling the cakes take about thirty minutes to an hour. Chilling the cakes after they have been filled and assembled also will take time. Some of the recipes, such as the Mocha Sponge Cake Roll, need only one to two hours of chilling time, but other recipes, such as the Strawberry Yogurt Cream Torte, need at least eight hours of chilling time. These cakes can be left to chill overnight, which allows the flavors even more time to settle and absorb. Feel free to make them the day before serving.

GENERAL TIPS AND TRICKS

A Reminder about Flour and Nut Meal

For sponge cake-based torte recipes, use a scant measure on the flour since it is easy to end up with too much flour. To get the scant measure, dip out a cup of flour and then shake off some of the flour so the cup measures somewhere between three-fourths full and full to the rim. Before getting started with sponge cake-based torte recipes, please read "Four Crucial Variables in Baking" starting on page 7, with special attention to "How to Measure Flour" (see page 7) and "Guidelines to Adjust Flour Amounts" (see page 9).

With sponge cake batters, if the flour or nut meal brand is more moisture absorbent or if working in a dry climate, start with a little less flour or nut meal than called for in the recipe. Sprinkling more flour or nut meal is always an option, but neither can be removed once added. Sponge cake batter should have a consistency like thick pancake batter. When scooped with a spoon and dropped onto a plate, the batter should flatten and spread slightly rather than stand like a dollop. If the batter maintains a dollop shape, it is too thick, and the cake will bake dry. Take note of how the batter looks before it goes into the oven and how it bakes up. Doing so will help with adjusting the flour or nut meal the next time, if need be.

Working with Gelatin

Several sponge cake recipes use gelatin to give fillings and toppings more integrity. That integrity prevents fillings and toppings from becoming loose and runny. Use unflavored ground gelatin.

Recipes that use gelatin include instructions, but the following is an overview of the process: Before combining with other ingredients, gelatin must first be mixed with cold water. This mixture then sits for five minutes, at which point the gelatin appears thick and firm. Next, melt the firm gelatin in a saucepan over low heat while stirring constantly, until the mixture is a flowing liquid. Remove from heat and allow to cool slightly, but not so much that it begins to gel up; the gelatin must stay in a liquid state. Once slightly cool, drizzle into the filling or topping. The drizzle should be a thin, slow, steady stream. Continue to stir constantly while drizzling in the gelatin.

For whipped cream fillings and toppings, gelatin is one option, but some recipes use whipped cream stabilizer instead. Whipped cream stabilizer is a common ingredient used in German baking. The whipped cream stabilizer does not need to be prepared the way gelatin does. Instead, it is simply

SPONGE CAKE-BASED TORTES

sprinkled in with the cream before whipping; always read the packet instructions, as specific techniques may vary depending on the brand. When whipping cream with whipped cream stabilizer, stop as soon as firm peaks are achieved, as it is easier to over-whip the cream. For recipes that give options of either the gelatin or the stabilizer, use one or the other for the whipped cream, but do not use both.

Keeping Air in the Egg Whites

Maintaining the air bubbles in the whipped egg whites is essential for a light texture in the sponge cake. When folding in the egg whites, do not stir to combine with the other ingredients, but rather use a whisk and a careful fold, lift, and turn motion to incorporate all ingredients. Once the egg whites are incorporated and the batter is ready, proceed with care when pouring it into the baking pan so the batter settles evenly. When all the batter has been poured, gently tilt the pan to distribute any uneven batter and then smooth the top with a light touch. These details are small but important with sponge cakes. If the batter is poured roughly, it loses air in the egg whites, and if the top of the batter is not smoothed, the cake will bake with a mound in the middle, which is a problem, especially with round sponge cakes. The mound shape, unless cut off, makes it difficult to smooth fillings, toppings, and decorations onto round cakes.

Choosing a Baking Pan

The round cakes in this chapter should bake in a ten-inch springform pan or cheesecake pan with a removable rim. If using a springform pan, the rim can hold the cake and filling in place during assembly and chilling time. Alternatively, if a springform pan is not used, have a 10 x 2-inch or 10 x 3-inch mousse cake ring mold on hand. Cakes that use sponge cake only (without a Mürbeteig crust as the cake's base) can also be assembled in a 9 x 2-inch or 9 x 3-inch mousse cake ring. Even though cakes bake in a ten-inch pan, sponge cakes shrink during baking and cooling, so the nine-inch mousse cake ring makes for a tighter fit during assembly. For more information, refer to "How to Cut and Assemble Layered Sponge Cakes" later in this chapter. (There is one round cake that is an exception in size. It is the double-layer version of the Hazelnut Sponge Cake. That cake bakes in two nine-inch layer cake pans. An eight-inch mousse cake ring is recommended for that cake.)

When choosing a pan, be it a springform pan, cheesecake pan, or another type, keep in mind that steel-based pans bake faster than aluminum pans. If using a carbon-coated steel pan, check the cake's doneness five to ten minutes before the end of the recipe's suggested bake time. Dark pans also bake faster than light pans.

Preparing the Baking Pan

Preparing the baking pan carefully is another small detail that can make a big difference in the success of a sponge cake, especially round sponge cakes. The base of the baking pan should be buttered and then lined with parchment paper; the butter helps the parchment stick and lie flat. But neither the butter nor the parchment should extend too far up the sides of the pan. As the cake bakes, it will stick a little to the pan's sides, but that is a benefit rather than a problem. The sticking helps to prevent the cake from deflating as it cools. Recipes include tips

CHAPTER 3

about how much to butter the pan and how big to cut the parchment paper.

Watch the Bake Time Carefully

Watching the baking time carefully is essential to maintaining the moisture of sponge cakes. Even a few minutes can overbake and dry out the cake. Get to know your oven, and if your oven bakes quickly, check the cakes a few minutes ahead of the recommended bake times. If the recipe offers a range for the baking time, always check the cake at the low end of the range. Remember that the cake will continue to set from the residual heat after it is pulled from the oven. If there is any doubt about the oven heating correctly, an inexpensive thermometer that hangs freely on a rack in the oven will show the temperature. Heating elements break or go out completely at times; should that be a concern, call for service.

How to Cut and Assemble Layered Sponge Cakes

Many of the sponge cakes in this chapter are cut in half horizontally before filling and layering. To cut easily and evenly, use a sharp knife and slice into the side of the cake about half an inch deep. Keeping the knife horizontal, move the cake counterclockwise (clockwise for lefthanded bakers) with one hand while the other hand cuts around the circumference. Then slip a sewing thread into the cut around the cake. When the thread meets, cross the ends over each other and pull them apart. Move arms outward, carefully but steadily, until the cake is sliced through horizontally. This chapter's video showcase includes a demonstration of this cutting technique.

VIDEO SHOWCASE
Sponge Cakes
vimeo.com/showcase/10470179

To assemble the cake, use the rim of the springform pan, cleaned from baking and freshly oiled with a bland-tasting oil like canola oil. An oiled mousse cake ring can be substituted. Place the pan's rim or the mousse cake ring around the base layer of the cake; the cake will be on a serving plate at this stage. From there, stack the cake layers and fillings according to the recipe directions and then refrigerate the cake accordingly. The pan's rim or mousse cake ring will help the cake keep its shape as it chills and sets. As you assemble the cake, there will likely be some extra space between the height of the cake and the top of the rim or ring. This space can make spreading the filling a little awkward. Select a spoon or an offset cake spatula that works best for you, and it should be just fine.

A showcase of sponge cake-based torte videos for inspiration and helpful technique demonstrations is available at vimeo.com/showcase/10470179.

SPONGE CAKE-BASED TORTES

RECOMMENDED TOOLS

- Two small cereal-type bowls for separating eggs
- Wire whisk, or silicone egg white whisk
- Large mixing bowl, clean of grease, preferably copper, for beating egg whites
- Two clean spatulas
- Large bowl for combining dry ingredients
- Stand mixer, or handheld electric mixer and large bowl for incorporating dry and wet ingredients
- Springform pan with a removable rim, or mousse cake ring (10 x 2- or 3-inch; 9 x 2- or 3-inch; or 8 x 2- or 3-inch depending on recipe)
- Double boiler or bain-marie
- Offset cake spatula, small and large sizes

SPONGE CAKE ROLL WITH LEMON BUTTERCREAM

This sponge cake roll is very versatile in the filling options. This recipe includes an easy lemon buttercream recipe made with raw pasteurized egg yolks. To make a lemon buttercream prepared in a double boiler with fresh-cooked eggs, refer to page 252, "Lemon or Lilikoʻi Buttercream." The buttercream must chill for two to three hours. Plan to make it before starting work on the cake or prepare it a day ahead of time. As another option in place of the buttercream, spread on your favorite jelly, about six to eight ounces, to create a classic jelly roll. My preference for jelly is red currant or raspberry, thinned with good-quality liqueur. Mixing a few tablespoons of a favorite liqueur, for example, orange liqueur or *kirschwasser* (German cherry brandy), with the jelly gives it a smooth texture and intensifies the flavor. Fresh whipped cream with fresh berries, like blueberries, strawberries, or red currants, or with fresh or canned cherries, makes a simple, light, and equally delicious filling.

SPONGE CAKE-BASED TORTES

BAKING PAN
12 x 17-inch rimmed cookie sheet, buttered and lined with parchment paper

BAKING TEMPERATURE
375°F

BAKE TIME
8 to 10 minutes

RACK PLACEMENT
middle of oven

YIELD
one rolled cake (10 to 12 servings)

INGREDIENTS

FOR CAKE

4 eggs, at room temperature

¾ cup sugar

¾ cup unbleached all-purpose flour (protein 3 grams per ¼ cup; see page 7)

¼ teaspoon baking powder

⅛ cup potato starch

¼ teaspoon lemon juice

2 tablespoons warm water

1 teaspoon vanilla powder, or ½ teaspoon vanilla extract

1 tablespoon orange liqueur

¼ cup powdered sugar, fine granulated baker's sugar, or granulated baker's sugar (for dusting kitchen towel before rolling)

FOR EASY LEMON BUTTERCREAM MADE WITH RAW PASTEURIZED EGG YOLKS
Yield: about 1 ½ cups

12 tablespoons (1 ½ sticks) unsalted butter, at room temperature

1 ¼ cups powdered sugar

3 egg yolks from pasteurized eggs, at room temperature

2 tablespoons lemon juice

Zest of 1 small lemon (about 2 teaspoons)

SPONGE CAKE ROLL WITH LEMON BUTTERCREAM

DIRECTIONS

1. Lemon buttercream needs to chill for 2 to 3 hours. If using buttercream, make it first, following the directions at the end of this recipe. Alternatively, the buttercream can be made the day before. Set it out on the counter the next day for an hour to warm to a spreadable consistency before filling the cake; stir every so often to ensure even softening.

2. When ready to start the sponge cake, position a rack in the middle of the oven and preheat to 375°F. Butter a rimmed cookie sheet and line with parchment paper in preparation for baking. Set aside.

3. Separate the eggs: Place egg whites into a large mixing bowl, preferably copper, and yolks into a small bowl (until mixing in step 5). Whip the whites until stiff peaks form, then slowly add half of the sugar and continue beating for 30 seconds until smooth and shiny. Set aside.

4. Sift the flour, baking powder, and potato starch into a bowl. Whisk briefly to incorporate evenly.

5. Make the batter: In a large mixing bowl with an electric mixer, cream the egg yolks, lemon juice, and warm water on medium to high for about 1 minute. Add the remaining sugar and the vanilla slowly while continuing to mix for 1 more minute. Drizzle in the orange liqueur. Slide the egg whites over the yolk mixture; resift and distribute the flour mixture on top. With a whisk, fold carefully to incorporate all ingredients without losing air bubbles in the egg whites. Do not stir and do not overmix. Stop as soon as the flour and egg white streaks have disappeared into the batter. Pour the batter onto the prepared cookie sheet. Smooth the top with a light touch.

6. Bake for 8 to 10 minutes, until a wooden skewer inserted through the center comes out clean. While the cake is baking, prepare a thin, cotton dish towel by sprinkling powdered sugar or baker's sugar over it. This is best done by hand. Once the cake is done, turn it over onto the sugared dish towel. Rub an ice cube over the parchment paper. This will create steam and loosen the paper. Carefully lift the paper away and discard.

7. Roll the cake: While the cake is still warm, grip one of the longer edges of the towel and begin to roll the cake tightly, as if rolling up a yoga mat. Roll the towel in with the cake; this can help prevent parts of the roll from sticking and tearing. Transfer the rolled cake onto a wire rack to cool. Position with the seam on the bottom to keep the roll from opening.

8. Assemble the roll: When the cake is completely cooled, gently unroll the cake along with the towel. Spread the buttercream over the cake. Leave ½ inch of bare space around the edges so the filling doesn't squeeze out. Roll the cake again; use the towel to help pull and roll but do not roll the towel in with the cake this time. Rather, lift the towel slightly and pull at an even pace so the cake rolls itself up. Transfer the cake onto a serving plate, seam down. Refrigerate to harden the buttercream, about

SPONGE CAKE-BASED TORTES

an hour. Cut ½ inch off each end for a clean-looking presentation. Dust with powdered sugar just before serving.

To Make Lemon Buttercream with Raw Pasteurized Egg Yolk

1. Cream the butter with an electric mixer for 10 minutes, until fluffy. Slowly sift in the powdered sugar. Whip the butter and sugar for 2 minutes on medium to high speed. Add the pasteurized egg yolks, lemon juice, and lemon zest and continue mixing, on slow to medium speed, until all ingredients are fully incorporated and the buttercream is uniform in color and fluffy in texture.

2. Refrigerate the buttercream for 2 to 3 hours before using as a filling. The buttercream should be set and firm but still spreadable. If the buttercream has chilled too long and firmed up too much, set it on the counter to warm until it reaches a spreadable consistency.

MOCHA SPONGE CAKE ROLL

The sponge recipe and technique for this cake roll resemble those of the Sponge Cake Roll with Lemon Buttercream, but this recipe adds the bold flavors of espresso, almond, and cocoa. To complement those flavors, the recipe suggests a filling of cherries and fresh whipped cream. There are two options for the cherries. One simply distributes sweet Bing cherries over whipped cream. The other creates a cooked sour cherry filling to spread over whipped cream. If preparing the cooked sour cherry option, use *kirschwasser* only in the cherries or in the whipped cream but not in both; decide which to suit individual taste. With either the Bing cherries or the cooked sour cherries, this cake is the perfect chocolate after-dinner dessert if time is a factor. Faster than many desserts and fancy looking, it will surely impress any guests. This sponge cake is very thin. Do not overbake this cake, or it will be dry. As you grow comfortable with this sponge cake roll, you may wish to experiment with the fillings. In *note 1* at the end of this recipe, there is a variation for a superb pistachio and whipped cream filling.

SPONGE CAKE-BASED TORTES

BAKING PAN
12 x 17-inch rimmed cookie sheet, buttered and lined with parchment paper

BAKING TEMPERATURE
375°F

BAKE TIME
8 to 10 minutes

RACK PLACEMENT
middle of oven

YIELD
one rolled cake (10 to 12 servings)

INGREDIENTS

FOR CAKE

4 eggs, at room temperature

¾ cup sugar

¾ cup unbleached all-purpose flour (protein 3 grams per ¼ cup; see page 7), sifted

3 tablespoons mocha frappé mix powder (for example, Ghirardelli makes a tasty mix with coffee added)

2 ½ tablespoons good-quality unsweetened Dutched cocoa (for example, Droste brand), sifted

¼ teaspoon espresso powder (see *note 2* at end of recipe)

¼ teaspoon baking powder

⅛ cup potato starch

½ teaspoon cinnamon

2 ounces baking chocolate or chocolate bar, 70% cocoa

¼ teaspoon lemon juice

2 tablespoons warm water

½ teaspoon vanilla extract

1 tablespoon almond extract

2 tablespoons coffee liqueur

¼ cup powdered sugar, fine granulated baker's sugar, or granulated baker's sugar (for dusting kitchen towel before rolling)

FOR BING CHERRY AND WHIPPED CREAM FILLING

7 to 8 ounces canned pitted Bing cherries (for example, Oregon brand)

1 ½ cups heavy whipping cream

4 grams (half an 8-gram envelope) whipped cream stabilizer

1 tablespoon kirschwasser, optional

2 tablespoons powdered sugar

Ingredients continued on next page

MOCHA SPONGE CAKE ROLL

FOR COOKED SOUR CHERRY AND WHIPPED CREAM FILLING
Yield: about 2 cups of filling

1 cup cherry juice, unsweetened organic

2 tablespoons cornstarch (for an opaque glaze), or 2 ½ tablespoons potato starch (for a translucent glaze)

3 teaspoons lemon juice

1 ½ tablespoons kirschwasser

⅓ cup sugar

10 ounces (1 very full cup) canned pitted tart or sour cherries (for example, Oregon brand), packed in water and drained

1 ⅛ cups heavy whipping cream

4 grams (half an 8-gram envelope) whipped cream stabilizer

2 tablespoons powdered sugar

OPTIONS FOR GARNISHING

Easy Chocolate Glaze (see page 261)

⅓ cup powdered sugar for dusting

DIRECTIONS

1. Position a rack in the middle of the oven and preheat to 375°F. Butter a rimmed cookie sheet and line with parchment paper in preparation for baking. Set aside.

2. Separate the eggs: Place egg whites into a large mixing bowl, preferably copper, and yolks into a small bowl (until mixing in step 4). Whip the whites until stiff peaks form, then slowly add half of the sugar and continue beating for 1 minute. Set aside.

3. Sift the flour, mocha frappé mix, cocoa, and espresso powder into a bowl. Add the baking powder, potato starch, and cinnamon and whisk briefly to incorporate evenly. Use a fine grater or pulse the blade in a coffee mill to grind the chocolate into coarse powder; some fine chunks are okay.

4. Make the batter: In a large mixing bowl with an electric mixer, cream the egg yolks, lemon juice, and warm water on medium to high for about 1 minute. Add the remaining sugar slowly while continuing to mix for 1 more minute. Add the vanilla extract and mix briefly, then add the almond extract and coffee liqueur. Mix again for 2 seconds only. Slide the stiff egg whites over the yolk mixture; resift and distribute the flour mixture over the egg whites, then distribute the ground chocolate on top. With a whisk, fold carefully to incorporate all ingredients without losing air bubbles in the egg whites. Do not stir and do not overmix. Stop as soon as the flour and egg white streaks

SPONGE CAKE-BASED TORTES

have disappeared into the batter. Pour the batter onto the prepared cookie sheet. Smooth the top with a light touch.

5. Bake for 8 to 10 minutes, until a wooden skewer inserted through the center comes out clean. While the cake is baking, prepare a thin, cotton dish towel by sprinkling powdered sugar or baker's sugar over it. This is best done by hand. Once the cake is done, turn it over onto the sugared dish towel. Rub an ice cube over the parchment paper. This will create steam and loosen the paper. Carefully lift the paper away and discard.

6. Roll the cake: While the cake is still warm, grip one of the longer edges of the towel and begin to roll the cake tightly, as if rolling up a yoga mat. Roll the towel in with the cake; this can help prevent parts of the roll from sticking and tearing. Transfer the rolled cake onto a wire rack to cool. Position with the seam on the bottom to keep the roll from opening.

7. Make the filling as the cake cools, then assemble. Filling preparation and cake assembly vary depending on whether the baker is making the Bing cherry filling or the cooked sour cherry filling.

For the Bing Cherry Filling and Assembly

1. Drain the cherries into a colander and set aside.

2. Sprinkle the whipped cream stabilizer in with the unwhipped heavy cream, then whip to almost stiff (or follow directions on the package). Mixing on low speed, drizzle in the kirschwasser (if using). Sift in the powdered sugar and beat just enough to incorporate the sugar and achieve stiff peaks; do not overmix. (Overmixing is easier with added whipped cream stabilizer; the whipped cream becomes rough looking, losing smoothness.)

3. When the cake is completely cooled, gently unroll the cake along with the towel. Spread the whipped cream over the cake. Leave ¾ inch of bare space on one of the long edges and ½ inch of bare space on the other three edges so the filling doesn't squeeze out. Flatten the Bing cherries by splitting them open. Lay the cherries in tight rows over the whipped cream. Starting at the long edge with ½ inch of space, roll the cake again; use the towel to help pull and roll but do not roll the towel in with the cake this time. Rather, lift the towel slightly and pull at an even pace so the cake rolls itself up. Transfer the cake onto a serving plate, seam down. Refrigerate to set the filling, about an hour. Cut ½ inch off each end for a clean-looking presentation. Dust with powdered sugar or pour on Easy Chocolate Glaze just before serving.

For the Cooked Sour Cherry Filling and Assembly

1. In a small bowl, whisk ¼ cup of the cherry juice with the cornstarch or potato starch until dissolved. Pour the remaining cherry juice, the lemon juice, and the kirschwasser (if using in the cooked sour cherries instead of in the whipped cream) into a medium-sized saucepan over medium-high heat. Add the cornstarch or

MOCHA SPONGE CAKE ROLL

potato starch mixture and the sugar. Whisking constantly, bring to a boil. Once the mixture boils, turn down the heat and continue to whisk vigorously, first with a whisk then with a wooden spoon, until it thickens to the consistency of jelly (see tip 1). Add the cherries and stir to coat; the cherries will release some liquid and thin the filling to a spreadable consistency. If the mixture is still too thick, add 1 to 2 tablespoons of juice and let cook briefly once more. Transfer to a bowl and refrigerate to cool (see tip 2).

~ TIP 1 ~

The juice mixture can bubble over or stick to the saucepan's bottom very quickly, so do not leave unattended at any time. Once the mixture boils, stir rapidly, making sure to scrape the bottom of the saucepan to avoid sticking and burning. A flat wooden spoon works best for this task. The mixture is nearly ready when it starts to bubble, which means that it has begun to gel up. At this point, turn off the heat or reduce it to low. Stir and scrape a few more times to prevent burning, and the mixture is ready. If the mixture boils too rapidly too early, remove from heat for a moment to prevent a spillover, then turn down heat before replacing the saucepan.

~ TIP 2 ~

To cool more quickly, spread the filling on a plate; a large, flat container; or even a frying pan and place in the freezer, stirring occasionally, while proceeding with making the whipped cream.

2. Sprinkle the whipped cream stabilizer in with the unwhipped heavy cream, then whip to almost stiff. Mixing on low speed, drizzle in the kirschwasser (if using in whipped cream instead of in the cooked sour cherries). Sift in the powdered sugar and beat just enough to incorporate the sugar and achieve stiff peaks; do not overmix. (Overmixing is easier with added whipped cream stabilizer; the whipped cream becomes rough looking, losing smoothness.)

3. When the cake is completely cooled, gently unroll the cake along with the towel. Spread the cherry filling over the cake. Leave ¾ inch of bare space on one of the long edges and ½ inch of bare space on the other three edges so the filling doesn't squeeze out. Spread the whipped cream on top of the cherry filling. Starting at the long edge with ½ inch of space, roll the cake again; use the towel to help pull and roll but do not roll the towel in with the cake this time. Rather, lift the towel slightly and pull at an even pace so the cake rolls itself up. Transfer the cake onto a serving plate, seam down. Refrigerate to set the filling, about 1 to 2 hours. Dust with powdered sugar or pour on Easy Chocolate Glaze just before serving.

SPONGE CAKE-BASED TORTES

Note 1: Experiment with other fillings of your imagination. This pistachio and whipped cream filling is just one of many delicious alternatives to the two cherry filling options.

Note 2: Use the amount of espresso powder to preferred taste. Many different brands are available, and they range in strength of espresso taste from mild to strong. Use ¼ to ½ teaspoon for brands with a strong espresso taste and up to 1½ teaspoons for mild-tasting brands.

INGREDIENTS FOR PISTACHIO AND WHIPPED CREAM FILLING

1 ⅛ cups heavy whipping cream

4 grams (half an 8-gram envelope) whipped cream stabilizer

2 tablespoons coffee liqueur

¼ cup powdered sugar

3 ounces chocolate, 70% cocoa

7.05 ounces (200 grams) Italian cream of pistachio (available online)

Prepare the heavy cream with the whipped cream stabilizer, coffee liqueur, and powdered sugar as in step 2 of either cherry filling option. Melt the chocolate in a microwave or double boiler (see page 15 for technique). Let cool slightly but not so much that it begins to harden. With a wire whisk, fold ½ cup of the whipped cream into the melted chocolate; this will cool the melted chocolate more. Add to the rest of the whipped cream by folding in carefully to preserve the air bubbles. Unroll the sponge cake. Spread the Italian cream of pistachio over the unrolled cake, then spread the chocolate whipped cream on top and roll up as per directions in step 3 of either cherry filling option. Refrigerate to set the filling, about 1 to 2 hours.

CHOCOLATE MOUSSE CAKE

Mousse has a reputation for being a difficult dessert for home bakers, but really all it takes is some patience in whipping the egg whites and cream, melting the chocolate, and folding the ingredients together. This recipe gives a choice for a Mürbeteig crust (shortcrust) or a hazelnut sponge cake crust to use as the base for the mousse. Pick one. You do not need to make both. The Mürbeteig is a crispier option; the sponge cake is softer and lighter.

The mousse uses sixty to sixty-five percent rich dark chocolate and seventy percent dark chocolate with mint as a refreshing flavor complement to the cool temperature and smooth texture. Raspberries are also layered into the mousse. To enhance the raspberry flavor, there are options for a raspberry jelly to spread over the crust during assembly and a raspberry syrup to pour on when serving. In *note 1* at the end of the recipe, there is a variation

SPONGE CAKE-BASED TORTES

to lay all the raspberries on top of the cake rather than layering within the mousse and then to finish with a simple glaze. Toy with the options to make the cake as simple or as elegant as you like. Even the simplest version, for example, Mürbeteig with just chocolate mousse on top, is divine. Once the cake is assembled, it should chill in the refrigerator for at least six hours and up to overnight.

BAKING PAN
10-inch springform pan; buttered and floured for Mürbeteig crust, or buttered and lined with parchment paper for sponge cake crust

BAKING TEMPERATURE FOR BOTH MÜRBETEIG AND SPONGE CAKE CRUSTS
325°F

BAKE TIME FOR MÜRBETEIG CRUST
20 to 22 minutes

BAKE TIME FOR SPONGE CAKE CRUST
20 minutes

RACK PLACEMENT FOR MÜRBETEIG CRUST
middle of oven

RACK PLACEMENT FOR SPONGE CAKE CRUST
top third of oven, one rung above middle

YIELD
one 10-inch cake

SPECIAL TOOLS
(for assembly)

10-inch rim from springform baking pan, or a 10-inch mousse cake ring

Offset cake spatula

CHOCOLATE MOUSSE CAKE

INGREDIENTS

FOR 10-INCH MÜRBETEIG CRUST

1 1/8 cups unbleached all-purpose flour (protein 3 grams per 1/4 cup; see page 7)

1/2 cup unblanched almond meal or hazelnut meal (can substitute finely milled blanched almond flour, but reduce to 1/3 cup)

2/3 cup powdered sugar

1/8 teaspoon salt

1 egg

7 tablespoons unsalted butter, cold

FOR HAZELNUT SPONGE CAKE CRUST

3 eggs, at room temperature

1/2 cup unbleached all-purpose flour (protein 3 grams per 1/4 cup; see page 7)

1/2 teaspoon baking powder

3 tablespoons warm water

1/2 cup sugar

Pulp of 1/2-inch piece of vanilla bean, or 1 teaspoon vanilla extract or almond extract

1/2 cup hazelnut meal

2 teaspoons hazelnut coffee liqueur, optional (for drizzling over the baked crust)

FOR MOUSSE

3.5 ounces (100 grams) dark mint chocolate, 70% cocoa

10.5 ounces (300 grams) dark chocolate, 60% or 65% cocoa

4 egg whites, or 1/2 cup pasteurized liquid egg whites plus 1 teaspoon cream of tartar (see *note 2* at end of recipe)

1 cup powdered sugar

2 1/2 cups heavy whipping cream

1 (7-gram) envelope ground gelatin, optional for use in whipping up the heavy cream

3 tablespoons cold water, if using optional gelatin

FOR RASPBERRIES

2 cups fresh or frozen raspberries, reserve 8 to 16 whole raspberries to place around edge of cake to indicate slices

FOR OPTIONAL RASPBERRY JELLY SPREAD (for use with Mürbeteig crust only)

1/4 cup raspberry jelly

1 teaspoon orange liqueur, raspberry schnapps, or kirschwasser

FOR OPTIONAL WHIPPED CREAM GARNISH

1/2 cup heavy whipping cream

2 tablespoons powdered sugar

FOR OPTIONAL RASPBERRY SYRUP (to drizzle over cake or onto slices when serving)

1 cup fresh or frozen raspberries

1/3 cup sugar

1 teaspoon lemon juice

SPONGE CAKE-BASED TORTES

DIRECTIONS

1. Position a rack in the middle of the oven for the Mürbeteig crust or in the top third of the oven (one rung above middle) for the sponge cake crust. Preheat to 325°F.

2. Make either the Mürbeteig crust or the hazelnut sponge cake crust.

For Mürbeteig Crust

Butter and flour the pan in preparation for baking. Set aside.

Set aside ¼ cup of the measured flour to use as needed while working the dough and pressing it into the form. Sift the remaining flour, nut meal, and powdered sugar onto a large marble or wooden board. Form a well in the middle and sprinkle the salt around the edge. Add the egg into the well. Cut the butter into small pieces, approximately ¼ to ½ inch (refer to page 21, "How to Cut Butter," in the Mürbeteige introduction). Distribute the pieces over and around the flour and nut meal. Using the tip of a metal dough scraper, stir the egg as if gently scrambling. Begin carefully pushing the dry ingredients into the well's center. Work to combine all ingredients, first with the dough scraper and then with your hands, until a ball of dough forms. Add flour sparingly or chill as necessary if the dough becomes too sticky (see tip 1). When finished, refrigerate the smooth ball of dough for 30 minutes.

~ TIP 1 ~

This dough has a high butter ratio. Small pieces of butter may be visible still before the dough is chilled. After chilling and when working the dough into the pan, the butter pieces will integrate. Some butter flecks may still show here and there; they will melt into the dough as it bakes. This dough makes a soft, delicate Mürbeteig (shortcrust).

After refrigerating, slice the dough horizontally into four discs. Lay the discs into the prepared pan. With flour-dipped fingers, mold the dough to cover the pan's bottom evenly by pushing it out rather than pressing it down. The crust should be flat and does not need to be pulled up the pan's sides to create a rim. Even out any thin spots to get the dough to a fairly consistent thickness.

Bake for 20 to 22 minutes, until firm. Place pan on a wire rack and remove the rim. Allow crust to cool completely, then remove from the pan's base with a *kuchenretter* (cake lifter) and place onto a serving dish. You can assemble the cake (step 5) on this same dish. If the crust baked in a springform pan, clean the pan's rim and set aside; you will need it to assemble the cake later (or a 10-inch mousse cake ring will work too).

For Hazelnut Sponge Cake Crust

Butter the pan and line with parchment paper in preparation for baking (see tip 2). Set aside.

CHOCOLATE MOUSSE CAKE

~ TIP 2 ~

Cut the parchment paper a little bigger than the circumference of the pan, by about ½ inch. The paper will fold and pleat nicely and still lie flat against the pan. Butter the base of the pan before laying the parchment paper to help it stick, but do not butter the sides. The cake will stick a little onto the sides. This sticking prevents the cake from deflating as it cools. If necessary, carefully run a wooden skewer around the edge to pry the cake loose when removing from pan.

Separate the eggs. Place egg whites into a large mixing bowl, preferably copper, and yolks into a small bowl (until time to mix with the warm water). Whip the whites until stiff peaks form. Set aside.

Sift the flour and baking powder into a bowl. Whisk briefly to incorporate evenly.

In a large mixing bowl with an electric mixer, cream the egg yolks and the warm water on medium to high for about 2½ minutes. Add the sugar and vanilla slowly while continuing to mix for 2 more minutes. Slide the stiff egg whites over the yolk mixture and distribute the flour mixture on top. Sprinkle the hazelnut meal over the flour mixture. With a whisk, fold carefully to incorporate all ingredients without losing air bubbles in the egg whites. Do not stir and do not overmix. Stop as soon as the flour and egg white streaks have disappeared into the batter. Pour the batter into the parchment-lined pan, tilting the pan so the batter settles more evenly. Smooth the top with an offset cake spatula and a light touch.

Bake for 20 minutes. Insert a wooden skewer into the cake's center to check for doneness. The skewer should come out with a few moist kernels stuck to it but no wet batter. Do not overbake the cake, or it will be dry. Cool the cake in the pan on a wire rack for 15 to 20 minutes. Remove the pan's rim and use a *kuchenretter* (cake lifter) to lift the parchment with the cake from the pan's base onto the cooling rack. When cool enough to handle, turn the cake upside down onto a serving dish. You can assemble the cake (step 5) on this same dish. Gently peel the parchment off the cake. Allow cake to cool completely. If the cake baked in a springform pan, clean the pan's rim and set aside; you will need it to assemble the cake later (or a 10-inch mousse cake ring will work too).

3. Make the components for the mousse.

Prepare the gelatin: If using gelatin in the whipped cream, mix the gelatin with the cold water in a small bowl or cup. Whisk until smooth and the lumps are gone (press lumps with the back of a spoon), then let sit for 5 minutes to firm up. Meanwhile, proceed with melting the chocolate and whipping the egg whites.

Melt the chocolate: Melt the dark mint chocolate and the dark chocolate in a double boiler. Remove from heat but keep chocolate in the double boiler so that it does not cool too quickly.

SPONGE CAKE-BASED TORTES

Whip the egg whites: If using raw egg whites, whip, preferably in a copper bowl, to almost stiff peaks. Sift half of the powdered sugar on top, then finish whipping to stiff peaks.

If using pasteurized liquid egg whites, add the cream of tartar and whip to almost stiff. Because the egg whites are pasteurized, this will take 2 minutes on high speed. Just short of stiff peaks, stop the mixer and sift half of the powdered sugar over the egg whites, then whip 30 seconds more.

Whip the heavy cream: If using gelatin in the whipped cream, skip this paragraph and proceed to "Melt the gelatin." If omitting gelatin, whip up the heavy cream to soft peaks, then sift the remaining powdered sugar on top and whip to stiff peaks. Proceed to "Combine all ingredients."

Melt the gelatin: Melt the now-firm gelatin into liquid in a small saucepan over low heat. Do not overheat. Remove from burner and set aside to cool slightly, but not so much that it begins to gel up; the gelatin must stay in a liquid state.

To combine the gelatin with the heavy cream, first whip the cream to soft peaks, then sift the remaining powdered sugar on top and whip to almost stiff peaks. Stop the mixer before adding the gelatin. Make sure the gelatin is still warm and liquid but not hot. With the mixer on low speed, drizzle the liquid gelatin into the cream—the slower this process, the better. Finish whipping the cream to stiff peaks on medium speed.

Combine all ingredients: Pour the melted chocolate into a large bowl; the chocolate should have cooled slightly but should still be liquid. With a wire whisk, partially fold in and combine ½ cup of the whipped cream to lower the chocolate's temperature a little more. This will prevent the still-warm chocolate from melting the rest of the whipped cream and the egg whites. Next fold in ½ cup of the whipped egg whites. Check for chocolate clinging to the bottom of the bowl; scrape the bottom with a spatula and gently fold the chocolate on top. Returning to the wire whisk, fold in and combine the rest of the whipped cream. Slide the remaining egg whites on top; fold carefully into the chocolate cream until just blended.

4. Make the optional raspberry jelly spread for the Mürbeteig crust, if using: Mix the raspberry jelly with the orange liqueur, raspberry schnapps, or kirschwasser.

5. Assemble the cake: If the cake is not already on a serving dish, place there now; assembly on the serving dish is easier than having to transfer the assembled cake later. For a Mürbeteig crust, either smooth on the optional jelly spread or leave the Mürbeteig plain. For a sponge cake crust, drizzle the optional hazelnut coffee liqueur over the cake (see tip 3).

From this point, proceed the same way for both crust types. Lightly oil the springform rim or mousse cake ring with a bland-tasting oil like canola oil and wipe off excess. Place the rim or ring around the crust (see tip 4). Spread one-third of the mousse over the crust and

CHOCOLATE MOUSSE CAKE

distribute the whole raspberries on top, reserving eight to sixteen raspberries for decorating later. Add the remaining mousse and gently smooth over. Refrigerate for at least 6 hours and up to overnight.

~ TIP 3 ~

Pour some of the hazelnut coffee liqueur into a teaspoon. Hold the spoon in one hand and tap on the spoon with the other hand while moving in a circular motion over the cake. Repeat with the second teaspoonful. It doesn't matter if the drizzling is not quite uniformly done. There will still be some of the flavor in each slice. There are also special decorating spoons, called drizzle spoons, available for perfecting the drizzle. They look like a spoon with a funnel at the tip.

~ TIP 4 ~

Secure plastic wrap around the bottom edge of the rim or ring to prevent filling from running out. Do not worry if some runs out. It will firm up as the cake chills. Remove the plastic wrap and the rim or ring just before serving the cake.

6. Prepare garnishes and decorate.

If using whipped cream to garnish, whip up the heavy cream, stopping just before achieving soft peaks. Add the powdered sugar and continue whipping. The peaks will soften but then begin to stiffen again. Transfer the stiff whipped cream into a pastry bag fitted with a star tip. Decorate the mousse with dots of whipped cream topped with raspberries.

If making the raspberry syrup, cook the raspberries with the sugar and lemon juice on medium heat while constantly stirring until thickened to the consistency of maple syrup. Strain through a mesh sifter to free the syrup of seeds and lumps. Drizzle over the entire cake just before serving or onto individual slices when serving.

SPONGE CAKE-BASED TORTES

Note 1: A variation is to omit layering the raspberries inside the mousse and instead cover the whole top of the cake with raspberries. You will need 25 ounces of fresh or thawed frozen raspberries to cover the cake. Wait to distribute the raspberries until after the cake has firmed in the refrigerator. Leave the springform rim or mousse cake ring around the cake when placing the raspberries. A glaze over the raspberries makes for a showy finish and is sure to awaken complementary taste buds.

INGREDIENTS FOR GLAZE

1 ½ cups fruit juice of choice; raspberry, cherry, or cran-raspberry juice work well

2 ¼ tablespoons potato starch

⅓ cup sugar

In a small bowl, whisk ½ cup of the juice with the potato starch until the potato starch dissolves. Pour remaining 1 cup of the juice into a medium-sized saucepan over medium-high heat. Add the potato starch mixture and the sugar. Whisking constantly, bring to a boil. Turn down the heat and continue to whisk, more vigorously now, first with a wire whisk, then continue with a wooden spoon, until the glaze starts to bubble up, thickens, and becomes clear, about 5 minutes (see tip 5). Drizzle the glaze over the raspberries with the help of a large spoon.

Refrigerate for another 2 to 4 hours to let the raspberries and glaze set before removing the rim.

~ TIP 5 ~

The glaze can bubble over or stick to the saucepan's bottom very quickly, so do not leave unattended at any time. Once the mixture boils, stir rapidly, making sure to scrape the bottom of the saucepan to avoid sticking and burning. A flat wooden spoon works best for this task. The glaze is nearly ready when it starts to bubble, which means that it has begun to gel up. At this point, turn off the heat or reduce to low. Stir and scrape a few more times to prevent burning, and the glaze is ready. If the glaze boils too rapidly too early, remove from heat for a moment to prevent a spillover, then turn down heat before replacing the saucepan. If the glaze appears too thick, add a little more juice and raise the heat to bring the mixture back to a low simmer. Turn down the heat and continue stirring to reach desired consistency.

Note 2: Mousse is traditionally made with fresh raw egg whites, but bakers uncomfortable with raw egg whites can choose pasteurized liquid egg whites. They will take considerably longer to whip and may seem to deflate more easily. Adding cream of tartar will help. There are some brands of pasteurized egg whites that have been heat treated to a temperature where they will not whip up at all. Some cartons specify whether the whites will whip up, but some do not. I do not recommend the egg whites that specifically state on the carton that they do not whip.

HAZELNUT SPONGE CAKE
(with Hazelnut Cream Filling or Cherry Cream Topping)
Two Versions: Double Layer and Quick

This recipe includes two variations of the same sponge cake: a Double-Layer Hazelnut Cream Cake and a Quick Hazelnut Cake with Cherry Cream Topping.

The Double-Layer Hazelnut Cream Cake is a nine-inch cake with a filling of whipped cream and toasted hazelnut between the layers. The recipe includes instructions to roast and grind hazelnuts at home, which adds richness to the filling. Alternatively, roasted hazelnuts can be bought through online stores. Pre-ground hazelnut meal is also available online and at some grocers if you prefer not to grind the nuts yourself (see *note 1* at end of Double-Layer Hazelnut Cream Cake directions). There are three topping options for this version of the cake: covering the cake with almond paste, spreading on a layer of fruit curd, or dusting with vanilla-flavored powdered sugar. The almond paste

SPONGE CAKE-BASED TORTES

option adds an extra rich dimension. The fruit curd option brings natural color and an added surprise to taste buds, with a delightful burst of citrusy flavor to finish the cake. Fruit curds are easily found in stores and available in many flavors. Mango, passion fruit, and lemon curd are always favorites. The vanilla-flavored powdered sugar option is fast and easy.

The Quick Hazelnut Cake with Cherry Cream Topping is a simpler alternative. This version is a single-layer ten-inch cake. If pressed for time or to divide the work, bake the cake one day and prepare the cherry cream topping the next. Alternatively, omit the cherry cream topping and simply top the cake with fresh fruit such as strawberries, raspberries, blueberries, kiwis, mangos, peaches, or pears. Fruit curd spread over the top is easy and refreshing too. Eight to nine ounces of fruit curd will cover a ten-inch cake.

Whether making a single ten-inch cake or two nine-inch cakes to layer, bakers can play and create fillings and toppings of their own, maybe even with ingredients they have on hand. This sponge cake matches well with a wide variety of fresh fruits, glazes, creams, frostings, and ice creams. For another simple variation, omit the sponge cake altogether and spread the hazelnut cream filling over a Mürbeteig (shortcrust) base. This crunchy base supports rich filling well. Use the nine-inch crust recipe in the Mürbeteige chapter introduction (see page 23) but bake it as a nine-inch flat bottom crust (do not pull the dough up the pan's sides to create a rim). Let the baked crust cool to room temperature. To assemble, spread jelly over the cooled Mürbeteig to prevent sogginess and add flavor contrast, then place a mousse cake ring around the Mürbeteig and spread the hazelnut cream filling on top. Refrigerate for three to six hours, or until set.

For Double-Layer Hazelnut Cream Cake
(a filled 9-inch cake)

BAKING PAN
two 9-inch layer cake pans, buttered and lined with parchment paper

Baking time may be shortened if steel-based pans are used rather than aluminum; dark pans bake faster than light pans.

BAKING TEMPERATURE
325°F

BAKE TIME
18 to 20 minutes

RACK PLACEMENT
top third of oven, one rung above middle

YIELD
two 9-inch cakes

SPECIAL TOOLS (FOR ASSEMBLY)
8-inch mousse cake ring (for a tighter fit as cake shrinks during baking; some trimming of the cake may be required)

Offset cake spatula

HAZELNUT SPONGE CAKE

INGREDIENTS

FOR HAZELNUT SPONGE CAKE

4 eggs, at room temperature

¾ cup sugar

¾ cup unbleached all-purpose flour (protein 3 grams per ¼ cup; see page 7)

1 ½ tablespoons cornstarch

½ teaspoon baking powder

4 tablespoons warm water

Pulp of ½-inch piece of vanilla bean, or 1 teaspoon vanilla extract or almond extract

1 teaspoon lemon juice

¾ cup hazelnut meal

FOR HAZELNUT CREAM FILLING

¾ cup whole hazelnuts (about 4 ounces), roasted and ground (makes 1 ½ cups nut meal) (see *note 1* at end of recipe)

2 cups heavy whipping cream

1 (8-gram) envelope whipped cream stabilizer

2 teaspoons vanilla sugar, or 1 teaspoon vanilla paste or extract

1 tablespoon almond or hazelnut liqueur, optional

½ cup powdered sugar, sifted

2 teaspoons raspberry brandy or raspberry schnapps, optional (to drizzle over bottom cake layer)

OPTIONS FOR TOPPING (choose one)

Cover cake in almond paste using
   12 ounces almond paste,
   ¼ cup powdered sugar for rolling, and
   12 whole hazelnuts to decorate top.

Spread top of cake with fruit curd spread of choice (6 to 7 ounces).

Simply dust with vanilla-flavored powdered sugar.

A Hazelnut Cream Cake on Mürbeteig or shortcrust, a variation from sponge crust. This is how it looks before it is covered with almond paste.

SPONGE CAKE-BASED TORTES

DIRECTIONS

1. Position a rack in the top third of the oven (one rung above middle) and preheat to 325°F. Butter the pans and line with parchment paper in preparation for baking (see tip 1). Set aside.

~ TIP 1 ~

Cut the parchment paper a little bigger than the circumference of the pan, by about ½ inch. The paper will fold up nicely and still lie flat against the pan. Butter the base of the pan before lining with the parchment paper to help it stick, but do not butter the sides. The cake will stick a little onto the sides. This sticking will prevent the cake from deflating as it cools.

---

2. Separate the eggs: Place egg whites into a large mixing bowl, preferably copper, and yolks into a small bowl (until mixing in step 4). Whip the whites until almost stiff peaks form. Add half the sugar and continue mixing until shiny and soft peaks form; the peaks will soften with the sugar. Set aside.

3. Sift the flour, cornstarch, and baking powder into a bowl. Whisk briefly to incorporate evenly. Set aside.

4. Make the batter: In a large mixing bowl with an electric mixer, cream the egg yolks and the warm water on medium for about 2 minutes. Add the vanilla, lemon juice, and the remaining sugar slowly while continuing to mix for 2 more minutes. Slide the egg whites over the yolk mixture; resift and distribute the flour mixture on top. Sprinkle the hazelnut meal over the flour mixture. With a whisk, fold carefully to incorporate all ingredients without losing air bubbles in the egg whites. A large spoon may be helpful at this point, but only fold the filling over itself to mix. Do not stir and do not overmix. Stop as soon as the flour and egg white streaks have disappeared into the batter. Pour the batter into the parchment-lined pans. Smooth the tops with a light touch.

5. Bake for 18 to 20 minutes. Insert a wooden skewer into the cakes' centers to check for doneness. The skewer should come out with a few moist kernels stuck to it but no wet batter. Do not overbake the cakes, or they will be dry. Cool the cakes in the pans on a wire rack for about 15 to 20 minutes.

   If necessary, carefully run a wooden skewer around the perimeter of each pan to loosen the cake from the edge. Carefully slide the skewer or a small flat spatula under the parchment paper, just enough to lift and grab the parchment, then slide a *kuchenretter* (cake lifter) under and transfer the cake with the parchment to the cooling rack. Allow cakes to cool completely.

6. Make the hazelnut cream filling: Roast whole hazelnuts on an ungreased cookie sheet at 350°F. Place on an upper third rack, one rung above middle, and bake for about 10 to 15 minutes. Shake and turn halfway through the roasting process. Let cool, then grind into nut meal (see page 14 for technique).

   Whip the heavy cream: Sprinkle the whipped cream stabilizer in with the unwhipped heavy

HAZELNUT SPONGE CAKE

cream and whip to soft peaks (or follow directions on the package). Mixing on low speed, add the vanilla sugar, paste, or extract and drizzle in the almond or hazelnut liqueur (if using). Add the sifted powdered sugar and beat just enough to incorporate the sugar and achieve stiff peaks; do not overmix. (Overmixing is easier with added whipped cream stabilizer; the whipped cream will get a rough texture and lose its smoothness.) By hand with alternating use of a wire whisk and a large spatula, carefully fold the hazelnut meal into the whipped cream.

7. Assemble the cake: Have a serving plate and an 8-inch mousse cake ring on hand for assembly. Lightly oil the ring with a bland-tasting oil like canola oil and wipe off excess. Place one cake upside down onto the serving plate and carefully lift off the parchment paper. Place the mousse cake ring over the cake and gently fit the cake into the ring; if necessary, trim the cake to fit. If using the raspberry brandy or schnapps, drizzle over the cake now (see tip 2).

~ TIP 2 ~

To drizzle, measure the raspberry brandy or schnapps into a jigger or shot glass; cover the opening with your fingers but create a small gap between two fingers so the liquid can sprinkle out while moving and shaking your hand over the cake.

Reserve some of the hazelnut cream filling (about ⅓ cup) in the refrigerator to cover the sides of the cake later, after the cake has been refrigerated. Spread the rest of the filling over the cake and level with an offset icing spatula. Dip the spatula into a tall glass of hot water to remove excess whipped cream and wipe dry before smoothing the filling. For the top layer, loosen the parchment paper at the edges of the second cake and peel back around the sides only. Place the second cake upside down over the filling and finish carefully peeling off the parchment paper. Push down gently

SPONGE CAKE-BASED TORTES

on the top cake, with a flat hand, to level any unevenness in the filling.

Refrigerate for 3 to 6 hours, or until set. Remove the mousse cake ring and spread the reserved filling around the outside of the cake (see tip 3). Dust the cake with vanilla-flavored powdered sugar or cover the top with a fruit curd. As an alternative, covering the entire cake with almond paste and decorating with twelve whole hazelnuts makes for a nice presentation as well (see *note 2* at end of recipe).

~ TIP 3 ~

Remove the ring by turning it while pulling upward in a slow motion.

Note 1: If using store-bought hazelnut meal instead of grinding the hazelnuts yourself, use the following directions to roast the nut meal: Heat a skillet over medium to medium-high. Add the hazelnut meal into the skillet and flatten it down with a spatula. Stir and flip the hazelnut meal regularly, for about 5 minutes, so it toasts evenly. If smoke starts to develop, the skillet is too hot. If that happens, remove from heat for a brief time and continue stirring, then return to heat, with the temperature reduced as needed. Aim for golden brown, not dark brown. If the nut meal darkens too much, it will become bitter. Spread out nut meal on a plate to cool.

Note 2: To cover the entire cake, roll out 12 ounces of almond paste to a diameter of 14 inches. Have ¼ cup powdered sugar on hand during rolling; sprinkle onto the work surface and rolling pin sparingly, using only as much as needed to keep the almond paste from sticking. Transfer by rolling the paste over the rolling pin as much as possible without having it stick to itself. Slide a metal dough scraper beneath the paste to loosen any portions stuck on the work surface. Lift the paste-draped rolling pin over the cake and gently unroll so the paste lies flat and even on the cake's top and sides. Gently push in place and tuck around the cake. Cut away any excess around the base of the cake. Decorate the cake's top with twelve whole hazelnuts evenly spaced.

Another method to roll out and drape the almond paste is to use strong-ply plastic wrap. Do not sprinkle the work surface with powdered sugar for this method. Place the almond paste between two pieces of the plastic wrap, then use a rolling pin to roll it out to a 14-inch diameter. Peel off the top piece of plastic wrap. Lift the bottom piece of plastic wrap (with the rolled out almond paste on top), hold it over the cake, and flip it over to transfer the almond paste onto the cake. Peel off the plastic and proceed with pushing and tucking the almond paste into place, cutting away any excess, and decorating the top with twelve whole hazelnuts.

HAZELNUT SPONGE CAKE

For Quick Hazelnut Cake with Cherry Cream Topping

(a single-layer 10-inch cake)

BAKING PAN
10-inch aluminum springform or cheesecake pan, buttered and lined with parchment paper

Baking time may be shortened if a steel-based pan is used rather than aluminum; dark pans bake faster than light pans.

BAKING TEMPERATURE
325°F

BAKE TIME
18 to 20 minutes

RACK PLACEMENT
top third of oven, one rung above middle

YIELD
one 10-inch cake

SPECIAL TOOL
(for assembly)

10-inch rim from springform baking pan, or a 9-inch mousse cake ring (for a tighter fit as cake shrinks during baking; some trimming of the cake may be required)

INGREDIENTS

FOR HAZELNUT SPONGE CAKE

3 eggs, at room temperature

½ cup sugar

½ cup unbleached all-purpose flour (protein 3 grams per ¼ cup; see page 7)

1 tablespoon cornstarch

½ teaspoon baking powder

3 tablespoons warm water

Pulp of ½-inch piece of vanilla bean, or 1 teaspoon vanilla extract or almond extract

½ cup hazelnut meal

CHERRY CREAM TOPPING

¾ cup cherry juice

2 tablespoons potato starch, or 1 ½ tablespoons cornstarch

2 teaspoons raspberry brandy or raspberry schnapps, optional (use either in the cherry topping or drizzle over cake during assembly; pick one but not both)

3 teaspoons lemon juice

⅓ cup sugar

1 (14- to 15-ounce) can pitted Bing or sour cherries, packed in water (or 12 ounces fresh raspberries for a flavor variation)

8 ounces (1 cup plus a scant ¼ cup) heavy whipping cream

1 (8-gram) envelope whipped cream stabilizer

1 tablespoon powdered sugar, sifted

SPONGE CAKE-BASED TORTES

DIRECTIONS

1. Position a rack in the top third of the oven (one rung above middle) and preheat to 325°F. Butter the pan and line with parchment paper in preparation for baking (see tip 1). Set aside.

~ TIP 1 ~

Cut the parchment paper a little bigger than the circumference of the pan, by about ½ inch. The paper will fold up nicely and still lie flat against the pan. Butter the base of the pan before lining with the parchment paper to help it stick, but do not butter the sides. The cake will stick a little onto the sides. This sticking will prevent the cake from deflating as it cools. If necessary, carefully run a wooden skewer around the edge to pry the cake loose when removing from pan.

A variation of the 10-inch single-layer Quick Hazelnut Cake: The sponge cake is cut in half and filled with cherry spread and hazelnut cream (from the 9-inch double-layer Hazelnut Cream Cake). Mango curd and piped whipped cream decorate the top.

HAZELNUT SPONGE CAKE

2. Separate the eggs: Place egg whites into a large mixing bowl, preferably copper, and yolks into a small bowl (until mixing in step 4). Whip the whites until almost stiff peaks form. Add half the sugar and continue mixing until shiny and soft peaks form; the peaks will soften with the sugar. Set aside.

3. Sift the flour, cornstarch, and baking powder into a bowl. Whisk briefly to incorporate evenly.

4. Make the batter: In a large mixing bowl with an electric mixer, cream the egg yolks and the warm water on medium for about 2 minutes. Add the remaining sugar and the vanilla slowly while continuing to mix for 2 more minutes. Slide the egg whites over the yolk mixture; resift and distribute the flour mixture on top. Sprinkle the hazelnut meal over the flour mixture. With a whisk, fold carefully to incorporate all ingredients without losing air bubbles in the egg whites. A large spoon may also be helpful at this point, but only fold the filling over itself to mix. Do not stir and do not overmix. Stop as soon as the flour and egg white streaks have disappeared into the batter. Pour the batter into the parchment-lined pan. Smooth the top with a light touch.

5. Bake for 18 to 20 minutes. Insert a wooden skewer into the cake's center to check for doneness. The skewer should come out with a few moist kernels stuck to it but no wet batter. Do not overbake the cake, or it will be dry. Cool the cake in the pan on a wire rack for about 15 to 20 minutes.

Remove the pan's rim and use a *kuchenretter* (cake lifter) to lift the cake (with the parchment) from the pan's base. Alternatively, hold on to the parchment and slide the cake from the pan's base onto the cooling rack. Allow cake to cool completely. When completely cool, turn the cake upside down onto a serving dish. Gently peel the parchment paper off the cake. You can assemble the cake (step 7) on this same dish. If the cake baked in a springform pan, clean the pan's rim and set aside; you will need it to assemble the cake later (or use a 9-inch mousse cake ring for a tight fit).

6. Make the cherry cream topping: In a small bowl, whisk ½ cup of the cherry juice with the potato starch until dissolved. Pour the remaining ¼ cup of cherry juice, the raspberry brandy or schnapps (if using in the topping), and the lemon juice into a medium-sized saucepan over medium-high heat. Add the potato starch mixture and the sugar. Starting with a whisk and continuing with a large wooden spoon, whisk and stir constantly and bring to a boil. Once the mixture boils, turn down the heat and continue to whisk vigorously until it thickens to the consistency of jelly (see tip 2). Add the cherries and stir to coat; the cherries will release some liquid and thin the filling to a spreadable consistency. Transfer to a bowl and refrigerate to cool (see tip 3). Once cooled, the filling should be thick but spreadable. If in doubt, leave the filling thicker rather than thinning it out. If the mixture is still too thick after cooling, add 1 to 2 tablespoons of juice and let cook briefly once more.

SPONGE CAKE-BASED TORTES

If the mixture is too thin after cooling, add more potato starch, 1 tablespoon at a time, and cook briefly.

~ TIP 2 ~

The juice mixture can bubble over or stick to the saucepan's bottom very quickly, so do not leave unattended at any time. Once the mixture boils, stir rapidly, making sure to scrape the bottom of the saucepan to avoid sticking and burning. A flat wooden spoon works best for this task. The mixture is nearly ready when it starts to bubble, which means that it has begun to gel up. At this point, turn off the heat or reduce it to low. Stir and scrape a few more times to prevent burning, and the mixture is ready. If the mixture boils too rapidly too early, remove from heat for a moment to prevent a spillover, then turn down heat before replacing the saucepan.

~ TIP 3 ~

To cool more quickly, spread the filling on a plate; a large, flat container; or even a frying pan and place in the freezer, stirring occasionally, while proceeding with making the whipped cream.

Sprinkle the whipped cream stabilizer in with the unwhipped heavy cream, then whip to almost stiff (or follow directions on the package). Add the sifted powdered sugar and beat just enough to incorporate the sugar and achieve stiff peaks; do not overmix. (Overmixing is easier with added whipped cream stabilizer.)

Fold one-third of the whipped cream into the cool cherry mixture. Reserve the rest of the whipped cream for decorating.

7. Assemble the cake: Lightly oil the springform rim or mousse cake ring with a bland-tasting oil like canola oil and wipe off excess. A 9-inch mousse cake ring makes a tighter fit; if necessary, trim the cake to fit. Place the rim or ring around the cake. If using the raspberry brandy or schnapps over the cake, drizzle on now (see tip 4). Spread the cherry whipped cream topping over the cake. Transfer the reserved whipped cream into a pastry bag fitted with a star tip. Decorate the top by piping out whipped cream rosettes to cover the cake. Let the assembled cake chill in the refrigerator for 6 hours before serving. Remove the rim or ring before serving.

~ TIP 4 ~

To drizzle, measure the raspberry brandy or schnapps into a jigger or shot glass; cover the opening with your fingers but create a small gap between two fingers so the liquid can sprinkle out while moving and shaking your hand over the cake.

STRAWBERRY YOGURT CREAM TORTE

During strawberry season, when strawberries have their full aroma and flavor, I make this cake often for my friends, one of whom thinks it should be renamed Strawberry Pink Dream. It is an airy, creamy cake, ideal for making the day before a gathering when you will need a light dessert. This recipe gives two topping options. One option covers the cake with whipped cream and then places nine strawberries for decoration—one in the middle and eight around the edge to indicate slices. The other option covers the entire top of the cake with strawberries drizzled with fruit glaze. Select the option that suits your tastes or invent a creative topping of your own.

SPONGE CAKE-BASED TORTES

BAKING PAN
10-inch aluminum springform or cheesecake pan, buttered and lined with parchment paper

Baking time may be shortened if a steel-based pan is used rather than aluminum; dark pans bake faster than light pans.

BAKING TEMPERATURE
350°F

BAKE TIME
18 to 22 minutes

RACK PLACEMENT
middle of oven

YIELD
one 10-inch cake

SPECIAL TOOLS (for assembly)
10-inch rim from springform baking pan, or a 10-inch mousse cake ring

Offset cake spatula

INGREDIENTS

FOR SPONGE CAKE

4 eggs, at room temperature

¾ cup unbleached all-purpose flour (protein 3 grams per ¼ cup; see page 7)

⅛ teaspoon baking powder

1/16 teaspoon salt

4 tablespoons warm water

⅔ cup sugar

1 teaspoon vanilla extract

FOR STRAWBERRY COMPONENT OF THE FILLING

3 (16-ounce) packages fresh strawberries (48 ounces total), plus additional package (16 ounces) if covering the finished cake with strawberries and glaze (see *note* at end of recipe)

2 cups sugar

3 tablespoons lemon juice

1 teaspoon lemon zest (about ½ small- to medium-sized lemon)

4 (7-gram) envelopes ground gelatin (28 grams total)

½ cup water

FOR CREAM COMPONENT OF THE FILLING

1 ½ cups very thick Greek yogurt

1 cup crème fraîche or mascarpone

1 ½ cups heavy whipping cream

FOR OPTIONAL WHIPPED CREAM TOPPING (use if decorating cake with nine strawberries)

1 cup heavy whipping cream

1 tablespoon powdered sugar

FOR OPTIONAL FRUIT GLAZE (see directions on page 258; use if covering entire cake top with strawberries)

1 cup fruit juice of choice

1 ½ tablespoons potato starch

3 tablespoons sugar

STRAWBERRY YOGURT CREAM TORTE

DIRECTIONS

1. Position a rack in the middle of the oven and preheat to 350°F. Butter the pan and line with parchment paper in preparation for baking (see tip 1). Set aside.

~ TIP 1 ~

Cut the parchment paper a little bigger than the circumference of the pan, by about ½ inch. The paper will fold and pleat nicely and still lie flat against the pan. Butter the base of the pan before laying the parchment paper to help it stick; do not butter past the parchment paper. The cake will stick a little onto the sides. The sticking will prevent the cake from deflating as it cools. If necessary, carefully run a wooden skewer around the edge to pry the cake loose when removing from pan.

2. Separate the eggs: Place egg whites into a large mixing bowl, preferably copper, and yolks into a small bowl (until mixing in step 4). Whip the whites until stiff peaks form. Set aside.

3. Sift the flour, baking powder, and salt into a bowl. Whisk briefly to incorporate evenly.

4. Make the batter: In a large mixing bowl with an electric mixer, cream the egg yolks and the warm water on medium to high for about 2½ minutes. Add the sugar and vanilla slowly while continuing to mix for 1 more minute. Slide the stiff egg whites over the yolk mixture and distribute the flour mixture on top. By hand with a whisk, fold carefully to incorporate all ingredients without losing air bubbles in the egg whites. Do not stir and do not overmix. Stop as soon as the flour and egg white streaks have disappeared into the batter. Pour the batter into the parchment-lined pan, tilting the pan in a circular motion so the batter settles more evenly; finish by smoothing the top with a light touch.

5. Bake for 18 to 22 minutes. Insert a wooden skewer into the cake's center to check for doneness. The skewer should come out with a few moist kernels stuck to it but no wet batter. Do not overbake the cake, or it will be dry. Cool the cake in the pan on a wire rack for about 15 to 20 minutes. Remove the pan's rim and use a *kuchenretter* (cake lifter) to lift the parchment with the cake from the pan's base onto the cooling rack. When cool enough to handle, turn the cake upside down onto a serving dish. You can assemble the cake (step 11) on this same dish. Gently peel the parchment off the cake. Allow cake to cool completely. When the cake has cooled, cut in half horizontally (see page 178, "How to Cut and Assemble Layered Sponge Cakes"). With a kuchenretter (cake lifter), lift the top half of the cake and transfer to a cooling rack. The bottom half remains on the serving dish. If the cake baked in a springform pan, clean the pan's rim. Place the rim or a mousse cake ring around the bottom half of the cake.

6. Prepare strawberries to use later for assembly and decoration: Start by setting aside nine

SPONGE CAKE-BASED TORTES

beautiful-looking strawberries of about the same size from one of the packages. These nine will be for decoration in step 12. Keep them in the refrigerator and do not wash until just before placing on cake, or they will get mushy. Wash and hull the remaining strawberries from this package. Cut each strawberry into slices (three slices if berries are small, four if they are large). Set aside until it is time to assemble the cake in step 11; the slices will be layered onto the cake just before it is filled.

7. Prepare the remaining two packages of strawberries for the filling: Wash and hull the strawberries. Place into a large-capacity blender layered with the sugar, lemon juice, and lemon zest (work in batches if the blender is small). Blend on medium-high for about 30 seconds or until a thick purée-like liquid is achieved. Set blender with purée aside.

8. Prepare the gelatin for the strawberry component of the filling: In a small bowl or cup, pour the gelatin into the water, stirring rapidly. Whisk until smooth and the lumps are gone (press lumps with the back of a spoon); set aside and let firm up for at least 5 minutes. The gelatin will be combined with the strawberry purée in step 10.

9. Prepare the cream component of the filling: Combine the Greek yogurt and crème fraîche (or mascarpone) in a large bowl (3 quarts). Whisk together until smooth. Set aside.

In a large bowl or stand mixer, whip the heavy cream until stiff peaks are achieved. Set aside.

10. Combine all filling components: In a small saucepan, melt the now-firm gelatin into a flowing liquid over low heat while stirring constantly. Once melted, turn the blender containing the strawberry purée on low speed; the strawberry purée should be churning visibly. With the blender running, drizzle the gelatin in a continuous stream into the strawberry purée.

Pour half of the blended strawberry purée into the large bowl containing the yogurt and crème fraîche or mascarpone; combine, folding and stirring slowly with a wire whisk. Repeat with the second half of the purée. Once incorporated, slide the whipped cream on top. Carefully fold the whipped cream into the strawberry mixture, keeping the whipped cream airy and fluffy. If you must, use a gentle whisking motion to blend. Set aside.

STRAWBERRY YOGURT CREAM TORTE

11. Assemble the torte: Remove the springform rim or mousse cake ring from around the cake's bottom half and lightly oil with a bland-tasting oil like canola oil and wipe off excess. Place back onto the serving dish over the cake's bottom half (see tip 2). Distribute the sliced strawberries over the cake half and then pour the strawberry and cream filling on top. Place the other half of the cake, cut-side down, over the filling. Press down lightly with a flat hand to level the top. Refrigerate for at least 8 hours until set; best refrigerated overnight.

~ TIP 2 ~

Secure plastic wrap around the bottom edge of the rim or ring to prevent filling from running out. Do not worry if some runs out. It will firm up as the torte chills.

12. After the cake has set in the refrigerator, remove the rim or ring and proceed to decorate, using one of the following two options.

For decorating with whipped cream topping and nine strawberries: Wash and hull the nine strawberries reserved in step 6. Set them aside. In a large bowl or stand mixer, combine the heavy cream with the powdered sugar. Whip until stiff peaks are achieved. Spread a thin layer of whipped cream on top of the cake with an offset metal cake spatula (see tip 3). Fill a pastry bag fitted with a drop-flower tip or open-star tip with the remaining whipped cream. Pipe one dollop of whipped cream in the middle of the cake and space eight more dollops evenly around the edge, indicating slices. Nestle a strawberry into the center of each dollop. If there is whipped cream left over, pipe a rim around the bottom of the cake or pipe rosettes around the strawberries.

~ TIP 3 ~

Occasionally, dip the spatula into a tall glass of hot water to remove excess whipped cream. This helps to avoid streaking or clumping and produces a smoother spread.

For covering the entire top of the cake with strawberries and a fruit glaze: Wash and hull the nine strawberries reserved in step 6 plus the additional 16 ounces of strawberries (use as many as will fit on the cake). Arrange whole strawberries by setting them upright over the cake. Alternatively, cut strawberries in half and lay on cake, cut-side down, in concentric circles. Prepare fruit glaze (see page 258 for directions) and drizzle over strawberries.

Note: When buying strawberries, decide which decorating option you prefer: decorating with whipped cream topping and nine strawberries or covering the entire top of the cake with strawberries and a fruit glaze. Three (16-ounce) packages of strawberries will allow for nine accent strawberries for decoration. Four (16-ounce) packages are needed if covering the entire cake.

QUARK CREAM TORTE WITH MANDARINS

This torte should really be called Aunt Käthi's Velvet Cheese Torte. The filling has a smooth, luxurious, light texture and a taste as refreshing as a summer breeze. It is one of the many creations my Aunt Käthi dreamed up in the small kitchen of the apartment she lived in with my uncle and three cousins. I always enjoyed watching as my aunt worked butter, sugar, eggs, and flour into delicious cakes. Her stove looked like the old-timey wood-fired ovens of my grandmother's day. It was probably one of the first gas models after the wood stoves became outdated. Except for the modernization to gas, the manufacturer had not changed much in the design. In the summer, Aunt Käthi's kitchen got very hot. On those sultry days, she thought it best to bake a crust at night or early in the morning and then later make a cool filling, like the quark cream in this recipe. We would carry these treats a few blocks from the apartment, where the fields started. My aunt and uncle had a garden plot there with a garden shed and a shady trellis spilling showering flowers. There was a garden table and wooden chairs nestled underneath. It was the perfect place for afternoon tea or coffee and a fresh slice of torte.

In this torte, mandarins from a can or jar are preferred since it is hard to gauge sweetness of fresh fruit. Canned or jarred mandarins also save bakers from having to remove the membrane from fresh fruit slices.

QUARK CREAM TORTE WITH MANDARINS

BAKING PAN
10-inch springform or cheesecake pan, buttered and lined with parchment paper

Baking time may be shortened if a steel-based pan is used rather than aluminum; dark pans bake faster than light pans.

BAKING TEMPERATURE
350°F

BAKE TIME
20 to 22 minutes

RACK PLACEMENT
middle of oven

YIELD
one 10-inch cake

SPECIAL TOOL
(for assembly)
10-inch rim from springform baking pan, or a 10-inch mousse cake ring

INGREDIENTS

FOR SPONGE CAKE

4 eggs, at room temperature

¾ cup unbleached all-purpose flour (protein 3 grams per ¼ cup; see page 7)

⅛ teaspoon baking powder

1/16 teaspoon salt

4 tablespoons warm water

⅔ cup sugar

1 teaspoon vanilla extract

FOR FILLING

1 (15- or 16-ounce) can mandarin oranges (or from a jar)

2 (7-gram) envelopes ground gelatin (14 grams total)

6 tablespoons cold water

16 ounces quark (if quark is hard to find, substitute 1 ½ cups ricotta and ⅔ cup sour cream)

8 ounces crème fraîche

1 cup fine sugar (caster or baking sugar is best)

2 teaspoons vanilla extract, or 2 ½ teaspoons vanilla sugar, or pulp of ½ of a vanilla bean

3 tablespoons lemon juice

1 teaspoon lemon zest (about ½ a small- to medium-sized lemon)

2 tablespoons passion fruit juice (also called liliko'i juice), optional

¼ teaspoon lemon oil, optional

1 cup heavy whipping cream

Ingredients continued on next page

SPONGE CAKE-BASED TORTES

3 tablespoons pasteurized egg whites, optional (for a lighter, fluffier filling)

½ teaspoon cream of tartar (to whip with optional egg whites)

OPTIONS FOR GARNISHING

⅓ cup powdered sugar (for dusting)

Whipped cream and mandarin decoration

FOR OPTIONAL WHIPPED CREAM AND MANDARIN DECORATION

½ cup heavy whipping cream

1 tablespoon powdered sugar

9 mandarin slices (from a can or jar)

*This makes enough to cover the cake with whipped cream. For fancier decoration with piping, double the amount of heavy whipping cream and powdered sugar.

DIRECTIONS

1. Position a rack in the middle of the oven and preheat to 350°F. Butter the pan and line with parchment paper in preparation for baking (see tip 1). Set aside.

~ TIP 1 ~

Cut the parchment paper a little bigger than the circumference of the pan, by about ½ inch. The paper will fold up and pleat nicely and still lie flat against the pan. Butter the base of the pan before laying the parchment paper to help it stick, but do not butter the sides. The cake will stick a little onto the sides, but that is not a problem. The sticking will prevent the cake from deflating as it cools. If necessary, carefully run a wooden skewer around the edge to pry the cake loose when removing from pan.

2. Separate the eggs: Place egg whites into a large mixing bowl, preferably copper, and yolks into a small bowl (until mixing in step 4). Whip the whites until stiff peaks form. Set aside.

3. Sift the flour, baking powder, and salt into a bowl. Whisk briefly to incorporate evenly.

4. Make the batter: In a large mixing bowl with an electric mixer, cream the egg yolks and the warm water on medium to high for about 2½ minutes. Add the sugar and vanilla slowly while continuing to mix for 1 more minute. Slide the stiff egg whites over the yolk mixture; resift and distribute the flour mixture on top. With a whisk, fold carefully to incorporate all ingredients without losing air bubbles in the egg whites. Do not stir and do not overmix. Stop as soon as the flour and egg white streaks have disappeared into the batter. Pour the batter into the prepared pan, tilting the pan so the batter settles more evenly. With an offset cake spatula, smooth the top with a light touch.

5. Bake for 20 to 22 minutes. Insert a wooden skewer into the cake's center to check for doneness. The skewer should come out with a

QUARK CREAM TORTE WITH MANDARINS

few moist kernels stuck to it but no wet batter. Do not overbake the cake, or it will be dry. Let the cake cool in the pan on a wire rack. Then remove the pan's rim and turn the cake upside down onto a serving dish. You can assemble the cake (step 9) on this same dish. Gently peel the parchment off the cake. If the cake baked in a springform pan, clean the pan's rim and set aside; you will need it to assemble the cake later (or a 10-inch mousse cake ring will work too).

6. Drain the mandarin oranges into a colander and set aside.

7. Prepare the filling components: Mix the gelatin and the cold water in a small bowl or cup. Whisk until smooth and the lumps are gone (press lumps with the back of a spoon), then let sit for 5 minutes to firm up.

Meanwhile, use an electric mixer to combine the quark, crème fraîche, sugar, vanilla, lemon juice, lemon zest, passion fruit juice (if using), and lemon oil (if using). Blend until smooth. Set aside.

Whip the heavy cream to stiff peaks. Set aside.

If using the pasteurized egg whites, add the cream of tartar and whip to stiff peaks. Set aside.

After the gelatin has set for at least 5 minutes and firmed up, transfer into a small saucepan over low heat and, while stirring constantly, melt to a flowing, liquid consistency. Do not overheat; remove from heat as soon as gelatin liquifies.

8. Combine the filling components: Pour the warm and liquid gelatin into 1 cup of the quark mixture in a slow stream while mixing continuously, then incorporate into the remaining quark mixture. Fold in the whipped cream until just combined; do not stir. If using whipped pasteurized egg whites, slide them on top of the mixture and fold in carefully.

9. Assemble the torte: Lightly oil the springform rim or mousse cake ring with a bland-tasting oil like canola oil and wipe off excess. Cut the cake in half horizontally (see page 178, "How to Cut and Assemble Layered Sponge Cakes"). Place half the cake, cut-side up, into the rim or ring and pour one-third of the filling on top (see tip 2). Make a layer with the mandarin oranges and then pour on the rest of the filling. Place the other half of the cake, cut-side down, over the filling. Press down lightly with a flat hand to level the top. Refrigerate for 6 hours or overnight to set.

~ TIP 2 ~

Secure plastic wrap around the bottom edge of the rim or ring to prevent filling from running out. Do not worry if some runs out. It will firm up as the torte chills.

10. Garnish or decorate: Remove the rim or ring and dust the cake with powdered sugar before serving or decorate with whipped cream and mandarins.

To decorate with whipped cream and mandarins, whip up the heavy cream with the powdered sugar to stiff peaks. With a metal icing spatula, spread the whipped cream to cover the top of the cake (see tip 3). Place one

SPONGE CAKE-BASED TORTES

mandarin in the center of the cake and space eight others evenly around the edge of the cake, indicating slices.

~ TIP 3 ~

Occasionally, dip the spatula into a tall glass of hot water to remove excess whipped cream. This helps to avoid streaking or clumping and produces a smoother spread.

For fancier decoration, double the amount of whipped cream and powdered sugar in the recipe. After covering the top of the cake with whipped cream, fit a piping bag with a star tip and fill with the remaining whipped cream. Pipe eight simple stars, evenly spaced around the edge of the cake, and one in the middle of the cake. Place a mandarin slice into each star around the edge or place the slices between the stars; place one mandarin slice into the star in the middle.

TIRAMISU

Ah, Italy, amore! Warm sun, sidewalk cafés, beaches, street vendors, and colors everywhere. That is what comes to mind when eating this cherished dessert, filled with rich flavors of cream and espresso. I had my introduction to tiramisu when I was only four years old. We had stopped in Italy on the way back from our family vacation in the south of France. Every year, we savored four weeks of camping, swimming, and basking in sunshine by the Mediterranean Sea after a year of mostly cloudy German weather.

The small Italian town we stopped in was called Sanremo. I loved the water, the scent of lemon and orange blossoms, and everything about the southern feel. Sanremo lies in a bay surrounded by houses and fishing huts painted in red, yellow, and orange, with terracotta roofs and green shutters. Striped sun umbrellas shade restaurant coffee tables along the sidewalks. There were also many street vendors with their décor of goods dangling in abundance from the roofs of their carts. Beautiful sandals with braided straps and a tiny heel caught my eye. As little girls do, I begged my parents for them. I still remember scuffing down the sidewalk, the shoes flip-flopping from my heels and clip-clopping along the stone. Afterward, my parents took me to one of the cafés where they had tiramisu with their afternoon coffee. I really wanted to stay longer, but we had a day and a half's drive to get back to Germany.

I took my recollections from that trip as I created a tiramisu recipe to make at home in my kitchen, many decades later. Sometimes, I make the ladyfingers from scratch. The ladyfinger recipe is included, but you can also buy them to shorten the time investment in the recipe considerably. If using store-bought ladyfingers, skip the first part of this recipe and go directly to the filling part. You will need two and a half packages of store-bought ladyfingers, about thirty ladyfingers in total.

The filling has some variations from traditional tiramisu. For the filling, this recipe makes *zabaglione*. I love zabaglione. It is an Italian and also French custard-type dessert (it is called *sabayon* in French). Zabaglione uses Marsala wine (I recommend sweet, not dry), whereas many variations of tiramisu often flavor the filling with brandy or liqueur, for example, orange, chocolate, or coffee liqueur. I ventured into combining these two delicious desserts, and this recipe's filling uses sweet Marsala wine, orange liqueur, and coffee liqueur. The zabaglione preparation also heats the egg yolks, which is another difference from traditional tiramisu filling. The traditional filling begins by mixing raw egg yolks with sugar and then incorporating mascarpone; raw egg whites are folded in to create the volume. The filling does not bake, so the eggs remain raw. This recipe opts not to use raw eggs. The zabaglione preparation takes care of pasteurizing the egg yolks, and whipped cream replaces raw egg whites to achieve the volume in the filling.

Plan ahead when making this tiramisu. Set aside three hours to prepare it, plus at least six hours for chilling time in the refrigerator. After chilling, the tiramisu is ready to dust with cocoa or mocha powder and serve.

SPONGE CAKE-BASED TORTES

TIRAMISU

For Making the Ladyfingers

BAKING PAN
two ladyfinger or twinkie-style pans, buttered then dusted with powdered sugar; or two cookie sheets small enough to fit on the same oven rack side by side, buttered and lined with parchment paper then dusted with powdered sugar

BAKING TEMPERATURE
400°F

BAKE TIME
8 to 9 minutes for ladyfinger pans; 9 to 11 minutes for twinkie-style pans or cookie sheets

RACK PLACEMENT
middle of oven

YIELD
When piping and baking on cookie sheets: 30 ladyfingers

When baking in twinkie-style pans: 16 ladyfingers (use two pans, each measuring 9 x 13 inches with eight 4 x 1 ½-inch molds); cut ladyfingers in half lengthwise to produce 32

When baking in ladyfinger pans: 32 ladyfingers (use two pans, each measuring 9 ¼ x 8 ¼ inches with eight 4 x 1 ¼-inch molds); bake two batches to produce the total yield of 32

SPECIAL TOOLS
Two cookie sheets, ladyfinger pans, or twinkie-style pans (available online)

Pastry bag fitted with large piping tip, for example, a Wilton 1A tip or a similar tip (important for shaping the ladyfingers if using cookie sheets)

Parchment paper (if using cookie sheets)

INGREDIENTS FOR LADYFINGERS

1 cup unbleached all-purpose flour (French T45 farine de blé is an excellent flour for making ladyfingers)

¼ cup cornstarch

¼ teaspoon baking powder

4 eggs, at room temperature

¾ cup sugar

4 tablespoons warm water

1 teaspoon vanilla sugar

Powdered sugar (for dusting pans or cookie sheets and for dusting ladyfinger tops before baking)

SPONGE CAKE-BASED TORTES

Directions for Ladyfingers

1. Position a rack in the middle of the oven and preheat to 400°F. If using ladyfinger or twinkie-style pans, butter the pans and dust each mold with powdered sugar. For cookie sheets, butter and line with parchment paper, then dust the parchment paper with powdered sugar. The ladyfingers will be piped out with a pastry bag onto the cookie sheets. It is helpful to have the two pans or cookie sheets ready and best if they fit onto the oven rack side by side. Keep batter in the refrigerator if baking in batches is necessary. Set the prepared pans aside.

2. Sift the flour, cornstarch, and baking powder into a bowl. Whisk briefly to incorporate evenly.

3. Separate the eggs: Place egg whites into a large mixing bowl, preferably copper, and yolks into a small bowl (until mixing in step 4). Begin whipping the egg whites. As the whites start to fluff, just before soft peaks form, add half the sugar. Continue whipping to soft peaks. The peaks should flop over like an elf's hat when scooped onto a whisk and turned over. Do not mix further. Set the egg whites aside.

4. In a large mixing bowl with an electric mixer, cream the egg yolks and the warm water on medium to high for about 1 minute. Add the rest of the sugar and the vanilla sugar and mix for 2 more minutes, until creamy and fluffy. Slide the whipped egg whites over the yolk mixture and sift the flour mixture on top. With a whisk, fold carefully to incorporate all ingredients without losing air bubbles in the egg whites. As soon as flour is incorporated, stop mixing.

5. Either spoon the batter into the molds of the prepared ladyfinger or twinkie-style pans or place into a pastry bag fitted with a large piping tip. Squeeze the batter into the pan molds or onto the prepared cookie sheets, about 4 inches long and ¾ inch apart. Stop squeezing before lifting and piping the next one. Dust with powdered sugar.

6. Bake until light golden brown—8 to 9 minutes for ladyfinger pans, or 9 to 11 minutes for twinkie-style pans or cookie sheets. If the ladyfingers have to bake in two batches, refrigerate the batter while the first batch bakes.

TIRAMISU

For Making the Filling and Assembling the Tiramisu

PAN FOR ASSEMBLY	**COOLING TIME**	**YIELD**	**SPECIAL TOOL**
9 x 13-inch glass or porcelain dish	6 hours or overnight	one 9 x 13-inch tiramisu	Bain-marie or double boiler

INGREDIENTS FOR FILLING

1 cup brewed espresso, or 1 cup brewed coffee and ½ teaspoon espresso powder (see *note 1* at end of recipe)

1 tablespoon good-quality unsweetened Dutched cocoa powder (for example, Droste brand)

2 (7-gram) envelopes ground gelatin (14 grams total)

¼ cup cold water, plus more if needed

16 ounces mascarpone, at room temperature

7 egg yolks

1 cup sugar

2 tablespoons lemon juice

Pulp of ½ of a vanilla bean

⅓ cup sweet Marsala wine

2 teaspoons orange liqueur (for example, Grand Marnier has a delicate and rounded flavor)

Zest of 1 small lemon (2 teaspoons)

2 tablespoons powdered sugar

2 cups heavy whipping cream

1 tablespoon coffee liqueur (for example, Kahlúa)

FOR DUSTING (choose one)

3 tablespoons cocoa powder mixed with 1 tablespoon powdered sugar

Or 2 tablespoons mocha frappé mix powder (for example, Ghirardelli makes a tasty mix with coffee added)

SPONGE CAKE-BASED TORTES

Directions for Filling and Assembly

1. Make 1 cup of espresso, or 1 cup of strong coffee, adding the espresso powder after the coffee is brewed. Mix the cocoa powder with 2 to 3 tablespoons of the espresso or coffee to dissolve (this helps to avoid lumps), then add to the remaining espresso or coffee. Set aside until it is time to dip the ladyfingers in step 8.

2. Soak the gelatin in ¼ cup cold water and let sit for 5 to 10 minutes. Add more water only if needed. The gelatin should be evenly moist and thick like a paste. Set aside until step 6.

3. Cream the soft mascarpone for 1 minute with an electric mixer. Set aside until step 6.

4. In a large bowl, whisk the egg yolks as if gently scrambling. Add the sugar and lemon juice and whisk to combine. Scrape the pulp from half of a vanilla bean, add to the egg yolk mixture, and mix well. Pour the mixture into the top pot of a bain-marie (double boiler); the bottom pot should have just enough water that it does not touch the upper pot (about 1 inch to 1¼ inches, depending on the size and space between pots). Bring water in the bottom pot to a simmer. The first part of the process to heat and whisk the mixture will take about 5 to 6 minutes. Whisk constantly throughout this process, as if whipping egg whites, to dissolve the sugar and fluff up the yolks. If your arm grows tired, rest briefly but take the entire bain-marie off heat so the yolks do not completely cook and firm up (see tip). Use a fast-read kitchen thermometer to watch the temperature as the mixture thickens; the egg yolk mixture must reach a temperature of 160°F/71°C (see *note 2* at end of recipe). This temperature ensures that any salmonellae are destroyed. The temperature may go up to 165.2°F/74°C at the end. Keep whisking vigorously toward the end of the process as the yolk mixture thickens. Without vigorous whisking, the bottom will start to set and clump.

~ TIP ~

A handheld mixer with a whisk attachment can come in handy for this task.

After the 5 to 6 minutes of beating, the sugar should be dissolved, and the mixture should look creamy and considerably larger in volume. At this point, remove the entire bain-marie from the heat but do not turn off the heat. While whisking, drizzle the Marsala wine and orange liqueur into the mixture, then place back on heat and whip for another 3 minutes. When the mixture is fluffy and thickened like a thin custard, remove from heat. Add the lemon zest and stir to distribute. Pour into a large bowl and continue whisking vigorously to cool the mixture and increase volume, about 1½ to 3 minutes. The mixture is now called zabaglione. Set aside until step 6.

5. Sift the 2 tablespoons of powdered sugar into the unwhipped heavy cream; whip to stiff peaks. Set aside.

TIRAMISU

6. Fold the creamed mascarpone into the zabaglione; set aside but keep on hand for step 7. Then, in a saucepan over low heat, melt the gelatin into a smooth, flowing liquid. Stir continuously while melting and do not overheat. Once melted, slowly pour the coffee liqueur into the gelatin while stirring. Briefly reheat if necessary.

7. Slowly pour the warm liquid gelatin, in a thin stream, into the zabaglione and mascarpone mixture. Fold in half of the whipped cream and set aside. The remaining half of the whipped cream will be spread over the tiramisu in step 9.

8. Divide the number of ladyfingers into two equal groups. Dip one group by quickly touching each ladyfinger, underside only, to the liquid of espresso or coffee. The dip should be just in and out. The ladyfingers are quick to soak up liquid and should not get soggy. Only dip the ladyfingers from one group. The other group remains dry.

9. Place the dipped ladyfingers into a 9 x 13-inch glass or porcelain dish to cover the bottom. Spread a little more than half of the zabaglione mixture over the ladyfingers. Lay the remaining ladyfingers, those that have not been dipped into the espresso or coffee, on top. Spread the rest of the zabaglione mixture over the second layer of ladyfingers and spread the remaining half of the whipped cream on top. Smooth out to a flat surface.

10. Refrigerate for 6 hours or overnight. Choose one option to dust over the tiramisu after refrigerating: either the cocoa powder mixed with powdered sugar or the mocha frappé mix powder. If using the cocoa powder and powdered sugar, sift together into a bowl and stir with a whisk to combine. With a small sifter, dust the cocoa mixture or the mocha frappé mix powder over the tiramisu just before serving.

Note 1: Use the espresso if you like a strong coffee taste. If you prefer a milder taste, make the tiramisu with the brewed coffee and espresso powder. Espresso powder is available at online baking stores. Different brands have varying strengths of taste. Add espresso powder according to the strength and individual taste. Start with less and taste test; a little goes a long way.

Note 2: Heating eggs to an internal temperature of 160°F/71°C is the FDA's guideline for food safety. The American Egg Board also uses this internal temperature in their recipes. For more information, see fda.gov/food/buy-store-serve-safe-food/what-you-need-know-about-egg-safety.

BLACK FOREST TORTE

Black Forest cakes are a quintessential German dessert. They are stacked chocolate cakes, with either two or three layers, and fillings of cherries and whipped cream. For the finishing touch, the tortes are decorated with piped whipped cream rosettes, maraschino cherries, and chocolate shavings. This recipe includes two layers of cake, plus a Mürbeteig crust (shortcrust) as the base. This Mürbeteig crust takes some additional time, but it is also more authentic, and it gives the torte extra flavor and a crunchy texture.

This recipe begins with an overview of the stages of preparation. Ingredients are listed as they are needed in each stage, including an ingredients list in the assembly stage. Be sure to look through all stages when gathering ingredients. If you would like to spread out the work, you can bake the Mürbeteig and the chocolate cake the day before preparing the fillings and assembling the torte. Allow the Mürbeteig to cool to room temperature, transfer onto a cake platter, and then cover until the next day. The chocolate cake can also be covered and left on the counter until the next day. The cherry filling can be prepared the day before assembly as well and stored in the refrigerator. When preparing the cherry filling, decide whether to use the *kirschwasser* (cherry brandy) to flavor the cherry filling or the whipped cream; it should flavor one or the other but not both. Keep in mind that the chocolate cake also is drizzled with kirschwasser. If bakers choose to prepare the filling without any kirschwasser, they may still drizzle it onto the cake during assembly to soak in the flavor. Clear Creek Distillery in Hood River, Oregon, makes a kirschwasser as tasty as German brands. Clear Creek Distillery's products are available in select liquor stores and online.

BLACK FOREST TORTE

Overview
Bake Mürbeteig
Bake chocolate cake
Make cherry filling
Make whipped cream filling/topping
Assemble and decorate the torte

For Mürbeteig

BAKING PAN
10-inch springform pan, buttered and floured

BAKING TEMPERATURE
325°F

BAKE TIME
20 to 22 minutes

RACK PLACEMENT
middle of oven

YIELD
one 10-inch crust

INGREDIENTS FOR MÜRBETEIG

1 cup unbleached all-purpose flour (protein 3 grams per ¼ cup; see page 7), plus ¼ cup more for working the dough

½ cup powdered sugar

¼ cup unblanched almond meal

Pinch of salt (about ⅛ teaspoon or less)

1 egg yolk

5 tablespoons unsalted butter, cold

Directions for Mürbeteig

1. Prepare the crust: Set aside ¼ cup of the measured flour to use as needed while working the dough and pressing it into the form. Sift the remaining flour and powdered sugar onto a large marble or wooden board. Sift and distribute the almond meal over the flour. Form a well in the middle and sprinkle the salt around the edge. Add the egg yolk into the well. Cut the butter into small pieces, approximately ¼ to ½ inch (refer to page 21, "How to Cut Butter," in the Mürbeteige introduction). Distribute the pieces over and around the flour. Using the tip of a metal dough scraper, stir the yolk as if gently scrambling. Begin carefully pushing the dry ingredients into the well's center. Work to combine all ingredients, first with the dough scraper and then with your hands, until a ball of dough forms. Add flour sparingly or chill as necessary if the dough becomes too sticky.

2. Refrigerate the dough for 30 minutes. About halfway through that time, position a rack in the middle of the oven and preheat to 325°F. Butter and flour the pan in preparation for baking.

3. Mold crust into pan: Remove the dough from the refrigerator. Slice horizontally into four discs. Lay the discs into the prepared pan. With flour-dipped fingers, push the dough out, rather than pressing it down, to cover the pan's bottom evenly. The crust should be flat and does not need to be pulled up the pan's sides to create a rim. Even out any thin spots to get the dough to a fairly consistent thickness.

4. Bake for 20 to 22 minutes, until firm and pale golden in color. Remove the pan's rim; place the pan's base with the crust on a wire rack and let cool completely. Then use a *kuchenretter* (cake lifter) to lift the crust from the pan's base onto the rack.

SPONGE CAKE-BASED TORTES

For Chocolate Cake

BAKING PAN
10-inch aluminum springform or cheesecake pan, buttered and lined with parchment paper

Baking time may be shortened if a steel-based pan is used rather than aluminum; dark pans bake faster than light pans.

BAKING TEMPERATURE
350°F

BAKE TIME
18 to 20 minutes

RACK PLACEMENT
top third of oven, one rung above middle

YIELD
one 10-inch cake

INGREDIENTS FOR CHOCOLATE CAKE

4 eggs, at room temperature

⅔ cup sugar

¾ cup unbleached all-purpose flour (protein 3 grams per ¼ cup; see page 7)

2 tablespoons potato starch

4 tablespoons good-quality unsweetened Dutched cocoa (for example, Droste brand)

4 tablespoons very warm to hot water

Pinch of salt (about ⅛ teaspoon)

2 teaspoons vanilla sugar, or 1 teaspoon vanilla extract

1 tablespoon coffee liqueur, optional

Directions for Chocolate Cake

1. Position a rack in the top third of the oven (one rung above middle) and preheat to 350°F. Butter the pan and line with parchment paper in preparation for baking (see tip 1). Set aside.

~ TIP 1 ~

Butter the pan's bottom and ½ inch up the sides. Use just enough butter to keep the parchment paper in place. Cut the parchment paper ½ inch bigger than the circumference of the pan. The paper will fold and pleat nicely and still lie flat against the pan. The cake will stick a little onto the sides of the pan, but that is not a problem. The sticking will prevent the cake from deflating as it cools. If necessary, carefully run a wooden skewer around the edge to pry the cake loose.

2. Separate the eggs: Place egg whites into a large mixing bowl, preferably copper, and yolks into a small bowl (until mixing in step 4). Whip the whites with half of the measured sugar until soft peaks form. The peaks will fall over but hold their shape. Set aside.

3. Sift the flour and potato starch into a bowl and mix with a wire whisk. Sift the cocoa into another bowl. Set aside.

4. Make the batter: In a mixing bowl with an electric mixer, cream the egg yolks and the very warm water on almost the highest setting for 1 minute. Lower speed to slow and add the remaining sugar and the salt in increments,

BLACK FOREST TORTE

then increase speed and mix 1½ minutes more. Scrape the sides of the bowl, if needed. The yolks will have increased in volume, and the mixture should be fluffy and frothy. Add the vanilla and optional coffee liqueur and mix briefly. Sift the cocoa (second sifting) directly over the egg yolk mixture and stir by hand to avoid a cocoa dust cloud. Then continue mixing on medium speed until the cocoa is just dissolved. Do not overmix. Transfer mixture into a large, wide bowl.

Slide the egg whites onto the cocoa and egg yolk mixture; sift the flour mixture (second sifting) directly over the egg whites. With a whisk, fold carefully to incorporate all ingredients without losing air bubbles in the egg whites. Do not stir and do not overmix. Stop as soon as the flour and egg white streaks have disappeared into the batter. Pour the batter into the parchment-lined pan, tilting the pan so the batter settles more evenly. Smooth the top with a light touch.

5. Bake for 18 to 20 minutes. Insert a wooden skewer into the cake's center to check for doneness. The skewer should come out with a few moist kernels stuck to it but no wet batter. Do not overbake the cake, or it will be dry. Let the cake cool in the pan on a wire rack for 10 minutes, then remove the pan's rim. Slide the cake with the parchment onto the cooling rack or use a *kuchenretter* (cake lifter) to lift the parchment with the cake from the pan's base onto the cooling rack. Once on the rack, allow cake to cool completely. If the cake baked in a springform pan, clean the pan's rim and set aside; you will need it to assemble the cake later (or a 10-inch mousse cake ring will work too).

6. After the cake has cooled, turn over onto a dish and peel off the parchment paper. Cut the cake in half horizontally (see page 178, "How to Cut and Assemble Layered Sponge Cakes"). Cut the top layer thicker and the bottom layer thinner; the top layer becomes the bottom during assembly and needs to be sturdier to support the torte. Keep together and set aside.

For Cherry Filling

INGREDIENTS FOR CHERRY FILLING

10 ounces (1 very full cup) canned pitted tart or sour cherries, packed in water

1 cup cherry juice, unsweetened organic

3 tablespoons cornstarch (for an opaque glaze), or 3 ½ tablespoons potato starch (for a translucent glaze)

1 teaspoon lemon juice

1 ½ tablespoons kirschwasser (if not using in the whipped cream filling/topping)

⅓ cup sugar

Directions for Cherry Filling

1. Drain the cherries into a colander and set aside until ready to use in step 3.

2. In a small bowl, whisk ¼ cup of the cherry juice with the cornstarch or potato starch until dissolved.

3. Pour the remaining cherry juice, lemon juice, and kirschwasser (if using) into a medium-sized saucepan over medium-high heat. Add

SPONGE CAKE-BASED TORTES

the cornstarch or potato starch mixture and the sugar. Whisking constantly, bring to a boil. Once the mixture boils, turn down the heat and continue to whisk vigorously until it thickens to the consistency of jelly (see tip 2). Add the cherries and stir to coat; the cherries will release some liquid and thin the filling to a spreadable consistency. Transfer to a bowl and refrigerate to cool (see tip 3). Once cooled, the filling should be thick but spreadable; it should not run over the edge when spread onto the cake. If in doubt, leave the filling thicker rather than thinning it out. If the mixture is still too thick after cooling, add 1 to 2 tablespoons of juice and let cook briefly once more. If the mixture is too thin after cooling, add more cornstarch or potato starch, 1 tablespoon at a time, and cook briefly.

~ TIP 2 ~

The juice mixture can bubble over or stick to the saucepan's bottom very quickly, so do not leave unattended at any time. Once the mixture boils, stir rapidly, making sure to scrape the bottom of the saucepan to avoid sticking and burning. A flat wooden spoon works best for this task. The mixture is nearly ready when it starts to bubble, which means that it has begun to gel up. At this point, turn off the heat or reduce it to low. Stir and scrape a few more times to prevent burning, and the mixture is ready. If the mixture boils too rapidly too early, remove from heat for a moment to prevent a spillover, then turn down heat before replacing the saucepan.

~ TIP 3 ~

To cool more quickly, spread the filling on a plate; a large, flat container; or even a frying pan and place in the freezer, stirring occasionally, while proceeding with making the whipped cream filling.

The decorating style of the slice of Black Forest torte shown above is my creative version, which is also shown on the cover of this book. In Germany, a Black Forest cake must be decorated in the traditional manner as shown on page 225.

BLACK FOREST TORTE

For Whipped Cream Filling/Topping

Prepare the whipped cream filling/topping using either gelatin or whipped cream stabilizer (see *note 1* at end of recipe).

INGREDIENTS FOR PREPARATION WITH GELATIN

1 ½ (7-gram) envelopes ground gelatin (10.5 grams total)

3 tablespoons cold water, or 1 tablespoon cold water plus 2 tablespoons kirschwasser (if not using in the cherry filling)

2 pints heavy whipping cream

¾ cup powdered sugar

*This amount makes enough for the filling and covering the cake's top and sides liberally.

INGREDIENTS FOR PREPARATION WITH WHIPPED CREAM STABILIZER

1 (8-gram) envelope whipped cream stabilizer

2 pints heavy whipping cream

3 tablespoons kirschwasser (if not using in the cherry filling)

¾ cup powdered sugar

*This amount makes enough for the filling and covering the cake's top and sides liberally.

Directions for Preparation with Gelatin

In a small bowl or cup, mix the gelatin with the cold water or the mixture of cold water and kirschwasser. Whisk until smooth and the lumps are gone (press lumps with the back of a spoon), then let sit for 5 minutes to firm up. In the meantime, whip the heavy cream until it starts to firm and shows a few ripples. Set aside. In a small saucepan, melt the now-firm gelatin into a flowing liquid over low heat while stirring constantly. Do not overheat. Pour into a small bowl and stir to cool down the liquid to warm, but do not cool so much that it begins to gel up again; the gelatin must stay in a liquid state. Return to the whipped cream. With the mixer on low speed, drizzle in the liquid gelatin in a thin stream—the slower this process, the better the distribution. Sift the powdered sugar over the whipped cream and continue whipping until stiff peaks are achieved. Store in refrigerator until ready to use.

Directions for Preparation with Whipped Cream Stabilizer

Sprinkle stabilizer in with the unwhipped heavy cream, then whip to almost stiff peaks (or follow directions on the package). Mixing on low speed, drizzle in the kirschwasser (if using). Sift in the powdered sugar. Continue whipping until stiff, then stop mixing. (Overmixing is easier with added whipped cream stabilizer; the whipped cream becomes rough looking, losing smoothness.) Store in refrigerator until ready to use.

SPONGE CAKE-BASED TORTES

For Assembling the Torte

SPECIAL TOOLS

10-inch rim from springform baking pan, or a 10-inch mousse cake ring

Offset cake spatula

INGREDIENTS FOR ASSEMBLING THE TORTE

For jelly mixture (to spread over Mürbeteig):
  7 ounces raspberry jelly or red currant jelly
  1 tablespoon kirschwasser

For drizzling over chocolate cake:
  1 to 2 jiggers kirschwasser

For garnish (see *note 2* at end of recipe):
  8 maraschino cherries or other cherries of choice
  Semi-sweet or dark baking chocolate or European chocolate bar, 70% cocoa, good quality

Directions for Assembling the Torte

1. Place the Mürbeteig on a serving plate. Mix the jelly with the kirschwasser and spread over the Mürbeteig. Lightly oil the springform rim or mousse cake ring with a bland-tasting oil like canola oil and wipe off excess. Place the rim or ring around the Mürbeteig (see tip 4).

~ TIP 4 ~

Secure plastic wrap around the bottom edge of the rim or ring to prevent filling from running out. Do not worry if some runs out. It will firm up as the torte chills.

2. Place the thicker half of the chocolate cake, cut-side up, on top of the jelly-covered Mürbeteig. Drizzle 1 to 2 jiggers of kirschwasser over the cake (see tip 5). When drizzling and filling, leave about ¼ inch of space around the cake's edge bare so that filling does not squeeze out. Spread all of the cooled cherry filling onto the kirschwasser-soaked cake. Take about 2 cups of the whipped cream filling and place into the refrigerator to use for decorating later. Spread the remaining whipped cream over the cherry filling. Lay the second half of the cake, cut-side down for a flat surface for decorating later, on top of the whipped cream filling and peel off the parchment paper.

~ TIP 5 ~

To drizzle, cover the opening of the jigger with your fingers but create a small gap between two fingers so the kirschwasser can sprinkle out while moving and shaking your hand over the cake.

3. Chill torte in the refrigerator for at least 6 hours.

4. Remove the rim or ring from the torte. Use the reserved whipped cream to cover the torte's top and sides. Pipe eight rosettes on top. Place a cherry into each rosette. Shave or rasp chocolate on top of the torte and around the sides.

BLACK FOREST TORTE

Note 1: If the assembled cake can remain in the refrigerator, the whipped cream will remain stiff without the gelatin or stabilizer. But if the cake is to stay out in a warm room for an extended time before or during serving, gelatin or stabilizer is recommended. Whipped cream tends to soften when left in a warm space.

Note 2: This recipe makes a Black Forest torte with traditional decoration. The book's cover photograph shows a Black Forest torte decorated with some creative, artistic expression. It has a white wine glaze made with agar agar (a plant-based alternative to gelatin made from algae). To replicate the cover photograph's decoration, use the following process after covering the torte with whipped cream in step 4 of assembly. Make the glaze with ½ cup white wine or water, 2 tablespoons sugar, and 1 teaspoon powdered agar agar (use a brand that indicates it is tasteless; I have good results with Living Jin brand). Follow the directions on the agar agar package to cook with the sugar and liquid. Pour into a cereal bowl and stir to cool for 1 minute. Place the desired number of cherries in the middle of the torte and pour the glaze over the cherries. The glaze will form a circle without running down the sides of the cake. Allow the glaze to cool completely after pouring (about 10 minutes). Proceed with piping rosettes and placing additional cherries. For instructions on how to make and pipe chocolate filigree, see the showcase of topping, filling, and garnish videos available at vimeo.com/showcase/10470112.

VIDEO SHOWCASE
Fillings and Garnishes
vimeo.com/showcase/10470112

CHOCOLATE IRISH CREAM CAKE

This cake was inspired while creating a more moist and intensely flavored chocolate cake for the Black Forest Torte recipe. I had baked the chocolate cake several times and finally found perfection. After trying out many different cocoas, I settled on a Dutched cocoa, which gives the cake the richest chocolate flavor. As I was assembling the Black Forest torte, an idea about a new kind of filling started forming in my head. I dreamed up a filling of roasted hazelnut meal to go along with the chocolate, complemented with Irish cream. I infused the liqueur into the cream filling, and it turned out to be one of my favorite cakes ever. The filling melts away in your mouth, and the chocolate sponge cake is moist and light. This cake freezes well when cut into slices, and it is easy enough to microwave a frozen piece for twenty seconds. The filling becomes semi-liquid similar to a lava cake but with elegant pizzazz. Drizzle with Raspberry Sauce for an unforgettable burst of flavor.

CHOCOLATE IRISH CREAM CAKE

BAKING PAN
10-inch springform or aluminum cheesecake pan, buttered and lined with parchment paper

Baking time may be shortened if a steel-based pan is used rather than aluminum; dark pans bake faster than light pans.

BAKING TEMPERATURE
350°F

BAKE TIME
18 to 20 minutes

RACK PLACEMENT
top third of oven, one rung above middle

YIELD
one 10-inch cake

SPECIAL TOOLS
(for filling and assembly)

Double boiler or bain-marie

10-inch rim from springform baking pan, or a 9-inch mousse cake ring (for a tighter fit as cake shrinks during baking; some trimming of the cake may be required)

Fast-read kitchen thermometer

Offset cake spatula

Culinary torch (optional to help remove the springform rim or mousse cake ring after cake chills)

INGREDIENTS

FOR CAKE

4 eggs, at room temperature

⅔ cup sugar

¾ cup unbleached all-purpose flour (protein 3 grams per ¼ cup; see page 7)

2 tablespoons potato starch

4 tablespoons unsweetened Dutched cocoa (for example, Droste brand)

4 tablespoons very warm to hot water

Pinch of salt (about ⅛ teaspoon or less)

2 teaspoons vanilla sugar, or 1 teaspoon vanilla extract, or pulp of ½ of a vanilla bean

1 tablespoon coffee liqueur, optional

FOR HAZELNUT MEAL COMPONENT OF THE FILLING

½ cup ground hazelnut meal (⅓ cup whole hazelnuts if grinding yourself, see page 14 for technique)

FOR CHOCOLATE SYRUP COMPONENT OF THE FILLING

½ cup sugar

½ scant cup water

7 ounces (200 grams) 70% dark chocolate, broken into pieces

1 jigger Irish cream liqueur

FOR WHIPPED CREAM COMPONENT OF THE FILLING

1 (7-gram) envelope ground gelatin

2 tablespoons cold water

1 ⅛ cups heavy whipping cream

FOR ASSEMBLY AND GARNISH

1 jigger Irish cream liqueur (to drizzle over cake)

4 ounces apricot or mango marmalade (to brush over cake)

Chocolate glaze of choice, such as Easy Chocolate Glaze (see page 261), Chocolate Mirror Glaze (see page 262), Tempered Chocolate Glaze (see page 263), or Tempered Chocolate Glaze the Easy Way (see page 265)

Raspberry Sauce (see page 259) or other red fruit syrup of choice

SPONGE CAKE-BASED TORTES

DIRECTIONS

For Cake

1. Position a rack in the top third of the oven (one rung above middle) and preheat to 350°F. Butter the pan and line with parchment paper in preparation for baking (see tip 1). Set aside.

~ TIP 1 ~

Butter the pan's bottom and ½ inch up the sides. Use just enough butter to keep the parchment paper in place. Cut the parchment paper a ½ inch bigger than the circumference of the pan. The paper will fold and pleat nicely and still lie flat against the pan. The cake will stick a little onto the sides of the pan, but that is not a problem. The sticking will prevent the cake from deflating as it cools.

---

2. Separate the eggs: Place egg whites into a large mixing bowl, preferably copper, and yolks into a small bowl (until mixing in step 4). Whip the whites with half of the measured sugar until soft peaks form. The peaks will fall over but hold their shape. Set aside.

3. Sift the flour and potato starch into a bowl and mix with a wire whisk. Sift the cocoa into another bowl. Set aside.

4. Make the batter: In a mixing bowl with an electric mixer, cream the egg yolks and the very warm water on almost the highest setting for 1 minute. Lower speed to slow and add the remaining sugar and the salt, then increase speed and mix 1½ minutes more. Scrape the sides of the bowl, if needed. The yolks will have increased in volume, and the mixture should be fluffy and frothy. Add the vanilla and optional coffee liqueur and mix briefly. Sift in the cocoa (second sifting) directly over the egg yolk mixture and stir by hand to avoid a cocoa dust cloud. Then continue mixing on medium speed until the cocoa is just dissolved. Do not overmix. Transfer mixture into a large, wide bowl.

Slide the egg whites over the cocoa and egg yolk mixture and sift the flour mixture (second sifting) directly over the egg whites. With a whisk, fold carefully to incorporate all ingredients without losing air bubbles in the egg whites. Do not stir and do not overmix. Stop as soon as the flour and egg white streaks have disappeared into the batter. Pour the batter into the parchment-lined pan, tilting the pan so the batter settles more evenly. Smooth the top with a light touch.

5. Bake for 18 to 20 minutes. Insert a wooden skewer into the cake's center to check for doneness. The skewer should come out with a few moist kernels stuck to it but no wet batter. Do not overbake the cake, or it will be dry. Let the cake cool in the pan on a wire rack for 10 minutes, then remove the pan's rim. If necessary, carefully run a wooden skewer around the edge to pry the cake loose. Slide the cake with the parchment onto a cooling rack or use a *kuchenretter* (cake lifter) to lift the parchment with the cake from the pan's base onto a cooling rack. Once on the rack, allow cake to cool completely. If the cake baked in a springform pan, clean the pan's rim and set aside; you will need it to assemble the cake later (or a 9-inch mousse cake ring will work too).

CHOCOLATE IRISH CREAM CAKE

6. After the cake has cooled, cut in half horizontally (see page 178, "How to Cut and Assemble Layered Sponge Cakes"). Cut the top layer slightly thicker; it will become the bottom layer during assembly and needs to be sturdier.

For Filling

1. Roasting the hazelnut meal is optional: Roasting brings out the robust flavor of the hazelnut. Heat a skillet over medium to medium-high. Add the hazelnut meal into the skillet and flatten it down with a spatula. Toast the hazelnut meal for about 5 minutes, until a light brown color, then stir and flip regularly to brown evenly. If smoke starts to develop, the skillet is too hot. If that happens, remove from heat for a brief time and continue stirring, then return to heat, with the temperature reduced as needed. Aim for golden brown, not dark brown. If the hazelnut meal darkens too much, it will become bitter. Spread nut meal out on a plate to cool.

2. Begin the chocolate syrup component of the filling: Cook the sugar and the water on a low simmer while stirring, until all sugar is dissolved. Continue cooking the syrup on medium to high for an additional minute. Set aside to cool. In a double boiler, melt the chocolate. Take the double boiler off heat; let chocolate cool while preserving liquidity. The melted chocolate and syrup will be combined in step 4.

3. Make the whipped cream component of the filling: Mix the gelatin and the cold water in a small bowl or cup. Whisk until smooth and the lumps are gone (press lumps with the back of a spoon), then let sit for 5 minutes to firm up. In the meantime, whip the heavy cream until it starts to firm and shows a few ripples. Set aside. In a small saucepan, melt the now-firm gelatin into a flowing liquid over low heat while stirring constantly. Do not overheat. Return to the whipped cream. Turn mixer on low speed and drizzle in the liquid gelatin in a thin stream—the slower this process, the better the distribution. Sift the powdered sugar over the whipped cream and continue whipping until stiff peaks are achieved. Store in refrigerator until ready to use.

4. Return to the chocolate syrup component: To mix the syrup and the melted chocolate, it is important for the syrup to be close to the same temperature as the chocolate, around 158°F/70°C works well. After making sure that the temperatures are close to the same, drizzle the syrup into the chocolate incrementally, using the following method: Pour a small amount of chocolate into a medium-sized bowl, then add a third of the syrup while stirring rapidly. Add more chocolate if the syrup is not absorbed. Repeat the process, alternating between adding more chocolate and more syrup, until all syrup and chocolate are blended. Pour back into the double boiler, bring water in lower pot to a strong simmer, and reheat while stirring continuously, until the mixture is of a smooth consistency. Pull off heat and set aside.

5. Combine the chocolate syrup, Irish cream liqueur, and hazelnut meal: In a medium-sized bowl, heat the jigger of Irish cream liqueur in the microwave for 20 seconds. While stirring and in increments, drizzle the chocolate syrup into the liqueur. Continue stirring until smooth

SPONGE CAKE-BASED TORTES

and all chocolate syrup is incorporated. Fold the hazelnut meal into the chocolate syrup. The chocolate syrup will cool down but do not allow to cool so much that the chocolate starts to set. If it sets, it could be hard to fold in the whipped cream in the next step.

6. Blend the whipped cream with the hazelnut chocolate syrup: Take one-third of the hazelnut chocolate syrup and place into a medium-sized bowl; incorporate ½ cup of the whipped cream by stirring gently. Some whipped cream may melt. Add this premix into the rest of the hazelnut chocolate syrup and gently combine. Slide the remainder of the whipped cream on top and, with a wire whisk, gently fold under the chocolate. As soon as the last speck of whipped cream is blended into the chocolate, stop mixing.

For Assembling

1. Place thicker half of the chocolate cake, cut-side up, on a serving plate and drizzle 1 jigger of Irish cream liqueur over the cake (see tip 2). Lightly oil the springform rim or mousse cake ring with a bland-tasting oil like canola oil and wipe off excess. Place the rim or ring around the cake (see tip 3). Spread the filling over the cake. Lay the second half of the cake, cut-side down and bottom-side up (the bottom side has a flatter surface for decorating later), on top of the filling. Press down lightly with a flat hand to level the top. Gently lift the parchment off the bottom of the cake.

~ TIP 2 ~
To drizzle, cover the opening of the jigger with your fingers but create a small gap between two fingers so the Irish cream can sprinkle out while moving and shaking your hand over the cake.

~ TIP 3 ~
Secure plastic wrap around the bottom edge of the rim or ring to prevent filling from running out. Do not worry if some runs out. It will firm up as the cake chills.

2. Chill cake in the refrigerator for at least 6 hours or overnight. Check filling for firmness; it may need to chill more than 6 hours.

3. Remove the rim or ring. To loosen, a culinary torch can be used, but move quickly around the outside rim, as the filling will melt. Remove the rim by twisting carefully while lifting. To garnish, strain the marmalade through a strainer and heat in a small saucepan for easy spreading. Spoon or brush over the top of cake. Let cool and firm up for about 10 minutes. Cover the cake with chocolate glaze of choice and serve with Raspberry Sauce or other red fruit syrup drizzled over individual slices.

A Chocolate Irish Cream Cake slice with Tempered Chocolate Glaze and white chocolate design.

TOPPINGS, FILLINGS, AND GARNISHES   4

Glazes, sauces, fillings, frostings, icings, and garnishes are versatile tools for any baker. They can spruce up a recipe with beautiful finishing touches, such as a casual drizzle of Fruit Glaze; fluffy swirls of Buttercream; or a smooth, glossy spread of Chocolate Mirror Glaze. These finishes can transform the look of the baked goods they complement, and they bring pops of flavor to dress up cakes, pies, cookies, and breads for different occasions. Adding a fresh sauce, glaze, filling, frosting, icing, or garnish can make an old recipe seem entirely new. Learning these recipes will give bakers more options for all their recipes.

Vanilla Sauce and Pudding	242
Chocolate Sauce and Pudding	247
Lemon, Liliko'i, or Chocolate Buttercream	252
Easy Lemon Buttercream	255
Cream Cheese Frosting	256
Royal Icing	257
Fruit Glaze	258
Raspberry Sauce	259
Sugar Glaze	260
Easy Chocolate Glaze	261
Chocolate Mirror Glaze	262
Tempered Chocolate Glaze	263
Tempered Chocolate Glaze the Easy Way	265
Caramelized Almonds	267

CHAPTER 4

PREPARATION TIME

The Sugar Glaze and Easy Chocolate Glaze take less than five minutes to prepare. The Fruit Glaze, Raspberry Sauce, Easy Lemon Buttercream, and Cream Cheese Frosting need only a few more minutes, usually ten minutes or less, total time. The Royal Icing, Chocolate Mirror Glaze, Tempered Chocolate Glaze, and Tempered Chocolate Glaze the Easy Way involve a little more time. They can be ready in under twenty minutes. The Chocolate and Vanilla Sauces and Puddings and the Lemon, Lilikoʻi, or Chocolate Buttercream are more time intensive with about twenty to thirty minutes of work, plus additional cooling time in the refrigerator.

GENERAL TIPS AND TRICKS

Try Easy Recipes First

Practice with easy glazes first: the Sugar Glaze, Fruit Glaze, Raspberry Sauce, Easy Chocolate Glaze, Easy Lemon Buttercream, and Cream Cheese Frosting. Then move on to the Royal Icing, Chocolate Mirror Glaze, Tempered Chocolate Glaze, and Tempered Chocolate Glaze the Easy Way. Finally, try the more involved Lemon, Lilikoʻi, or Chocolate Buttercream and the Vanilla and Chocolate Sauces and Puddings. Working from easy to hard will boost confidence and skills for success.

Pay Attention to Ingredient Temperature

Always have eggs (whole, whites, or yolks), butter, and cream cheese at room temperature for cream fillings, frostings, and icings. Butter should be soft but not melted.

Invest in a Fast-Read Thermometer and a Bain-Marie (a Professional Double Boiler)

A reliable thermometer is very handy, even necessary, for creams prepared over heat and for the Tempered Chocolate Glaze. Do not waste money on regular kitchen thermometers; buy a fast-read thermometer instead. A slow thermometer can be frustrating. By the time it registers, ingredients may already be a few degrees hotter, which can result in curdled eggs or over-crystallized cocoa butter. Curdled eggs may mean a baker has to start over on the recipe. Over-crystallized cocoa butter will

TOPPINGS, FILLINGS, AND GARNISHES

require the baker to reduce the temperature of the chocolate, add new chocolate pieces or new cocoa butter chunks, and repeat the process.

A bain-marie gives extra leeway for temperature in sauces prepared on the stovetop. The two pots with water in between create a cushion that helps to guard sauces with chocolate, eggs, and/or dairy from burning, seizing, or curdling. For example, with the Chocolate and Vanilla Sauce and Pudding recipes, it is harder to burn the sauce/pudding and have it lump up when using a bain-marie versus a single saucepan.

A showcase of topping, filling, and garnish videos for inspiration and helpful technique demonstrations is available at vimeo.com/showcase/10470112.

VIDEO SHOWCASE
Fillings and Garnishes
vimeo.com/showcase/10470112

RECOMMENDED TOOLS
- Double boiler or bain-marie
- Fast-read kitchen thermometer
- Strainer
- Sifter
- Bowls
- Whisks
- Spatulas
- Wooden spoons

VANILLA SAUCE AND PUDDING

Vanilla sauce and pudding are versatile staples. The ingredients and preparation are the same for both sauce and pudding, but the difference is in the amount of cornstarch. The sauce has less cornstarch than the pudding and will therefore be thinner. When refrigerated, the sauce will firm up but is easily reheated to a pourable consistency. The pudding will set up to be thicker. If you have never used whole vanilla beans before, this recipe is a good time to try. The vanilla bean adds a fresh and intense flavor to the cream. Two preparation methods are given. The first method uses a bain-marie (double boiler) and is a reliable way to achieve a smooth, non-lumpy sauce or pudding without burning the milk. The second method uses a regular saucepan but be aware that the danger of burning the milk and getting lumpy sauce or pudding is higher with this method.

YIELD
2 cups of sauce, or 1 ¾ cups of pudding (smaller yield because it thickens more than sauce)

SPECIAL TOOLS
Bain-marie or double boiler

Fast-read kitchen thermometer

Timer

Wooden spoon

Whisk

INGREDIENTS

FOR VANILLA SAUCE

2 egg yolks, at room temperature

1 ½ cups milk, cold

1 teaspoon almond extract, optional

1 ½ tablespoons cornstarch (see page 12)

½ cup heavy whipping cream

Dash of salt

⅓ cup sugar

1 vanilla bean, or 1 teaspoon vanilla paste

FOR VANILLA PUDDING

2 egg yolks, at room temperature

1 ½ cups milk, cold

1 teaspoon almond extract, optional

3 tablespoons cornstarch (see page 12)

½ cup heavy whipping cream

Dash of salt

⅓ cup sugar

1 vanilla bean, or 1 teaspoon vanilla paste

TOPPINGS, FILLINGS, AND GARNISHES

Directions for Bain-Marie (Double Boiler)

1. Whisk the egg yolks in a small bowl. Set aside until step 5.

2. Measure out the cold milk and add the optional almond extract, if using. Mix ⅓ cup of the milk with the cornstarch in a small bowl; stir until the cornstarch is dissolved.

3. Pour water into the bottom of a bain-marie, just enough so the water does not touch the upper pot (about 1 inch to 1¼ inches, depending on the size and space between pots). Place onto a burner and turn the heat to medium to high.

4. In the top pot of the bain-marie, stir together the rest of the milk, the heavy whipping cream (unwhipped), the salt, and the sugar. Add the cornstarch and milk mixture. Split the vanilla bean down the middle and scrape the pulp into the mixture or add the vanilla bean paste. Cook over medium to high heat while stirring for about 2 minutes. Remove the entire bain-marie from the heat. Turn the burner to medium so it cools down for step 5.

5. Place the bain-marie back on the burner over medium heat and continue cooking while stirring with a wooden spoon and/or wire whisk. Cook and stir for about 10 minutes more. At this point, the mixture will be hot to the touch; keep stirring for about 2 more minutes. The mixture will start to thicken; stir more vigorously to prevent the cornstarch from clumping.

If the mixture clumps, take off heat and use a wire whisk vigorously to dissolve all clumps, then place back on heat and continue cooking. The mixture should thicken enough that a wooden spoon or whisk, when drawn through the mixture, will reveal the bottom of the pot. From start to finish, this process will take about 20 minutes.

When the cream mixture is a satisfactory consistency, turn off the heat and remove the bain-marie from the burner. Remove the top pot from the bottom; place a lid on the bottom pot to keep the water hot. Stir the mixture in the upper pot for about 2 minutes, or longer if necessary, to cool down to below 150°F/65°C. The temperature is important when combining the cream mixture with the egg yolks; the yolks in cream mixtures should not be heated too quickly or the protein in the yolk separates and the cream will curdle. It is best to work with a fast-read kitchen thermometer. When a temperature below 150°F/65°C is achieved, scoop out 2 tablespoons of the cream mixture and blend it into the egg yolks. Next, scoop out ½ cup of the cream mixture and gradually add into the egg yolks while stirring. Gradually add this egg yolk mixture into the bain-marie and combine with the remaining cream. Stir with a quick, consistent motion to prevent the yolks from clumping. The temperature will be around 135°F/57°C now. With this process, the yolks warm gradually and will not curdle.

Place the bain-marie's top pot back over the bottom pot holding the water. Set stovetop heat

VANILLA SAUCE AND PUDDING

to 5 (on a 1 to 10 dial); heat the cream mixture and stir rapidly for 2 to 4 minutes. The cream must reach a temperature of 160°F/71°C (see *note* at end of directions for the bain-marie method). This temperature ensures that any salmonellae are destroyed. The temperature may go up to 165.2°F/74°C at the end of the heating time. Because of the milk in the mixture and the indirect heat from the bain-marie's steam, the egg yolks heat more gently and evenly and can be raised over the normal curdle temperature of 164°F/73.3°C. With vigorous stirring, the egg yolks should not curdle; rather, they will bind the sauce or pudding.

To test that the cream has finished cooking, pull off heat and check the consistency: Turn a big wooden spoon over with the back of the spoon facing up, dip into the cream to coat the spoon's back, and blow onto the cream to see if it creates ripples, much like water droplets would make when splashed onto still water. If the cream ripples, it is done. Another test to check for doneness is to scoop a spoonful of cream onto a cold plate, let it cool for a minute, and then tilt the plate. The cream should hold a firm consistency, like that of yogurt. Drawing a wire whisk through the cream in the pot should leave ripples. Remember, the pudding or sauce will firm up more after cooling.

6. Pour the sauce or pudding into a cold bowl and cover right away with plastic wrap, pushing the plastic onto the surface of the mixture to prevent a skin from forming. Let cool completely in the refrigerator (see tip). Serve the pudding cold. For the sauce, heat to serve over fruit, strudel, cake, or chocolate pudding. Heat in a microwave (make sure to remove plastic wrap), saucepan, or bain-marie. Use low-medium heat. Keep a close watch and stir frequently if heating in the microwave; stir constantly if heating on the stovetop. The sauce warms up fast and can burn quickly.

~ TIP ~

Pour the cream into a porcelain bowl for quicker cooling.

Note: Heating eggs to an internal temperature of 160°F/71°C is the FDA's guideline for food safety. The American Egg Board also uses this internal temperature in their recipes. For more information, see fda.gov/food/buy-store-serve-safe-food/what-you-need-know-about-egg-safety.

TOPPINGS, FILLINGS, AND GARNISHES

Directions for Saucepan

1. Whisk the egg yolks in a small bowl. Set aside until step 4.

2. Measure out the cold milk and add the optional almond extract, if using. Mix ⅓ cup of the milk with the cornstarch in a small bowl; stir until the cornstarch is dissolved.

3. In a saucepan, stir together the rest of the milk, the heavy whipping cream (unwhipped), the salt, and the sugar. Add the cornstarch and milk mixture. Split the vanilla bean down the middle and scrape the pulp into the mixture or add the vanilla bean paste. Cook over medium heat while stirring with a large wooden spoon; set dial to 6 (on a 1 to 10 dial). Do not allow the mixture to boil. Keep stirring for about 10 minutes. At this point, the mixture will be hot to the touch; keep stirring for about 2 more minutes. The milk will start to thicken; stir more vigorously to prevent the cornstarch from clumping. Here you might want to switch to a wire whisk. If the mixture clumps too rapidly, take off heat and use a wire whisk vigorously to dissolve all clumps, then place back on the heat and continue cooking. After an additional 2 to 3 minutes, the mixture will get even thicker, and a wooden spoon or whisk, when drawn through the mixture, will reveal the bottom of the pan. From start to finish, this process will take about 15 to 20 minutes.

4. When the cream mixture is a satisfactory consistency, remove the saucepan from the heat. Stir the mixture for about 2 minutes, or longer if necessary, to cool down to below 150°F/65°C. Make sure the cream mixture is still hot but not steaming hot (below 150°F/65°C). The temperature is important when combining the cream mixture with the egg yolks; the yolks in cream mixtures should not be heated too quickly or the protein in the yolk separates and the cream will curdle. It is best to work with a fast-read kitchen thermometer. When a temperature below 150°F/65°C is achieved, scoop out 2 tablespoons of the cream mixture and blend it into the egg yolks. Next, scoop out ½ cup of the cream mixture and gradually add into the egg yolks while stirring. Add the egg yolk mixture back into the pot with the remaining cream. Stir with a quick, consistent motion to prevent the yolks from clumping. With this process, the yolks warm gradually and will not curdle.

Place the pot back onto the heat and set to 5 (on a 1 to 10 dial). Heat the mixture and stir rapidly for 2 to 4 minutes. The cream must reach a temperature of 160°F/71°C (see *note* at end of directions for the bain-marie method). This temperature ensures that any salmonellae are destroyed. The temperature may go up to 165.2°F/74°C at the end; make sure to continue vigorous stirring. With vigorous stirring, the egg yolks should not curdle; rather, they will bind the sauce or pudding. When in danger of excessive heat or burning the bottom, pull off heat and keep stirring. Reduce the heat, then place back on the burner and continue stirring.

VANILLA SAUCE AND PUDDING

To test that the cream has finished cooking, pull off heat and check the consistency: Turn a big wooden spoon over with the back of the spoon facing up, dip into the cream to coat the spoon's back, and blow onto the cream to see if it creates ripples, much like water droplets would make when splashed onto still water. If the cream ripples, it is done. Another test to check for doneness is to scoop a spoonful of cream onto a cold plate, let it cool for a minute, and then tilt the plate. The cream should hold a firm consistency, like that of yogurt. Drawing a wire whisk through the cream in the pot should leave ripples. Remember, the pudding or sauce will firm up more after cooling.

5. Pour the sauce or pudding into a cold bowl and cover right away with plastic wrap, pushing the plastic onto the surface of the mixture to prevent a skin from forming. Let cool completely in the refrigerator (see tip). Serve the pudding cold. For the sauce, heat to warm and serve over fruit, strudel, cake, or chocolate pudding. Reheat in a microwave (make sure to remove plastic wrap) or saucepan. Use low-medium heat. Keep a close watch and stir frequently if heating in the microwave; stir constantly if heating on the stovetop. The sauce warms up fast and can burn quickly.

~ TIP ~

Pour the cream into a porcelain bowl for quicker cooling.

CHOCOLATE SAUCE AND PUDDING

Homemade chocolate sauce and pudding with real chocolate taste much better than those from a bottle or box with preservatives and coloring. The preparation method and ingredients are the same for both the sauce and the pudding with only a difference in the amount of cornstarch. The sauce has less cornstarch because it is thinner than the pudding. We start by making a vanilla sauce or pudding and then incorporate the melted chocolate. The result is a smooth, velvety treat that will delight your family. The added chocolate means that less cornstarch is needed than in the Vanilla Sauce and Pudding recipe. The chocolate makes the consistency firmer.

Two preparation methods are given. The first method uses a bain-marie (double boiler) and is a reliable way to achieve a smooth, non-lumpy sauce or pudding without burning the milk. The second method uses a regular saucepan but be aware that the danger of burning the milk and getting lumpy sauce or pudding is higher with this method.

YIELD
2 ⅔ cups of sauce, or 2 ¼ cups of pudding (smaller yield because it thickens more than sauce)

SPECIAL TOOLS
Bain-marie or double boiler

Fast-read kitchen thermometer

Timer

Wooden spoon

Whisk

INGREDIENTS

FOR CHOCOLATE SAUCE

2 egg yolks, at room temperature

1 ½ cups milk, cold

1 teaspoon almond extract, optional

1 tablespoon cornstarch (see page 12)

½ cup heavy whipping cream

Dash of salt

½ cup sugar

1 vanilla bean, or 1 teaspoon vanilla paste

4 ounces 60% or 70% dark chocolate bar, or ⅔ cup Belgian 54% to 55% dark chocolate callets (for example, Callebaut No. 811)

FOR CHOCOLATE PUDDING

2 egg yolks, at room temperature

1 ½ cups milk, cold

1 teaspoon almond extract, optional

2 ½ tablespoons cornstarch (see page 12)

½ cup heavy whipping cream

Dash of salt

½ cup sugar

1 vanilla bean, or 1 teaspoon vanilla paste

4 ounces 60% or 70% dark chocolate bar, or ⅔ cup Belgian 54% to 55% dark chocolate callets (for example, Callebaut No. 811)

CHOCOLATE SAUCE AND PUDDING

Directions for Bain-Marie (Double Boiler)

1. Whisk the egg yolks in a small bowl. Set aside until step 5.

2. Measure out the cold milk and add the optional almond extract, if using. Mix ⅓ cup of the milk with the cornstarch in a small bowl; stir until the cornstarch is dissolved.

3. Pour water into the bottom of a bain-marie, just enough so the water does not touch the upper pot (about 1 inch to 1¼ inches full, depending on the size and space between pots). Place onto a burner and turn the heat to medium to high.

4. In the top pot of the bain-marie, stir together the rest of the milk, the heavy whipping cream (unwhipped), the salt, and the sugar. Add the cornstarch and milk mixture. Split the vanilla bean down the middle and scrape the pulp into the mixture or add the vanilla bean paste. Cook over medium to high heat while stirring for about 2 minutes. Remove the entire bain-marie from the heat. Turn the burner to medium so it cools down for step 5.

5. Place the bain-marie back on the burner over medium heat and continue cooking while stirring with a wooden spoon and/or wire whisk. Cook and stir for about 10 minutes more. At this point, the mixture will be hot to the touch; keep stirring for about 2 more minutes. The mixture will start to thicken; stir more vigorously to prevent the cornstarch from clumping. If the mixture clumps, take off heat and use a wire whisk vigorously to dissolve all clumps, then place back on heat and continue cooking. The mixture should thicken enough that a wooden spoon or whisk, when drawn through the mixture, will reveal the bottom of the pot. From start to finish, this process will take about 20 minutes.

When the cream mixture is a satisfactory consistency, turn off the heat and remove the bain-marie from the burner. Remove the top pot from the bottom; place a lid on the bottom pot to keep the water hot. Stir the mixture in the upper pot for about 2 minutes, or longer if necessary, to cool down to below 150°F/65°C. The temperature is important when combining the cream mixture with the egg yolks; the yolks in cream mixtures should not be heated too quickly or the protein in the yolk separates and the cream will curdle. It is best to work with a fast-read kitchen thermometer. When a temperature below 150°F/65°C is achieved, scoop out 2 tablespoons of the cream mixture and blend it into the egg yolks. Next, scoop out ½ cup of the cream mixture and gradually add into the egg yolks while stirring. Gradually add this egg yolk mixture into the bain-marie and combine with the remaining cream. Stir with a quick, consistent motion to prevent the yolks from clumping. The temperature will be around 135°F/57°C now. With this process, the yolks warm gradually and will not curdle.

Place the bain-marie's top pot back over the bottom pot holding the water. Set stovetop heat to 5 (on a 1 to 10 dial); heat the cream mixture and stir rapidly for 2 to 4 minutes. The cream

TOPPINGS, FILLINGS, AND GARNISHES

must reach a temperature of 160°F/71°C (see *note* at end of directions for the bain-marie method). This temperature ensures that any salmonellae are destroyed. The temperature may go up to 165.2°F/74°C at the end of the heating time. Because of the milk in the mixture and the indirect heat from the bain-marie's steam, the egg yolks heat more gently and evenly and can be raised over the normal curdle temperature of 164°F/73.3°C. With vigorous stirring, the egg yolks should not curdle; rather, they will bind the sauce or pudding.

To test that the cream has finished cooking, pull off heat and check the consistency: Turn a big wooden spoon over with the back of the spoon facing up, dip into the cream to coat the spoon's back, and blow onto the cream to see if it creates ripples, much like water droplets would make when splashed onto still water. If the cream ripples, it is done. Another test to check for doneness is to scoop a spoonful of cream onto a cold plate, let it cool for a minute, and then tilt the plate. The cream should hold a firm consistency, like that of yogurt. Drawing a wire whisk through the cream in the pot should leave ripples. Remember, the pudding or sauce will firm up more after cooling.

. . . .

Note: Heating eggs to an internal temperature of 160°F/71°C is the FDA's guideline for food safety. The American Egg Board also uses this internal temperature in their recipes. For more information, see fda.gov/food/buy-store-serve-safe-food/what-you-need-know-about-egg-safety.

6. Break up the chocolate into small pieces. In a glass measuring cup or microwave-safe container, heat the chocolate for 30 seconds, stir, and heat for 30 seconds more. Stir until all chocolate pieces are melted. Spoon some vanilla cream mixture into the melted chocolate and stir, then add to the rest of the vanilla cream. With a wire whisk, stir until all chocolate is incorporated and the mixture looks smooth.

7. Pour the sauce or pudding into a cold bowl and cover right away with plastic wrap, pushing the plastic onto the surface of the mixture to prevent a skin from forming. Let cool completely in the refrigerator (see tip). Serve the pudding cold. For the sauce, heat to warm and serve over cake, fresh berries for a light dessert, or vanilla pudding to offset the flavors as a special treat. Heat in a microwave (make sure to remove plastic wrap), saucepan, or bain-marie. Use low-medium heat. Keep a close watch and stir frequently if heating in the microwave; stir constantly if heating on the stovetop. The sauce warms up fast and can burn quickly.

~ TIP ~

Pour the cream into a porcelain bowl for quicker cooling.

CHOCOLATE SAUCE AND PUDDING

Directions for Saucepan

1. Whisk the egg yolks in a small bowl. Set aside until step 4.

2. Measure out the cold milk and add the optional almond extract, if using. Mix ⅓ cup of the milk with the cornstarch in a small bowl; stir until the cornstarch is dissolved.

3. In a saucepan, stir together the rest of the milk, the heavy whipping cream (unwhipped), the salt, and the sugar. Add the cornstarch and milk mixture. Split the vanilla bean down the middle and scrape the pulp into the mixture or add the vanilla bean paste. Cook over medium heat while stirring with a large wooden spoon; set dial to 6 (on a 1 to 10 dial). Do not allow the mixture to boil. Keep stirring for about 10 minutes. At this point, the mixture will be hot to the touch; keep stirring for about 2 more minutes. The milk will start to thicken; stir more vigorously to prevent the cornstarch from clumping. Here you might want to switch to a wire whisk. If the mixture clumps too rapidly, take off heat and use a wire whisk vigorously to dissolve all clumps, then place back on the heat and continue cooking. After an additional 2 to 3 minutes, the mixture will get even thicker, and a wooden spoon or whisk, when drawn through the mixture, will reveal the bottom of the pan. From start to finish, this process will take about 15 to 20 minutes.

4. When the cream mixture is a satisfactory consistency, remove the saucepan from the heat. Stir the mixture for about 2 minutes, or longer if necessary, to cool down to below 150°F/65°C. Make sure the cream mixture is still hot but not steaming hot (below 150°F/65°C). The temperature is important when combining the cream mixture with the egg yolks; the yolks in cream mixtures should not be heated too quickly or the protein in the yolk separates and the cream will curdle. It is best to work with a fast-read kitchen thermometer. When a temperature below 150°F/65°C is achieved, scoop out 2 tablespoons of the cream mixture and blend it into the egg yolks. Next, scoop out ½ cup of the cream mixture and gradually add into the egg yolks while stirring. Add the egg yolk mixture back into the pot with the remaining cream. Stir with a quick, consistent motion to prevent the yolks from clumping. With this process, the yolks warm gradually and will not curdle.

Place the pot back onto the heat and set to 5 (on a 1 to 10 dial). Heat the mixture and stir rapidly for 2 to 4 minutes. The cream must reach a temperature of 160°F/71°C (see *note* at end of directions for the bain-marie method). This temperature ensures that any salmonellae are destroyed. The temperature may go up to 165.2°F/74°C at the end of the heating time; make sure to continue vigorous stirring. With vigorous stirring, the egg yolks should not curdle; rather, they will bind the sauce or pudding. When in danger of excessive heat or burning the bottom, pull off heat

TOPPINGS, FILLINGS, AND GARNISHES

and keep stirring. Reduce the heat, then place back on the burner and continue stirring.

To test that the cream has finished cooking, pull off heat and check the consistency: Turn a big wooden spoon over with the back of the spoon facing up, dip into the cream to coat the spoon's back, and blow onto the cream to see if it creates ripples, much like water droplets would make when splashed onto still water. If the cream ripples, it is done. Another test to check for doneness is to scoop a spoonful of cream onto a cold plate, let it cool for a minute, and then tilt the plate. The cream should hold a firm consistency, like that of yogurt. Drawing a wire whisk through the cream in the pot should leave ripples. Remember, the pudding or sauce will firm up more after cooling.

5. Break up the chocolate into small pieces. In a glass measuring cup or microwave-safe container, heat the chocolate for 30 seconds, stir, and heat for 30 seconds more. Stir until all chocolate pieces are melted. Spoon some vanilla cream mixture into the melted chocolate and stir, then add to the rest of the vanilla cream. With a wire whisk, stir until all chocolate is incorporated and the mixture looks smooth.

6. Pour the sauce or pudding into a cold bowl and cover right away with plastic wrap, pushing the plastic onto the surface of the mixture to prevent a skin from forming. Let cool completely in the refrigerator (see tip). Serve the pudding cold. For the sauce, heat to serve over cake, fresh berries for a light dessert, or vanilla pudding to offset the flavors as a special treat. Heat in the microwave (make sure to remove plastic wrap) or a saucepan. Use low-medium heat. Keep a close watch and stir frequently if heating in the microwave; stir constantly if heating on the stovetop. The sauce warms up fast and can burn quickly.

~ TIP ~

Pour the cream into a porcelain bowl for quicker cooling.

LEMON, LILIKOʻI, OR CHOCOLATE BUTTERCREAM

This buttercream comes in very handy for layered sponge cakes, sponge cake rolls (jelly rolls), or even pound cakes that can be cut horizontally and layered. The recipe makes a lemon buttercream with a chocolate variation. For the chocolate variation, omit the lemon juice and lemon zest in step 3 and follow step 5 to incorporate the chocolate. The buttercream is easily adaptable to other flavors too. For example, there is an option to add fresh lilikoʻi (also called passion fruit) juice to the lemon buttercream. The lilikoʻi simply goes in with the lemon zest, and it creates a pleasing, delicate flavor. Regardless of the variation, this buttercream is not very sweet, so it will not overpower a cake or pie, and the only secret is patience in creaming the butter and whisking the eggs. Bakers will need to cream the butter and whisk the eggs for several minutes. Really get in there and enjoy yourself, especially with the whisking. Two hours before beginning the recipe, place the butter on the counter so that it has time to soften to room temperature (see *note 1* at end of recipe). The finished buttercream needs to chill for one and a half to two hours to cool to a firm but spreadable consistency. Plan your recipe accordingly. As an alternative to this lemon buttercream made in a bain-marie (double boiler), make the Easy Lemon Buttercream prepared with raw pasteurized egg yolks (see page 255).

YIELD
1 ½ cups of lemon or lilikoʻi buttercream, or 2 cups of chocolate buttercream

SPECIAL TOOLS
Bain-marie or double boiler

Fast-read kitchen thermometer

INGREDIENTS

LEMON OR LILIKOʻI BUTTERCREAM

14 tablespoons (1 ¾ sticks) unsalted butter, at room temperature and very soft (see *note 1* at end of recipe)

2 eggs, at room temperature

⅓ cup sugar

4 teaspoons lemon juice

1 whole vanilla bean (or at least ½ of a vanilla bean), split down the middle

Zest of 1 small lemon (about 2 teaspoons)

5 teaspoons fresh lilikoʻi (passion fruit) juice, optional (see *note 2* at end of recipe)

CHOCOLATE BUTTERCREAM

14 tablespoons (1 ¾ sticks) unsalted butter, at room temperature and very soft (see *note 1* at end of recipe)

2 eggs, at room temperature

⅓ cup sugar

1 whole vanilla bean (or at least ½ of a vanilla bean), split down the middle

¾ cup dark or semi-sweet chocolate chips or European chocolate bar (broken into pieces), 60% or 70% cocoa

TOPPINGS, FILLINGS, AND GARNISHES

DIRECTIONS

1. Cream the butter with an electric mixer on medium for 10 minutes, until smooth and fluffy. Set aside.

2. Fill the bottom of a bain-marie with about 1 to 2 inches of water and place on the stovetop over high heat. There should be enough water in the bottom that it will heat the pot above, but the water should not touch the pot above.

3. Whisk together the eggs, sugar, and lemon juice (omit lemon juice for chocolate buttercream) and pour into the top pot of the bain-marie. Scrape the pulp from the vanilla bean and add to the egg mixture. Whisk constantly throughout this step. Egg mixtures for cream should not be heated too quickly or the protein in the eggs separates and the cream will curdle. Bring water in the bottom pot to a simmer. Keep whisking the mixture, as if whipping egg whites, to dissolve the sugar and fluff up the eggs, about 5 to 6 minutes. Use a fast-read kitchen thermometer to watch the temperature as the mixture thickens while whisking; the egg mixture must reach a temperature of 160°F/71°C. This temperature ensures that any salmonellae are destroyed (see *note 3* at end of recipe). The temperature may go up to 165.2°F/74°C at the end. Keep whisking constantly and vigorously toward the end of the process as the egg mixture thickens. Without vigorous whisking, the bottom will start to set and clump. As soon as the mixture has thickened enough that the pot becomes visible when running a wooden spoon over the bottom, remove from heat. Add the lemon zest and optional lilikoʻi juice (omit both for chocolate buttercream) and continue whisking vigorously to get the mixture cool and even fluffier, about 2 minutes.

4. Once cooled to lukewarm, use a whisk to fold one-third of the creamed butter into the egg mixture. Continue with the rest of the butter, one-third at a time, until all is fully incorporated.

5. Optional step for chocolate buttercream: Melt the chocolate in a microwave or double boiler (see page 15 for technique). Pour the melted chocolate into a large porcelain bowl and stir to cool. The temperature should be as low as possible to avoid melting the buttercream but warm enough that the chocolate stays fluid and does not set up. With a whisk, incorporate the chocolate into the buttercream.

6. Refrigerate the buttercream for 1½ to 2 hours before using as a frosting or filling. The buttercream should be set and firm but still spreadable. If the buttercream has chilled too long and firmed up too much, set it on the counter to warm until it reaches a spreadable consistency; stir every so often to ensure even softening.

LEMON, LILIKOʻI, OR CHOCOLATE BUTTERCREAM

Note 1: Letting the butter soften slowly on the counter is better than microwaving or melting it in a pot, especially over high heat. Heating too fast may cause the butter to melt and the milk solids to separate; the butter will appear curdled. If overheated melted butter is used in the recipe, the eggs may not incorporate correctly, and the buttercream will look curdled and not smooth. (This would occur in step 4 or later.) If separation occurs at that stage, save the buttercream by adding 2 tablespoons of cornstarch and 2 egg yolks. Do so by placing ½ cup of the buttercream into a mixing bowl. Sift in the cornstarch and mix until smooth, then add the egg yolks and mix well. Add this mixture back into the rest of the buttercream. In the bain-marie, stir the buttercream over medium heat until it thickens and the bottom of the pot shows when dragging a wooden spoon across. Remove from heat and proceed with cooling.

Note 2: For fresh lilikoʻi (passion fruit) juice, cut the fruit in half and push the pulp through a strainer to separate seeds; discard the seeds. Depending on size, one fruit will yield between 1 to 2 tablespoons of juice. Fresh lilikoʻi juice is very tart; taste it and add sugar, a tablespoon at a time, before adding the juice to the mixture. For a video demonstration of making lilikoʻi juice, see vimeo.com/showcase/10470112.

VIDEO SHOWCASE
Fillings and Garnishes
vimeo.com/showcase/10470112

Note 3: Heating eggs to an internal temperature of 160°F/71°C is the FDA's guideline for food safety. The American Egg Board also uses this internal temperature in their recipes. For more information, see fda.gov/food/buy-store-serve-safe-food/what-you-need-know-about-egg-safety.

EASY LEMON BUTTERCREAM

This recipe is a simple variation on buttercream, using pasteurized raw egg yolks. The buttercream needs to chill for two to three hours. Plan to make it a few hours before baking the cake that will be frosted or filled. Alternatively, make the buttercream a day ahead. The next day, let the buttercream soften on the counter for an hour to warm to a spreadable consistency before applying to the cake. Use good-quality 10x (sifted 10 times) powdered sugar for excellent and consistent results (see page 12).

YIELD
about 1 ½ cups

INGREDIENTS

12 tablespoons (1 ½ sticks) unsalted butter, at room temperature

1 ¼ cups powdered sugar

3 egg yolks from pasteurized eggs, at room temperature

2 tablespoons lemon juice

Zest of 1 small lemon (about 2 teaspoons)

DIRECTIONS

1. Cream the butter with an electric mixer for 3 minutes, until fluffy. Slowly sift in the powdered sugar. Whip the butter and sugar for 2 minutes on medium to high speed. Add the pasteurized egg yolks, lemon juice, and lemon zest and continue whipping until all ingredients are fully incorporated and the buttercream is uniform in color and fluffy in texture.

2. Refrigerate the buttercream for 2 to 3 hours before using as a frosting or filling. The buttercream should be set and firm but still spreadable. If the buttercream has chilled too long and firmed up too much, set it on the counter to warm until it reaches a spreadable consistency; stir every so often to ensure even softening.

CREAM CHEESE FROSTING

Adapt this frosting to bring more or less sweetness as desired. Restrain the amount of powdered sugar to highlight the tangy cream cheese. On the other hand, be liberal with the sugar to enhance the sweetness and downplay the cream cheese's savory side. Use as a topping for muffins and breads, or as a filling and frosting for cakes and quick (sweet) breads such as carrot cake, zucchini bread, and pumpkin bread. The frosting should be thick enough that it does not run down the sides of the bread or cake. Before adding more powdered sugar to thicken a runny frosting, first determine the sweetness of the powdered sugar brand being used. Different brands have varying cornstarch to powdered sugar ratios. Some powdered sugars are less sweet than others. With most powdered sugar brands, the cornstarch to powdered sugar ratio is fine for sweetness. Use good-quality 10x (sifted 10 times) powdered sugar for excellent and consistent results (see page 12).

YIELD
2 ½ cups of frosting

DIRECTIONS

1. Cream the butter in a mixer. Add the soft cream cheese and whip to combine. After the butter and cream cheese are blended, add the vanilla and the sifted powdered sugar. Mix to achieve a thick but spreadable consistency.

2. Check the consistency. If it is too thin, add more powdered sugar or chill for 30 minutes to 1 hour. If it is too thick, add more cream cheese, starting with ½ to 1 ounce at a time.

INGREDIENTS

8 tablespoons (1 stick) unsalted butter, at room temperature

8 ounces cream cheese (⅓ less fat or regular), at room temperature

3 teaspoons vanilla extract, or pulp of ½ of a vanilla bean

16 ounces powdered sugar (about 3 ½ to 4 cups), sifted

ROYAL ICING

This icing is glossy and sticky. Icing can be thickened by simply adding more powdered sugar. It is perfect for spreading over *schnecken* (cinnamon rolls), decorating cookies, or smoothing onto quick (sweet) breads like banana bread. If you prefer not to use the liquid egg whites whipped with cream of tartar, meringue powder is commercially available as an alternative. It consists of dried egg white with some added sugar and can be whipped up with water to create icing. If using meringue powder, follow the instructions on the packaging. (I have good success with Wilton brand meringue powder; substitute two teaspoons of meringue powder and two tablespoons of water per egg white.) For the powdered sugar, taste for sweetness before beginning. With most powdered sugar brands, the cornstarch to powdered sugar ratio is fine for sweetness. Use good-quality 10x (sifted 10 times) powdered sugar for excellent and consistent results (see page 12).

YIELD
1 very full cup of icing

INGREDIENTS

2 ⅓ cups sifted powdered sugar

4 tablespoons pasteurized liquid egg whites, at room temperature (equals whites from 2 large eggs)

¼ teaspoon cream of tartar

1 tablespoon lemon juice

DIRECTIONS

1. Sift the powdered sugar before measuring. Measure and set aside.

2. Whip the egg whites with the cream of tartar until soft peaks form. When the whisk is lifted and turned over, the peak should be as stiff as possible. Pasteurized egg white does not whip up to the same firm stiffness as unpasteurized egg white. Whipped pasteurized egg white should hold its shape, but the top will flop over like a very droopy elf's hat.

3. Add the sifted powdered sugar to the egg whites and keep beating until a soft, shiny icing forms.

4. Add the lemon juice and mix briefly.

5. Check the consistency. If it is too thin, add more powdered sugar or chill for 30 minutes to 1 hour. If it is too thick, add more lemon juice, just a few drops at a time.

FRUIT GLAZE

This glaze is the perfect finish for pies and cakes that are topped with fresh fruit. Spread some of the glaze over a bare cake or empty pie shell to prevent it from growing soggy, then cover with fruit and drizzle the rest of the glaze on top. Be creative and use the glaze with other types of cakes and pies as well. Any kind of fruit juice will work to make a glaze. Experiment to find the perfect accompaniment for your recipe. An interesting juice flavor in the glaze is an easy way to add extra dimension. For desserts with light-colored fruit, use white grape or apple juice to make a light glaze. For desserts with red-colored fruit, make the glaze with red-colored fruit juices such as cherry or raspberry. Dark juice works well with dark fruit like blackberries. For any type of juice, it is important to use potato starch and not cornstarch. The potato starch will dissolve into a translucent glaze as it cooks, but the cornstarch will have an opaque look.

YIELD
1 ½ cups of glaze

INGREDIENTS

1 ½ cups juice, such as cherry or raspberry (for red glazes), or apple or white grape (for clear glazes)

2 tablespoons potato starch

¼ cup sugar

DIRECTIONS

In a small bowl, whisk ⅓ cup of the juice with the potato starch and sugar until dissolved. Pour the remaining juice into a medium-sized saucepan set over medium-high heat. Add the potato starch mixture. Stirring constantly, bring to a boil. Turn down the heat and continue to stir, more vigorously now, until the glaze starts to thicken (see tip 1). Make sure to scrape the bottom of the saucepan to avoid sticking and burning. The glaze is ready when a wooden spoon pulled along the bottom of the saucepan leaves a trail. It should make a slurping sound when stirred, and it will be slightly thicker than maple syrup (see tip 2). Finished glaze should pour or spoon over pies and cakes in a steady, thick stream while hot. Work quickly to spread or spoon hot glaze before it sets.

~ TIP 1 ~

The glaze can bubble over or stick to the saucepan's bottom very quickly, so do not leave unattended at any time.

~ TIP 2 ~

As a helpful test to gauge the proper consistency, drizzle a few drops of glaze onto a cold plate and tilt the plate. The glaze should gel up slightly rather than run loosely over the plate.

RASPBERRY SAUCE

This sauce is bright, tart, and sweet. The black currant liqueur is highly recommended. It intensifies the raspberry's natural flavor. The directions add the liqueur after the sauce is strained in step 2; alternatively, it can be added with the other ingredients in step 1 to give the alcohol extra time to cook out. *Kirsch* (cherry), raspberry, or pear brandy are worth experimenting with and lend aromatic flavors as well. This sauce is for drizzling over a cake or pie in a few decorative strokes or for dolloping next to an individual slice when serving. It is not a sauce for spreading to cover an entire cake.

YIELD
1 ½ cups of sauce

INGREDIENTS

4 cups frozen raspberries (about 16 ounces)

1 ⅓ cups sugar

2 tablespoons lemon juice

2 teaspoons black currant liqueur

DIRECTIONS

1. Combine the raspberries, sugar, and lemon juice in a medium saucepan. Stir over high heat until the mixture begins to bubble, then reduce to medium-high. Stir until the raspberries have dissolved into juice. After about 3 minutes, the sauce develops a consistency like syrup and should start to pull away from the bottom of the saucepan when stirred. Keep stirring, a little faster now, and let bubble for about 5 more minutes, until seeds separate from the fruit (see tip).

~ TIP ~

As a helpful test to gauge the proper consistency, drizzle a few drops of glaze onto a cold plate and tilt the plate. The glaze should gel up slightly rather than run loosely over the plate.

2. Place a large sifter or strainer over a ceramic bowl. Pour in the sauce and use a large spoon to press and strain, leaving the seeds behind. Using a spatula, scrape off sauce that clings to the underside of the sifter or strainer. Pour the sauce back into the pot and add the liqueur. Cook for 1 more minute to let the alcohol evaporate. Let cool in a ceramic bowl for 5 minutes; stir once to avoid skin build up, then cover with plastic wrap, pushing the plastic onto the sauce's surface to prevent a thick layer of skin from forming. Let cool to room temperature before drizzling onto cake or pastry.

SUGAR GLAZE

This recipe provides an extremely simple glaze. Spread it over any pastry to provide a sweet finish. It is also good for brushing over cookies. Increase the lemon taste as desired by using all lemon juice instead of the rum or water. Decrease the lemon taste by substituting water for some of the lemon juice. Other liquids can be used or combined, such as passion fruit juice in place of some or all of the lemon juice or water. If a thinner glaze is desired, add more liquid, one-fourth to one-half teaspoon at a time. Just a little liquid will change the consistency considerably. Powdered sugar has added starch, and different brands of powdered sugar may need more or less liquid depending on the amount of starch they contain. Powdered sugar brands also vary in sweetness. With most brands, the cornstarch to powdered sugar ratio is fine for sweetness. Use good-quality 10x (sifted 10 times) powdered sugar for excellent and consistent results (see page 12).

YIELD
about ½ cup of glaze

INGREDIENTS

1 cup powdered sugar (see *note* at end of recipe)

7 teaspoons lemon juice

7 teaspoons rum or water, or 3 ½ teaspoons of each

DIRECTIONS

1. Whisk all ingredients. If using lemon juice, adjust to taste. Substitute water if less lemon taste is preferred.

2. Check the consistency. Feel at liberty to thin or thicken the glaze to suit your needs. If too thin, add more powdered sugar. If too thick, add drops of water or lemon juice, a little at a time. Powdered sugar will thin surprisingly fast with just a little liquid. Some bakers like a thin, see-through glaze with a hint of sugar; some bakers add more sugar to achieve a thick coating on the pastry.

Note: To make a smaller batch of glaze with only ½ cup sugar, the ratio of liquid will be less for the same consistency. Use the following measurements:

½ cup powdered sugar

2 to 2 ⅛ teaspoons lemon juice

2 to 2 ⅛ teaspoons rum or water

EASY CHOCOLATE GLAZE

The two ingredients in this recipe melt into a reliable glaze for any baked good. Pour over cakes, drizzle onto pancakes, dunk cookies into it—the possibilities abound. The chocolate glaze's texture will vary with the amount of time that passes between pouring the glaze over the pastry and serving. If a warm and loose glaze is preferred, prepare and pour over the pastry close to serving time, just before if possible. As time passes and the glaze cools, the texture will become firmer and denser. Prepare the glaze in either a microwave or a double boiler (or bain-marie). The recipe includes directions for both methods.

YIELD
1 cup of glaze

INGREDIENTS

1 cup dark chocolate chips (60% to 70% cocoa) or dark European chocolate bar broken into small pieces (see page 11)

2 tablespoons coconut oil

DIRECTIONS

For Microwave

Microwave the coconut oil in a small microwave-safe glass or cup for 25 seconds. Set aside. Place the chocolate chips into a microwave-safe bowl or glass measuring cup. Microwave for 40 seconds. Stop and stir. Heat for another 30 to 40 seconds. Some pieces will remain, but they will dissolve while stirring. The chocolate is done when it stirs easily and has a smooth consistency. Chocolate will not be usable if it overheats and seizes (balls up). Start with the lower heating time and increase if necessary. Depending on the microwave, time can vary by 10 seconds. Ensure the coconut oil and melted chocolate are about the same temperature before stirring the coconut oil into the chocolate; this ensures the chocolate stays smooth and liquid.

For Double Boiler (or Bain-Marie)

Fill the bottom of a double boiler with about 1 to 2 inches of water. The water should not touch the bottom of the upper pot. Bring water to a simmer. Turn back heat to medium-low or low. Add the chocolate and coconut oil into the top pot. Watch closely to make sure the chocolate does not seize (ball up) and stir regularly to achieve the smooth consistency. Remove from heat sooner rather than later. A few small lumps may remain, but they will melt easily while stirring the chocolate off the heat. Chocolate will seize if water splashes in from the double boiler. Take care not to get any water into the chocolate.

CHOCOLATE MIRROR GLAZE

Mirror glazes get their name from their glossy shine. When done properly, these glazes throw back a reflection. In this recipe, the sunflower liquid lecithin is essential for the shine, so do not omit it if you are after a lustrous sheen. This glaze makes a dazzling finish on frozen desserts and ice cream, but do not refrigerate the glazed cake. Refrigeration makes the glaze dull looking. This recipe offers an option to use the glaze as both a filling and a top covering. If using as both a filling and covering, cut the cake horizontally into two layers. Place each cake on a flat surface (supportive cardboard round cake circles work well and are available online) and freeze for thirty minutes to an hour to have the cake surfaces cold. Fifteen minutes before serving, fill and pour the glaze over the cake.

INGREDIENTS

FOR 1 CUP OF GLAZE (enough to cover a 10-inch cake)

⅓ cup water

⅓ cup sugar

166 grams (6 ounces) 60% to 70% cocoa chocolate bar (broken into pieces) (see page 11)

½ teaspoon sunflower liquid lecithin

⅛ cup heavy cream

FOR 1 ½ CUPS GLAZE (enough for both filling and covering a 10-inch cake)

½ cup water

½ cup sugar

250 grams (9 ounces) 60% to 70% cocoa chocolate bar (broken into pieces) (see page 11)

¾ teaspoon sunflower liquid lecithin

¼ cup heavy cream

DIRECTIONS

1. Add the water and sugar into a saucepan. Heat over medium-high and stir until sugar is dissolved. Reduce heat and let simmer for 5 more minutes. Dip the end of a wooden skewer into the syrup; the syrup should be thick enough to coat the skewer. Take off heat and let sit for 2 minutes.

2. As the syrup sits, melt the chocolate in a double boiler (or bain-marie).

3. Keep heat for chocolate on low. It is important that the melted chocolate and the syrup are close to the same temperature (see tip). Pour the syrup into the chocolate all at once. Stir quickly until smooth. Then drizzle in the sunflower liquid lecithin and stir once more to incorporate.

~ TIP ~

The melted chocolate will thicken if the syrup is colder than the chocolate. Have both at about the same temperature for smooth mixing.

4. Heat the cream in a separate saucepan over medium-low heat until it barely starts to bubble.

5. Remove from heat and add one-third of the cream into the chocolate mixture; stir to blend. Add the remaining cream; stir until smooth and blended.

TEMPERED CHOCOLATE GLAZE

The only ingredient needed to make a tempered chocolate glaze is couverture chocolate. Couverture is made from dark or bittersweet chocolate. It has a higher cocoa butter content but is not necessarily higher in cocoa. Choose couverture from a high-quality brand to help the success of the glaze. This recipe offers a traditional tempering method of melting the chocolate over low heat, cooling in a water bath, and then briefly heating again, all while monitoring the temperature with a fast-read thermometer. Extra caution has to be taken to prevent accidental water drops from falling into the chocolate or the chocolate will seize (ball up) and be useless. As a precaution, wipe the bottom of the pot when lifting out of the water. Also take care to watch the thermometer closely and adhere to the temperature ranges in each step. Tempered chocolate glaze makes a thin and snappy coating.

YIELD
1 ¾ to 2 cups of glaze, enough to cover a cake's top and sides

SPECIAL TOOLS
Double boiler or bain-marie

Fast-read kitchen thermometer

Large bowl of cold water at the ready

INGREDIENTS
9 ounces dark couverture chocolate (about 1 ¾ cups), high-quality brand recommended, for example, Belgian 54% to 55% dark chocolate callets (see page 11)

DIRECTIONS

1. Prepare a cold water bath by filling a large bowl with cold water. Set aside until step 3.

2. Fill the bottom of a double boiler with water, just enough so the water doesn't touch the upper pot. Place the double boiler onto a burner and turn the heat to low to medium to a steady simmer. Place the chocolate pieces into the top pot. Make sure no droplets of water splash into the chocolate during the process, or the chocolate will seize up and become unusable. Stir constantly as the chocolate melts until it reaches 38°C to 46°C (100.4°F to 114.8°F).

3. Once the chocolate is smooth and liquified, remove the entire double boiler from heat. Lift the upper pot off the bottom pot carefully so as not to get any water drops into the chocolate. Place a lid on the bottom pot to keep the water warm. Place the pot containing the chocolate into the cold water bath and keep stirring. Take care not to let any water splash into the chocolate (see tip). Stir the chocolate rapidly. The fast motion will cool the chocolate and also upset the chocolate's cocoa butter crystals and help them reorganize to make a smoother glaze. As stirring continues and the chocolate cools, it will start to thicken a bit and have a drag. Keep stirring until the chocolate has come down to 27°C to 28°C (80.6°F to 82.4°F).

TEMPERED CHOCOLATE GLAZE

~ TIP ~

It helps to wipe away any condensation or drops of water from the top and sides of the bath bowl before transferring the pot with the chocolate. That way, water will not get on the spoon or hands and drip into the chocolate.

4. This step may only take 5 seconds depending on the temperature of the water in the double boiler, so be on your toes. Remove the lid from the bottom pot and place back over low to medium heat to a steady simmer. Place the pot containing the chocolate back over the bottom pot. Allow the chocolate to rise to 31°C to 32°C (87.8°F to 89.6°F). Make sure the temperature does not go above 32°C (89.6 °F). If it does, you will have to start over. Watch for fat streaks in the chocolate; if any appear, reduce the heat some and stir until they are gone.

5. Pour the chocolate over the cake for glazing. Make sure the cake is placed on a cooling rack with a cookie sheet or a large plate underneath to catch the excess chocolate.

TEMPERED CHOCOLATE GLAZE THE EASY WAY

The Tempered Chocolate Glaze recipe before this one gives a traditional method of tempering by melting, cooling, and then reheating the chocolate, all while using a thermometer to watch the temperature. This recipe provides an alternate preparation with cocoa butter wafers. There will still be heating and cooling of the chocolate, which are necessary for tempering chocolate; however, this recipe uses timing instead of a thermometer. Choose high-quality products to help the success of the glaze. The chocolate chips should be Belgian dark chocolate with 54% to 55% cocoa solids. The wafers should be organic cocoa butter. Tempered chocolate glaze makes a thin and snappy coating.

YIELD
about 1 ¾ to 2 cups, enough to cover a cake's top and sides

SPECIAL TOOLS
Double boiler or bain-marie

Timer

Offset metal icing spatula

INGREDIENTS
9 ounces dark couverture chocolate (about 1 ¾ cups), high-quality brand recommended, for example, Belgian 54% to 55% dark chocolate callets (see page 11)

1 ounce organic cocoa butter wafers

DIRECTIONS

1. Fill the bottom of a double boiler with water, just enough so the water doesn't touch the upper pot. Place onto a burner and bring water to a simmer, then reduce to low heat.

2. Place the chocolate pieces into the top pot. Make sure no droplets of water splash into the chocolate during the process, or the chocolate will seize up and become unusable. Keep the water temperature around simmering or just below (about medium heat, start with dial on 6 then turn down to 4 on a 1 to 10 dial). Stir constantly as the chocolate melts, about 2 to 3 minutes; the time depends on the heat. Once melted, reduce heat some and stir an additional 2 to 3 minutes.

3. Once the chocolate is smooth and liquified, remove the entire double boiler from heat. Lift the upper pot off the bottom pot carefully so as not to get any water drops into the chocolate. Place a lid on the bottom pot to keep the water warm. In the top pot, stir the chocolate rapidly. The fast motion will cool the chocolate and also upset the chocolate's cocoa butter crystals and help them reorganize to make a smoother glaze. As stirring continues and the chocolate cools, it will start to have a drag and thicken a bit. Keep stirring for approximately 3 minutes, until the chocolate starts to firm up visibly. Test the chocolate by dragging a spoon through

TEMPERED CHOCOLATE GLAZE THE EASY WAY

it. The spoon should leave a trail, making the bottom of the pot visible for a second or so before the chocolate slides back into place.

4. Place the top pot back over the bottom and, on medium heat (dial on 5 to 6), bring the water back to a simmer. Once back to a low simmer, add the cocoa butter wafers and keep stirring at a medium fast pace until they melt. Watch for fat streaks; if any appear, reduce the heat some and keep stirring until they are gone, about 2½ minutes. Remove from heat.

5. Stir the chocolate off heat to cool further and achieve a smooth flowing consistency. Pour the chocolate over the cake for glazing (see *note* at end of recipe). Make sure the cake is placed on a cooling rack with a cookie sheet, parchment paper, or a large plate underneath to catch the excess chocolate.

. . . .

Note: When covering a cake with this chocolate, pour the glaze onto the middle, circling over the top toward the edge. Stop short of the edge to keep chocolate from running down the sides randomly. To control the flow of the chocolate, grip the cooling rack and use your thumbs and the edge of your hands to secure the cake; tilt and roll the rack so the glaze can run over the cake's top and drip down the sides. Use an offset metal icing spatula to spread the glaze evenly around the sides only; avoid touching the cake's top.

CARAMELIZED ALMONDS

Caramelized almonds can be prepared days ahead of time and stored in a cool place. Crush them up and use in a cake batter for more flavor and a surprise of crunchiness when savoring the cake. To use as a garnish, press the crushed caramelized nuts around the circumference of frosted or glazed cakes, making for an extra treat in the last bite. This recipe uses slivered almonds, but hazelnuts are also very good; hazelnuts need to be chopped into small pieces with a blender or by hand first. Make sure to use a large frying pan when preparing the caramel, even though the amount of sugar is small. There needs to be enough space to spread out the almonds in the caramel. If they are crowded, they will not roast and brown. For a video demonstration of making caramelized almonds, see vimeo.com/showcase/10470112.

VIDEO SHOWCASE
Fillings and Garnishes
vimeo.com/showcase/10470112

YIELD
¾ cup of crushed caramelized almonds

INGREDIENTS

¼ cup sugar

⅛ teaspoon salt, optional

½ cup slivered almonds

1 tablespoon unsalted butter, at room temperature and soft

DIRECTIONS

1. In a large frying pan, spread and melt the sugar (also add in the optional salt, if using): Select the appropriately sized burner to match the pan size and set the stovetop dial to 4 to 6 (on a 1 to 10 dial). Every stovetop is different, so adjust heat accordingly throughout this step.

After 4 to 5 minutes, the sugar will start to melt and liquify. A few puddles will begin to form, mostly in the middle of the pan. When that happens, gently push the outside sugar inward so that the sugar melts evenly. Use a heat-resistant spatula to scrape down the sides of the pan efficiently. Stirring may create lumps. Flatten these lumps with the spatula, let them melt, and then stir as more of the sugar liquifies. Once the sugar has liquified completely, keep stirring until the liquid turns an amber color, about 1 to 2 more minutes (see tip). Timing is crucial at this stage so the caramel does not become bitter. If smoke appears during the browning process, move the pan off the burner and examine the color. Reduce heat and brown more if needed. When a dark amber color is achieved, pull the pan from the burner. Keep the burner on but reduce heat to 3 on the dial. Allow the burner to cool down while continuing to work in the pan off the heat.

CARAMELIZED ALMONDS

~ TIP ~

One important detail to know is that however brown the sugar is before the butter goes in, that is the color the caramel will stay. Do not add the butter while the sugar is still very light. Doing so will produce a pale caramel.

With the pan off the heat, stir in the soft butter. Add the slivered almonds and stir until all almonds are coated. Place pan back on heat; the dial should still be at 3. Stir until all almonds are roasted and a light brown color, about 1½ minutes. Spread out onto a plate and let cool.

2. When thoroughly cooled, crush the almonds into small pieces by placing them into a sandwich bag, sealing the bag with little air remaining, and using a rolling pin to smash them.

3. Add these delicate almonds into cake batter before baking or use them to decorate the edge of glazed and frosted cakes. To apply as decoration, take small handfuls and press into and around the cake. It helps to tilt the cake slightly and to use a cake spatula to lift dropped nuts and push them back into place.

ACKNOWLEDGMENTS

A big thank you to my husband and children for their positivity and support throughout writing and creating this book.

To my sons, Derek and Jared, who thoroughly enjoyed the cakes I baked while they were growing up. They have grown into beautiful and lovely young men. I am thankful for their encouragement to finish my baking book so they can bake what they are missing in their own kitchens. I heard you when you said: "Mom, please finish the book! There is nothing out there that I can buy like your desserts." Thank you to Jared for the continuous support and baking my desserts to share with friends. Inevitably, he was asked to bake a cake for an engagement party, which he happily did. He inspired many of his generation to learn how to bake. Thank you, Derek, for loving the sweets I bake without flour and reminding me that there are other people who enjoy flourless baked goods. Thank you to Derek's wife, Linh, who helped me bake on their visits to Hawaii and is an awesome cookie decorator.

To my loving husband, Jason, the world's best dessert taste tester, who took his job very seriously and says his delicate palate and sound suggestions were a most essential and important part of the book. Thank you for the patience and support throughout my work on writing this book, baking for days, and for understanding my need for space and quiet in the kitchen so my creativity could blossom.

A big thank you and heartfelt appreciation to my mother, grandmother, and aunt, my first baking teachers.

To my late grandmother: Oma could make the best sweet yeast sheet crumb cake. When asked how she did it, she would exclaim: "All from my wrist!"

My mother carries on with the baking tradition and also is especially fond of yeast crumb cake with fruit. She is now teaching her grandchildren how to bake. She taught me the basics and how to bake with flavorful fruit and lightness in pound cakes. Being around her

ACKNOWLEDGMENTS

when she baked was always exciting, and watching her put her own twist into a recipe inspired me to not be afraid to create my own.

To my Aunt Käthi: Her experiments with new recipes and invitations for me to try them with her were my inspiration to bake cream-filled layer tortes.

I am also thankful for our many family gatherings when all the women brought their creations to our large table. It was a smorgasbord of desserts and so hard to pick which one to eat first because they all tasted so incredible.

I especially want to thank my ghostwriter and editor, Rebecca Morris, who stuck with me through thick and thin and ups and downs. This book would not have been possible without her. Rebecca's professionalism, support, and expertise were unequivocal. I remember when I was about two-thirds through writing this book and I experienced a doubting phase. Should I even finish this book? Rebecca quickly told me that it is very common for writers to go through this phase and to keep going. Rebecca helped shape this book with her attention to detail and ability to condense my instructions and explanations into a shorter and precise form while not losing important details. She helped me patiently with editing and revisions for more than five years and baked almost all the recipes because she wanted to understand the process. A big thank you to her extended family and friends who graciously tested desserts and did a marvelous job baking them.

And a special thank you to my close friends who also tested my recipes. Cheers to my friends who live close by and helped me eat the many test cakes and always loved them, even though I thought some could be better and had to remake them, inevitably asking for their help with eating another cake, which only resulted in delightfulness.

I wish to thank Jennifer Jas for her suggestions during the proofreading and editing. Thank you for doing such a thorough job. I am also thankful to 1106 Design LLC for the thorough and excellent indexing. Much appreciation goes to my book designer, Michelle M. White, who took great care in the recipe layout and designing the cover to represent the book's interior.

BAKING UTENSILS

1. Cake decorating icing spatulas
2. Apple coring knife
3. Bread knife
4. Flexible silicone whisk (works well for beating egg whites) and metal whisks
5. Chocolate rasp
6. Fast-read thermometer
7. Mixing bowls, small to large sizes
8. Decorating bag and piping tips
9. Set of measuring cups
10. Fine mesh sifter/strainer
11. Spatulas of varying strength and size
12. Set of measuring spoons
13. Metal dough scraper/cutter and plastic dough scraper
14. Lemon or orange zester
15. Cooling rack
16. Bamboo rolling pin
17. Pastry brushes
18. Cookie dough scoop
19. Cookie cutters
20. Pie lattice cutter
21. *Spekulatius* cookie mold

BAKING PANS

22. Cookie sheet without rim, 16 x 12 inches
23. Copper tarte Tatin pan, lined with stainless steel, 9.5 inches
24. Carbon-coated steel pie pan with removeable bottom, 10 inches
25. *Kuchenretter*, or large cake lifter/spatula, with stenciled out hearts for when dusting cake with powdered sugar
26. Aluminum pan with removable bottom, used for cheesecake and other cakes with long baking times, 10 inches
27. Copper bowl for whipping egg whites
28. Cookie sheets with rims, 17 x 12 inches, 15 x 10 inches, 12 x 9 inches
29. German Fresh Fruit Tart pan with moat creating a rim when crust is turned over, 11.5 inches (used in Volume II)
30. Ceramic pie dish, 10 inches
31. Carbon-coated steel springform pan, 10 inches

INDEX

A

Almond Hazelnut Mini Tarts, 85–88
Almond or Hazelnut Crust, 109–111
almond paste, 11
Almond Paste Crescents, 121–124
almonds
    Almond Hazelnut Mini Tarts, 85–88
    Almond or Hazelnut Crust, 109–111
    Almond Paste Crescents, 121–124
    Apricot Almond Cream Tart, 77–80
    blanching, 13–14
    Caramelized Almonds, 267–268
    Pear Frangipane Tart, 72–76
    Raspberry Almond Tart, 81–84
    Vanillekipferl (Vanilla Almond Crescents), 125–127
Apfelstrudel (Apple Strudel), 102–108
apple
    Apfelstrudel (Apple Strudel), 102–108
    Apple Crumb Pie, 25–28
    Apple Pie, 33–37
    Covered Apple Pie, 29–32
    Tarte Tatin, 94–101
Apple Crumb Pie, 25–28
Apple Pie, 33–37
apricot
    Apricot Almond Cream Tart, 77–80
    Apricot Nut Cookies, 157–159
    Ricotta Cheesecake, 56–59
Apricot Almond Cream Tart, 77–80
Apricot Nut Cookies, 157–159

B

bains-marie, 241
baking pans
    illustration, 271
    for Mürbeteig, 22–23
    properties of various kinds, 10
    for sponge cake-based tortes, 177–178
baking powder, 11
Black Forest Torte, 225–232
blanching almonds, 13–14
brownies
    Candied Ginger Brownies, 143–145
    Coffee Liqueur Brownies, 146–148
    Nut Brownies, 149–151
butter, how to cut, 21
Butter Cookies, 140–142

C

cakes
    Black Forest Torte, 225–232
    Chocolate Irish Cream Cake, 233–237
    Chocolate Mousse Cake, 190–197
    Hazelnut Sponge Cake, 198–207
    Liliko'i Cheesecake, 64–68
    Mocha Sponge Cake Roll, 184–189
    Pumpkin Cheesecake, 69–71
    Quark Cream Torte with Mandarins, 213–217
    Ricotta Cheesecake, 56–59
    Sponge Cake Roll with Lemon Buttercream, 180–183
    Traditional German Cheesecake with Quark, 60–63
Candied Ginger Brownies, 143–145
Caramelized Almonds, 267–268
cheesecake
    Liliko'i Cheesecake, 64–68
    Pumpkin Cheesecake, 69–71
    Ricotta Cheesecake, 56–59
    Traditional German Cheesecake with Quark, 60–63
Cherry Turnovers, 112–115
chocolate
    about, 11–12
    Almond Paste Crescents, 121–124
    Black Forest Torte, 225–232
    Candied Ginger Brownies, 143–145
    Chocolate Buttercream, 252–254
    Chocolate Irish Cream Cake, 233–237
    Chocolate Mirror Glaze, 262
    Chocolate Mousse Cake, 190–197
    Chocolate Sauce and Pudding, 247–251
    Coffee Liqueur Brownies, 146–148
    Easy Chocolate Glaze, 261
    melting, 15–16
    Mocha Sponge Cake Roll, 184–189
    Nut Brownies, 149–151
    Tempered Chocolate Glaze, 263–264
    Tempered Chocolate Glaze the Easy Way, 265–266
Chocolate Buttercream, 252–254
Chocolate Irish Cream Cake, 233–237
Chocolate Mirror Glaze, 262
Chocolate Mousse Cake, 190–197
Chocolate Sauce and Pudding, 247–251
Cinnamon Stars, 128–131
Coconut Macaroons, 132–133

coffee
    Coffee Liqueur Brownies, 146–148
    Mocha Sponge Cake Roll, 184–189
    Tiramisu, 218–224
Coffee Liqueur Brownies, 146–148
cookie sheets, 119
cookies
    about, 117–118
    Almond Paste Crescents, 121–124
    Apricot Nut Cookies, 157–159
    baking in batches, 119
    baking times, temperatures for, 118–119
    Butter Cookies, 140–142
    Candied Ginger Brownies, 143–145
    Cinnamon Stars, 128–131
    Coconut Macaroons, 132–133
    Coffee Liqueur Brownies, 146–148
    cookie sheets and, 119
    flour measurements for recipes, 118
    Gingerbread House, 160–173
    Hazelnut and Jelly Sandwich Cookies, 152–156
    Hazelnut Macaroons, 134–135
    Nut Brownies, 149–151
    preparation time for, 118
    recommended tools for, 120
    Spekulatius Cookies, 136–139
    tips and tricks for, 118–120
    Vanillekipferl (Vanilla Almond Crescents), 125–127
    yields of, 120
cornstarch, 12
Covered Apple Pie, 29–32
cream cheese
    about, 12
    Cream Cheese Frosting, 256
    Liliko'i Cheesecake, 64–68
    Pumpkin Cheesecake, 69–71
    Ricotta Cheesecake, 56–59
Cream Cheese Frosting, 256
crumbs, browning, 15
crusts
    Almond or Hazelnut Crust, 109–111
    nine-inch pie crust recipe, 23
    special crust recipe for sturdy lattice, 23

E

Easy Chocolate Glaze, 261
Easy Lemon Buttercream, 255

INDEX

egg whites, whipping, 16–17, 177
eggs, 12

F

fast-read thermometers, 240–241
fillings
    Chocolate Buttercream, 252–254
    Chocolate Mirror Glaze, 262
    Cream Cheese Frosting, 256
    Easy Lemon Buttercream, 255
    Lemon or Liliko'i Buttercream, 252–254
flour
    extra for Mürbeteig recipes, 20
    guidelines for adjusting amounts of, 9
    how to measure, 7, 20, 118, 176
    liquid absorption of, 7–9, 20, 118, 176
    measuring for cookie recipes, 118
    measuring for Mürbeteig recipes, 20
    measuring for sponge cake-based torte recipes, 176
frostings
    Cream Cheese Frosting, 256
    Easy Lemon Buttercream, 255
    Lemon, Liliko'i, or Chocolate Buttercream, 252–254
    Royal Icing, 257
Fruit Glaze, 258

G

gelatin, working with, 176–177
ginger
    Candied Ginger Brownies, 143–145
    Gingerbread House, 160–173
Gingerbread House, 160–173
glazes
    Chocolate Mirror Glaze, 262
    Easy Chocolate Glaze, 261
    Fruit Glaze, 258
    Sugar Glaze, 260
    Tempered Chocolate Glaze, 263–264
    Tempered Chocolate Glaze the Easy Way, 265–266

H

Hazelnut and Jelly Sandwich Cookies, 152–156
Hazelnut Sponge Cake
    Cherry Cream Topping for, 204–207
    Hazelnut Cream Filling for, 200–202
hazelnuts
    Almond Hazelnut Mini Tarts, 85–88
    Almond or Hazelnut Crust, 109–111
    Chocolate Mousse Cake, 190–197
    Hazelnut Sponge Cake, 198–207

Linzer Torte, 89–93
Pear Frangipane Tart, 72–76

J

jams, jellies
    about, 12
    straining, 16

K

kirschwasser, 12

L

Lemon, Liliko'i, or Chocolate Buttercream, 252–254
lemons
    Easy Lemon Buttercream, 255
    Lemon, Liliko'i, or Chocolate Buttercream, 252–255
    Sponge Cake Roll with Lemon Buttercream, 180–183
    zesting, 17
liliko'i (passion fruit)
    Lemon, Liliko'i, or Chocolate Buttercream, 252–255
    Liliko'i Cheesecake, 64–68
Liliko'i Cheesecake, 64–68
Linzer Torte, 89–93

M

macaroons
    Coconut Macaroons, 132–133
    Hazelnut Macaroons, 134–135
marmalade, straining, 16
Mixed Berry Pie, 38–42
Mocha Sponge Cake Roll, 184–189
Mürbeteig
    about, 19
    Almond Hazelnut Mini Tarts, 85–88
    Almond or Hazelnut Crust, 109–111
    Apfelstrudel (Apple Strudel), 102–108
    Apple Crumb Pie, 25–28
    Apple Pie, 33–37
    Apricot Almond Cream Tart, 77–80
    bakeware for, 22–23
    Cherry Turnovers, 112–115
    Covered Apple Pie, 29–32
    cutting butter for, 21
    extra filling from, 23–24
    flour measurements for recipes, 20
    Liliko'i Cheesecake, 64–68
    Linzer Torte, 89–93
    Mixed Berry Pie, 38–42
    Pear Frangipane Tart, 72–76

Pecan Pie, 52–55
pie crust recipes for, 23
pie crust shields for, 22
preparation time for, 20
Pumpkin Cheesecake, 69–71
Pumpkin Pie, 48–51
Raspberry Almond Tart, 81–84
recommended tools for, 24
Ricotta Cheesecake, 56–59
Strawberry Rhubarb Pie, 43–47
Tarte Tatin, 94–101
technique for preparing dough, 21–22
tips and tricks for, 20–24
Traditional German Cheesecake with Quark, 60–63
work surfaces for, 22

N

nine-inch pie crust recipe, 23
Nut Brownies, 149–151
nut flour, 14–15, 118, 176
nut meal, 14–15, 118, 176
nuts
    grinding whole nuts into nut meal and nut flour, 14
    liquid absorption of nut flour, 14
    liquid absorption of nut meal, 14, 118, 176
    Nut Brownies, 149–151
    roasting nut meal and nut flour, 15
    roasting whole nuts, 15

O

oven rack placement, adjusting, 10

P

passion fruit. *see* liliko'i (passion fruit)
Pear Frangipane Tart, 72–76
Pecan Pie, 52–55
pecans
    Apricot Nut Cookies, 157–159
    Coffee Liqueur Brownies, 146–148
    Nut Brownies, 149–151
    Pecan Pie, 52–55
pie crust shields, 22
pie dishes, for Mürbeteig, 22–23
pies
    Apple Crumb Pie, 25–28
    Apple Pie, 33–37
    Covered Apple Pie, 29–32
    Mixed Berry Pie, 38–42
    Pecan Pie, 52–55
    Pumpkin Pie, 48–51
    Strawberry Rhubarb Pie, 43–47

INDEX

potato starch, 12
powdered sugar, 12
preserves, straining, 16
pumpkin
    Pumpkin Cheesecake, 69–71
    Pumpkin Pie, 48–51
Pumpkin Cheesecake, 69–71
Pumpkin Pie, 48–51

Q

quark
    about, 12–13
    Pumpkin Cheesecake, 69–71
    Quark Cream Torte with Mandarins, 213–217
    Traditional German Cheesecake with Quark, 60–63
Quark Cream Torte with Mandarins, 213–217

R

raspberries
    Chocolate Mousse Cake, 190–197
    Linzer Torte, 89–93
    Raspberry Almond Tart, 81–84
    Raspberry Sauce, 259
Raspberry Almond Tart, 81–84
Raspberry Sauce, 259
Ricotta Cheesecake, 56–59
Royal Icing, 257

S

sauces
    Chocolate Sauce and Pudding, 247–251
    Raspberry Sauce, 259
    Vanilla Sauce and Pudding, 242–246
special crust recipe for sturdy lattice, 23
Spekulatius Cookies, 136–139
Sponge Cake Roll with Lemon Buttercream, 180–183
sponge cake-based tortes
    about, 175
    bake times for, 178
    Black Forest Torte, 225–232
    Chocolate Irish Cream Cake, 233–237
    Chocolate Mousse Cake, 190–197
    choosing baking pans for, 177
    cutting and assembling layered sponge cakes, 178
    flour measurements for recipes, 176
    gelatin for, 176–177
    Hazelnut Sponge Cake, 198–207
    keeping air in the egg whites for, 177
    Mocha Sponge Cake Roll, 184–189
    preparation time for, 176
    preparing baking pans for, 177–178
    Quark Cream Torte with Mandarins, 213–217
    recommended tools for, 179
    Sponge Cake Roll with Lemon Buttercream, 180–183
    Strawberry Yogurt Cream Torte, 208–212
    tips and tricks for, 176–178
    Tiramisu, 218–224
strawberries
    Strawberry Rhubarb Pie, 43–47
    Strawberry Yogurt Cream Torte, 208–212
Strawberry Rhubarb Pie, 43–47
Strawberry Yogurt Cream Torte, 208–212
streusel, browned, 15
Sugar Glaze, 260

T

Tarte Tatin, 94–101
tarts
    Almond Hazelnut Mini Tarts, 85–88
    Linzer Torte, 89–93
    Pear Frangipane Tart, 72–76
    Raspberry Almond Tart, 81–84
    Tarte Tatin, 94–101
Tempered Chocolate Glaze, 263–264
Tempered Chocolate Glaze the Easy Way, 265–266
Tiramisu, 218–224
toppings, fillings, garnishes
    about, 239
    bains-marie for, 240–241
    Caramelized Almonds, 267–268
    Chocolate Mirror Glaze, 262
    Chocolate Sauce and Pudding, 247–251
    Cream Cheese Frosting, 256
    Easy Chocolate Glaze, 261
    Easy Lemon Buttercream, 255
    fast-read thermometers for, 240–241
    Fruit Glaze, 258
    ingredient temperature for, 240
    Lemon, Lilikoʻi, or Chocolate Buttercream, 252–254
    preparation time for, 240
    Raspberry Sauce, 259
    recommended tools for, 241
    Royal Icing, 257
    Sugar Glaze, 260
    Tempered Chocolate Glaze, 263–264
    Tempered Chocolate Glaze the Easy Way, 265–266
    tips and tricks for, 240–241
    Vanilla Sauce and Pudding, 242–246
Traditional German Cheesecake with Quark, 60–63

U

utensils, baking, 271

V

Vanilla Sauce and Pudding, 242–246
vanilla sugar, 13
Vanillekipferl (Vanilla Almond Crescents), 125–127

Y

yogurt
    Lilikoʻi Cheesecake, 64–68
    Strawberry Yogurt Cream Torte, 208–212

Z

zesting lemons, 17

ABOUT THE AUTHOR

Heidrun Metzler is a German-born baker and author with a degree in social pedagogy and early childhood education. With a passion for baking passed down from her mother, aunt, and grandmother, she began creating recipes at the age of ten. Travels to other European countries and relocation to the United States fueled her baking inspirations. Aside from baking, Heidrun enjoys spending time with her horses, trick training and practicing natural horsemanship. She is also a published children's book author and photographer. Heidrun currently resides with her husband on a farm in Hawaii.

German Heritage Baking, Volume I, is Metzler's first cookbook. Metzler's second cookbook is the companion volume, *German Heritage Baking, Volume II*. Volume II includes Pound Cakes, Yeast Sweet Doughs, Yeast and Sourdough Breads, Quick (Sweet) Breads, Breakfast Items, and Toppings and Fillings.

Connect with Heidrun on her website, heidrunmetzler.com, and on her Vimeo channel, vimeo.com/channels/bakingwithheidrunmetzler/videos, where bakers can find instructional videos with tips for successful baking.

VIDEO SHOWCASE
Baking with Heidrun
vimeo.com/showcase/6576524

OUR BAKING FAMILY

Baking has always been a passion of mine, and it brings me great joy to share my skills and knowledge with my family, especially the younger members who are eager to learn. I love teaching my tricks of the trade and passing down the recipes and techniques that my teachers have perfected over generations.

My favorite part of baking is the freedom to create a one-of-a-kind treat with my personal touch, tweaking recipes by adding more spice or a little more butter, a touch of milk, another half teaspoon of cinnamon or cardamom, or by swapping out some almond meal for some hazelnut meal for a more robust flavor.

I gained the confidence to add my personal touches by watching the women in my family make their own creative variations.

Baking is a great family activity; we all have fun together while making memories that will last a lifetime. And when the baking is done, there's nothing better than enjoying the delicious treats with the whole family.

Photos at right:

Top row, left to right:

My mother, Antonie Metzler, proudly presents her Champagne Peach Torte. At 89 years old, she is still baking cakes and exclaims, "Cakes that you bake yourself always taste better!"

In the backcountry forest, our family of bakers enjoy a hike: Aunt Käthi, Katharina Werner; our son, Jared, wearing my father's hat and jacket; my mother; and myself, Heidrun Metzler.

Middle row, left to right:

A cherished moment with my grandmother, Susanna Schmidt, as she holds my eight-month-old son, Derek, alongside my mother.

A snapshot of my mother and me in the house, where she passed down her baking skills to me.

Bottom left:

A family portrait at our Hawaiian home featuring our daughter-in-law Linh, sons Derek and Jared, myself, and my husband, Jason, with our beloved dog, Kayla.

Bottom right:

Our son Jared, embodying the next generation of family bakers, as he prepares a carrot cake for my birthday.